ALSO BY PAUL ALEXANDER

Ariel Ascending: Writings About Sylvia Plath (editor)

Rough Magic

Boulevard of Broken Dreams

DEATH AND DISASTER

The Rise of

the Warhol

Empire and

the Race

for Andy's

Millions

DEATH AND DISASTER

Paul Alexander

Villard Books

New York

1994

VILLARD BOOKS is a registered trademark
of Random House, Inc.

Frontispiece: The Menil Collection, Houston

Library of Congress Cataloging-in-Publication Data
Alexander, Paul.
Death and disaster: the rise of the Warhol empire and the race
for Andy's millions/by Paul Alexander.—1st ed.
p.   cm.
ISBN 0-679-43273-6
1. Warhol, Andy, 1928–   —Death and burial.   2. Warhol, Andy,
1928–   —Estate.   I. Title.
N6537.W28A78   1994
700'.92—dc20   93-46789
[B]

9 8 7 6 5 4 3 2
First Edition

FOR LAUREN ELIZABETH ALEXANDER

A lady friend of mine asked me,
"Well, what do you love most?"
That's how I started painting money.

—Andy Warhol

We only begin to live when we conceive
life as tragedy.

—W. B. Yeats,
    quoted by Sylvia Plath
    as an epigraph to her journal

CONTENTS

DEATH

1

AN UNEASY STILLNESS FILLED THE ROOM. THE TELEVISION SET ATTACHED TO the swing hinge on the wall had been turned off for two or three hours, maybe longer. The telephone sat quietly; the last calls had been made sometime before midnight. The overhead lights had been dimmed, so that the room was illuminated by a block of light spilling in through the door that led into the hallway, a faint glow of moonlight filling the window, and a lamp beside the yellow Naugahyde chair in which a nurse now sat. The only noises that broke the room's silence were the expected minor disturbances that occur in any hospital at four o'clock in the morning—an orderly clanging a tray down the hall, a nurse walking past the doorway, an announcement crackling softly over the public address system. It was so quiet and peaceful in the hospital room, number 1204 of Baker Pavilion—one of the nicer private rooms New York Hospital had to offer—that the private-duty nurse, who had spent most of her time sitting in the yellow chair since she had come on duty at eight o'clock, should have easily been able to hear any noise made by her only patient as he lay motionless a few feet away. At this time, though, she noticed nothing unusual about him; as a result, she just kept on doing what she was doing. Periodically she turned one page and then another while she read—no, studied, with an intensity common among highly religious people—the copy of the Bible she held in her hands.

The nurse was a woman named Min Cho. Born in Korea on April 8, 1935, she had been educated at the Seoul Sanitarium School of Nursing, where she was awarded a diploma in nursing in 1954, and at Sung Kyun

Swan University, where she took a degree in social work after she had transferred out of a literature program because, in her own words, "literature don't think help." After working at different hospitals in Korea, among them the Severance Hospital in Seoul—she was a registered nurse in the surgery department—Min Cho relocated with her husband to New York City in 1970 and got a job at New York Hospital. From there she moved on to Montefiore Hospital; in 1974, she returned to New York Hospital to work for the next decade or so. Even though she had spent much of her adult life in America, as of February 1987 she still spoke English so badly that a person could get a headache from a long and complicated conversation with her. For example, this is how she described a job she once held in Korea: "No, it is not really lab technician. Because like in gynecology, like you have to do service. That is in Jinhai. Many prostitutes we have to examine like discharge. It is very simple way we do exam. Then you can look at it, whether they have disease or not. We can analyze. Anything we see, we tell the doctors. He examine and we have to treat them." As unconcerned as she was with mastering the English language, Min Cho had a similar lack of interest in learning about American culture. She had absolutely no idea who her patient on this night actually was.

In the future everyone will be world famous for fifteen minutes.

I think everyone should be a machine; I think everyone should be like everybody.

If you want to know all about [me], just look at the surface: of my paintings and films and me, and there I am.

I like boring things. I like things to be exactly the same over and over again.

It wasn't just that Min Cho did not recognize these statements or understand what they meant in a larger cultural context. Before she walked into room 1204 of the Baker Pavilion on Saturday, February 21, 1987, Min Cho had never even heard of Andy Warhol, the man who had made these statements—a fact hard to imagine, considering that Warhol was so well known he had been not only a spokesman for Pontiac (in typical Warhol fashion, in the thirty-second commercial he made for the company he did not speak but merely held a dog as he stared at the camera) but also a guest star on *The Love Boat*, playing himself. All Min Cho knew when she came on duty that Saturday was what another nurse had told her about why her patient was using a pseudonym. Because Warhol was a famous artist—maybe the most famous artist in America—the nurse had told Min Cho, he had checked into the hospital under an assumed name, Bob Robert.

That had been on Friday, in the late morning. Andy arrived at the admission department accompanied only by Ken Leland, his personal assistant, to whom he referred either as his "walker" or his "bodyguard." Mostly, his job, held previously by Benjamin Liu, was simply to be with Andy. At the admission desk, Andy joked with a woman named Barbara, who was in charge of helping patients check in. "Any big stars in the hospital?" he wanted to know. "You're the biggest," Barbara answered. Then Barbara asked Andy, who had requested the use of a pseudonym, what name he wanted to be registered under. "Oh, make it Barbara," he said. When Barbara told him she couldn't do that, Andy answered, "Just make it Bob Robert." After that, he and Barbara filled out the rest of the routine admission form. As his next of kin Andy listed Fred Hughes, the person with whom he had had the single most complicated relationship of his adult life. A business associate since 1967, Fred, more than anyone else in Andy's circle of friends and advisors, had helped shape fundamentally the way Andy handled his career as a creative artist and the kinds of financial investments he made outside the field of art. On the admission form, Andy also had to give the name of his admitting physician, Dr. Denton Cox, a man who had treated him for so long—twenty-seven years—that they had become close friends. Finally, Andy had to provide Barbara with his insurance number. Andy Warhol, Barbara later told one of his biographers, was the only patient she had ever checked into New York Hospital who actually knew his insurance number by heart. He had the number memorized.

There was a reason why Warhol had committed the number to memory. On some basic level, it had come to represent to Warhol the very act of checking into the hospital, and while this is an unpleasant event for most people, for Andy it was, even as a concept, an event that filled him with such apprehension and uncertainty—such outright terror—that he had avoided this moment (and willfully ignored his medical condition) for years. Through some queer cerebral twist, the dread number must have emblazoned itself in his memory. For Andy had a unique phobia of hospitals. The origin of the fear could be traced back to June 3, 1968, the day an obsessed feminist who had worked as an actress for Warhol in one of his experimental underground films walked with Andy into the Factory (his studio), pulled out a revolver, and shot him in the abdomen at point-blank range. One bullet ripped through six internal organs. By the time an ambulance got him to Columbus Hospital, just a few blocks away, he was so close to death that a surgeon had to cut open his chest and massage his heart before a team of doctors could operate on him. He was in surgery for five hours. At one point early on, a doctor pronounced Warhol clinically dead, a comment that he would insist he remembered hearing even though he was under anesthesia at the time. He spent the next two months in the hospital recovering. Even so, from June 1968 on he would be terrified of entering a hospital. His fear of hospitals was so severe that when he walked up York Avenue toward Sotheby's, where he often attended auctions, he would cross the street to avoid walking on the sidewalk next to New York Hospital. Some days, particularly if he was feeling unusually nervous, he would turn his head away from the building; that way he wouldn't even have to catch a glimpse of it.

By February 1987, Andy's physical condition had deteriorated so much—he had an infected gallbladder that needed to be removed—that he relented and agreed to check into New York Hospital, the very place he had so often gone out of his way to avoid. This didn't mean that he was happy about it. Denton Cox had referred him to Dr. Bjorn Thorbjarnarson, a highly regarded Manhattan surgeon known for operating on some of the most famous people in the world (among them the Shah of Iran) and an expert in gallbladder surgery. Andy saw him for the first time on Thursday, February 19. After a ten-minute examination in his office, Thorbjarnarson told Andy that he had to have his gallbladder removed; what's more, the gallbladder was infected so badly that the surgery needed to be done right away. There was no room to negotiate on this critical medical point. When Andy told him that he didn't want to go into a hospital, Thorbjarnarson reassured him, attempting as best as he could to relieve some of Andy's concerns. "I'm not going to make it," Andy said, his voice, normally whiny yet controlled, brittle with emotion. "Oh, don't worry, Andy," Thorbjarnarson said, again trying to calm him down. "You'll make it." That Andy believed he could be killed from a routine gallbladder operation seemed silly to Thorbjarnarson; no one died from gallbladder surgery. "No, no," Andy said, sure of what he was saying. "I'm not going to make it."

In fact, the surgery did *not* kill him. At eight o'clock on Saturday morning, February 21, Andy was wheeled on a gurney from his private room to the operating room. At ten after eight, before he was taken out of preop, a Nurse Cannon asked him if he was allergic to any drugs. Only penicillin, he told her. Next she asked him if he had ever had surgery before. "Yes," he said, but did not elaborate about the shooting in 1968. From eight forty-five until ten after twelve, Warhol was in surgery. During that time, Thorbjarnarson not only took out his gall-bladder (which was more difficult than usual since the gallbladder was gangrenous and Thorbjarnarson had to be careful not to rupture the organ and release poisons into the abdominal area that could cause peritonitis to set in), but he also repaired a hernia Andy had had since 1968, a result of the shooting. From a little past noon until three forty-five, Andy stayed in the recovery room. Around four, he was returned to room 1204. Between four and eight, Andy was watched over by Nurse Ellen McDonald, a feisty, hardworking private-duty nurse who, like Min Cho, had been hired by Warhol's business office through a referral service recommended by the hospital. McDonald had been there since eight o'clock in the morning when Andy went into surgery, so she had spent most of the day waiting for him to come back from recovery. After he was returned to his room, she was determined to help him get back on his feet as soon as possible—literally. More than once, she made him get out of bed, sit in a chair, and do a set of deep-breathing exercises that were designed, she explained, to help prevent fluid from collecting in his lungs, a complication that occasionally occurs with patients following surgery. At some time between six-thirty and seven, McDonald also helped Andy urinate into a plastic container. After the operation, Andy had experienced some pain, for which he had been given two moderate-sized doses of morphine, but all in all he was doing extremely well. It looked like he was going to make it. Despite his paralyzing fear, Andy had done it: He had checked into the hospital, gone through surgery, come out of it, and appeared to be recovering just fine. If he had not been so incapacitated, he might actually have been proud of himself.

There was one detail to this story that even he would have thought ironic. Throughout his ordeal, during the preop, the surgery, the recovery, and the postop, no member of the medical staff at New York Hospital had forced Andy to take off his wig. The image is incongruous and in many ways telling: Andy lying on the operating table, the midsection of his body cut wide open, and the famous white fright wig still stuck to his head. Who would beg his doctors to operate on him not in a hospital but at home—originally Andy had done this until the doctors made it clear they wouldn't go along with his scheme—and then, when he did relent and check into the hospital, insist on wearing his wig even during surgery? No one but Andy Warhol.

This particular wig, whiter and bushier than some he had worn in previous years, was from a new batch he had ordered only a few months ago from Mr. Bocchicchio, his wigmaker out in Queens. Andy had been wearing wigs since the sixties. As he began to go bald, he decided he "needed a wig," so he simply bought one and started to wear it. Then again, he was always one to embrace the literal. When he did a silkscreen in 1962 of 210 Coca-Cola bottles, he entitled the painting *210 Coca-Cola Bottles,* a naming procedure he used throughout his career. At any rate, beginning around the time he started wearing that first wig, he would buy a new group of wigs from Mr. Bocchicchio about once a year; they would arrive at the Factory in big green boxes. Andy threw few of his old wigs away. As a matter of fact, Andy didn't like to throw *anything* away. He was such a hoarder and collector that he would not even allow his employees to throw away used batteries; sometimes he actually dug dead batteries out of the garbage. "You never know if copper is going to go up in value," he would say. So he kept the wigs. By February 1987 he had so many that they filled an entire closet in his townhouse on East Sixty-sixth Street.

Under normal circumstances, Andy took off his wig at night before he went to bed, always careful to make sure he was alone in his bedroom when he removed it. In all of the years he had been wearing wigs, Andy's friends and associates could recall only a single instance in which he'd been seen without one. On this day, Andy was signing books at a store in downtown Manhattan when a crazed fan snuck up behind him and yanked the wig off his head. Luckily Andy was wearing a hooded jacket, so he quickly pulled the hood up over his head. Through the years, Andy had not even allowed Jed Johnson or Jon Gould to see him without his wig, and they had both been his boyfriends. Of all the affairs and one-night stands Andy had had in his life, Jed, in the seventies, and then Jon, in the eighties, represented Andy's only two serious attempts at long-term relationships. And if Andy had not allowed either of them to see him without his wig, he surely was not going to let some doctor or nurse at New York Hospital.

On August 20, 1969, a little over a year after he was shot, Andy went to Richard Avedon's studio in New York City, where Avedon took pictures of his exposed chest and abdomen. The photographs, which would become famous for their gruesome starkness, show the aftermarks of Andy's wounds—the healed puncture, the patchwork of scars, the map of tiny holes that had been stitches. Andy was more than willing to let Avedon snap this series of painfully revealing, uniquely intimate pictures. But he would never—*never*—have allowed Avedon to photograph him without his wig.

Min Cho had not noticed Andy's wig. Then again, since she had no idea who Warhol was, she was unaware of its significance. It was never really clear what she did or did not know about Andy. Earlier in the evening, she had helped him make some telephone calls, dialing the numbers for him and then handing him the receiver. Like Nurse McDonald, she had coached him through some deep-breathing exercises. Also, she would later claim that while he was awake she took his vital signs about once an hour. But otherwise Min Cho had had little to do. Though Andy had been afraid of the operation, he had come through it with no complications. After spending the evening dozing on and off while he watched television, he finally went to sleep for good around two in the morning.

It was now four o'clock, and Min Cho was looking at Andy from the chair where she was sitting. Andy lay in the hospital bed sleeping. He had a single IV drip connected to his arm. There was no catheter; no other tubes; no machine to monitor any of his vital signs, not even his heartbeat. The hospital medical personnel had deemed his physical condition good enough that he did not need any form of monitoring other than the sort that his private-duty nurse and the staff nurses could provide. Years later, Min Cho offered a description of the vigil she kept over her patient. "I was sitting face-to-face," she said. "I can look at his face. I almost stare at him almost every minute. And I check IV, and I check tube and I check—I look at him and he is sleeping soundly. First time I can hear a snore, analyze of snoring. To me, just normal."

The overall implication of what she is saying comes through. Min Cho claimed that from the time Andy went to sleep until sometime much later, she diligently stared at him "face-to-face." Unfortunately, this does not seem to be entirely true. Besides reading her Bible, she also left the room. Somewhere between four-thirty and five o'clock in the morning (she would never be sure about the precise time), she went down the hall to the nurses' station to pick up Warhol's morning medication. At any rate, even if she was sitting in her chair watching Andy hour after hour, never leaving the room, never letting her attention stray from him in the least, she did not see everything. For at some point between four forty-five and five o'clock, when she got out of her chair to go over and check on Andy, Min Cho realized that something was wrong. Andy looked pale. He was unusually quiet. He lay eerily motionless. And as soon as Min Cho touched him, as soon as she placed the tips of her fingers to his wrist to check his pulse, she could tell that his skin was cold—cold even for Andy, whose skin always tended to be pasty and clammy.

2

ANDY'S GALLBLADDER CONDITION HAD FIRST BEEN DIAGNOSED BACK IN APRIL 1973 by Denton Cox, whom Andy had gone to originally in 1960 for a case of warts. A graduate of Yale and of Columbia College of Physicians and Surgeons, a veteran of the navy, and a doctor known for his international practice, his empathy for his patients, and his warm bedside manner, Denton Sayer Cox was an unusually skillful diagnostician. When Warhol was admitted through the emergency room to New York Hospital on April 13, 1973, he was told by the staff doctors that he was suffering from a kidney stone, but as soon as Cox got involved in the case a little later he knew that Andy's pain was the result not of a kidney stone but a gallstone. Once a gallbladder X-ray was finally taken on May 31 (Warhol had stayed in the hospital for just two days), Cox was proved right. Andy did have a gallbladder condition, Cox explained to him, which could be cured only by surgery. Andy, however, refused to have the operation, no matter how badly he needed it. He would do anything, he said, *except* be operated on—and that was the end of the discussion.

So, over the years, instead of submitting to surgery, Andy tried almost anything he could to get some relief. From 1978 until 1984, he took Actigall, a gallbladder medication recommended to him by Cox, which one day would be considered standard treatment for controlling a gallbladder condition but in 1978 was still thought to be so experimental that Andy had to buy it from a pharmaceutical manufacturer in Japan. He also maintained a low-fat diet. Then, in 1984, at the suggestion of Jon Gould, Andy began trying alternatives to traditional medicine, going to chiropractors, nutritionists, crystal healers, physical therapists—any professional or semiprofessional except a surgeon. In short, Andy pursued every alternative to surgery, and for well over a decade he was successful in keeping his condition from becoming serious enough that he could not continue to live with it.

Warhol probably was not thinking about his medical problem—he often went for long periods of time when the gallbladder did not bother him at all—as he lay in his antique Federal-period four-poster bed one morning in the early fall of 1986, planning his schedule for the day. Already he had spoken on the telephone with Pat Hackett, a friend who through the years had helped him write his books. Each morning for more than a decade now, Andy called Pat (or Pat called Andy), and during their conversation he described to her in as much detail as possible what he had done the day before. He had started this routine as a way of keeping a record of his expenses for income tax purposes, but over time Pat's growing document had become what amounted to Warhol's diary. Just as he needed help with almost everything else in his life, Andy could not even keep his own diary. And what a diary! At this point in Warhol's life, the document had grown so large that it was now approaching twenty thousand pages.

After talking with Pat, Andy called the Factory to check in with Paige Powell, the advertising manager at his *Interview* magazine and, for the last several years, one of his closest friends. They talked for a few minutes, as they did almost every morning; as part of their chat, Paige reminded him of what he had to do for the day. Usually Andy arrived at the Factory in the early afternoon; on most days he got there just in time to attend the Factory lunch. (These days, almost all of the lunches were for business purposes.) Following lunch, Andy spent the rest of the afternoon painting, either a commissioned portrait or part of a series. At this stage of his career, Warhol rarely started a canvas unless it had been expressly commissioned—even a series of paintings had a buyer or gallery lined up beforehand—and he almost never worked on a canvas alone. Sometimes he had as many as three or four assistants in the studio painting with him. Nearly always the last person to leave the Factory, Warhol stopped working around seven o'clock. At that time, he proceeded to the first stop on his agenda for the night. And Andy went out just about every night of the week—to a party, a dinner, a gallery opening, a movie, a play. Indeed, Andy went to so many events that, among the New York publicists, who were always trying to attract celebrities, it was said that Andy would come to the opening of an envelope if he knew the press was going to be there.

Andy ended his evening by going home around midnight or a little after. He would make a few phone calls while he relaxed in bed—he and Paige regularly spent time talking on the telephone late at night—then he would turn off the lights around one o'clock and go to sleep, usually with the help of a Valium or a sleeping pill. The next morning, Andy woke up and followed basically the same schedule he had the day before. The names and the places were different, but the routine rarely changed.

This morning, though, Andy's business and social calendar would have to wait, at least for a few hours. For during the late morning and early afternoon, he would be doing what had become one of the main focuses of his life: He was going shopping. He had always been a collector, from as far back as the early fifties when he first started making enough money to buy what he wanted. Over time, however, it was not so much the acquisitions that he loved as the act of acquiring them. From the beginning, one of the main themes of his work had been money, or, on a somewhat more general basis, commerce. In the early seventies, in the wake of his near-fatal shooting, he became even more intent on accumulating material objects—furniture, jewelry, paintings by other artists, collectibles—and when Jed Johnson was living with Andy during the seventies, he found a way to keep order among all the objects Andy was buying. Then, in 1980, Andy and Jed broke off their relationship. After that, Andy not only stopped caring about organizing his acquisitions but started to increase dramatically the volume of his purchases.

In the early eighties, Andy had become friends with Stuart Pivar. An independently wealthy inventor who had made his fortune in plastics, Stuart collected and sold art. He also loved to shop—about as much as Andy did, if that was possible. The two of them could go shopping together every day, and for several years they nearly did. They hit the shops on Madison Avenue, the jewelry stores in the Diamond District, the antique stores uptown and downtown, and the big and not-so-big auction houses: Christie's, Sotheby's, Christie's East, Doyle's, Lubin's, Tepper. On weekends, they went to flea markets and antique shows. Andy especially liked the antique shows held on the West Side piers because they were so large, but for that same reason Stuart sometimes dreaded going there with him. "Andy was interested in every single category of an auction," Pivar later said, "from classical antiquities to stamps. He'd look at every lot. When you'd go to the pier antique show with him, it was like being kidnapped in Lebanon. He'd study every single thing. It'd take three or four hours at least."

Stuart would pick Andy up at the townhouse in his black Chrysler limousine, which was driven by Stuart's chauffeur, Beso. Then Andy and Stuart would head out on the route they had decided on for the day. As they made their rounds, Beso would wait in the car while Stuart and Andy went inside a store to shop; after they made their purchases, they came outside and piled the packages in the trunk of the car. In this manner, they proceeded from store to store during the two hours or so they spent shopping. Almost everything Warhol bought ended up back in his townhouse, where his trove of collectibles spilled out of closets, cluttered hallways and staircases, and filled up room upon room—in bags, in boxes, loose. Several rooms—a sitting room, two bedrooms, a study—were so jammed with bags and boxes that they were no longer functional. Of all the rooms in the house, though, the worst was the dining room. Andy had crammed so many bags and boxes in the room that, chest-high, they now completely hid the dining room table. The only way to get from one end of the room to the other was to squeeze through the narrow path that Andy had cleared through the junk.

Why would Warhol go out almost every day, buy item after item, bring them all back home, and then not even bother to take most of them out of the wrappings he brought them home in? "There is nothing so thrilling as encountering something for sale," Stuart liked to say, and that seemed to be what most captivated Andy as well. He was much more fascinated by the act of buying than he was by actually owning the object. In fact, Andy seemed to be addicted to the rush he got when he made a purchase. The high was intense but brief. Perhaps that was why he had to go out shopping as often as he did.

Today, Stuart picked Andy up in his limousine just as he had on so many other mornings over the last few years. Dressed in black jeans, a black turtleneck, a jacket, and, of course, his silvery wig, Andy descended the steps from his townhouse, got into the back of the limousine with Stuart, and waited for Beso to head off. Andy always carried with him a stack of *Interview* magazines. As he shopped, he liked to give away free copies to store owners, clerks, even strangers, especially if that person recognized him.

Andy and Stuart passed the time by gossiping as Beso drove them along. When they reached their first stop, Seaman Schepps, the jewelry store located on the corner of Park Avenue and Fifty-eighth Street, Andy and Stuart got out of the car and walked inside. Andy had been in the store many times before. Because Schepps was one of his favorite jewelry designers, Andy had collected numerous pieces of his work through the years; he continued to buy jewelry at Seaman Schepps even though Schepps himself had died back in 1972 and the shop was now being run by his daughter, Patricia Vaill.

Though Andy had been in the store often, this morning he still got a buzz when he walked through the front door. Imagine—all of the jewelry in every case was there for someone to buy! He crossed over to a case and began to look. Patricia Vaill came from the back of the store to greet him. Andy had bought from her so much through the years that in the late seventies he ran a profile of her in *Interview.* For that profile, Andy had had Vaill photographed by someone he used for the magazine on occasion despite the fact that he didn't like the man personally—Robert Mapplethorpe.

"Oh, Pat," Andy said, handing her a copy of *Interview,* "do you have any masterpieces?"

By "masterpiece" Andy meant anything that he might be interested in buying. For Andy, a masterpiece could be the cheapest piece of costume jewelry—*if* he liked it—or the most expensive diamond ring in the store. It simply didn't matter.

Vaill, a cultured, elegant woman who had once been a model—just the sort of sophisticated woman Andy liked to do business with—showed him a new piece he hadn't seen.

And so Andy started searching for his next masterpiece to buy, if not right now at Seaman Schepps, then at the next store or the one after that.

It was rare, as Stuart Pivar would later remember, for Andy to have a "masterpieceless" day.

3

TRUMAN CAPOTE ONCE CALLED ANDY WARHOL "A SPHINX WITH NO SECRET." The comment could not have been further from the truth, for Warhol was nothing if not full of secrets. Throughout much of his life, especially during the last several years, he allowed almost no one to come inside his townhouse, and those few who did rarely made it past the front entryway. It was unusual for him to give parties—and they were never held at his home—even though he had the reputation of being the ultimate socializer. There were, however, more fundamental contradictions to his personality than this. Warhol was a millionaire countless times over, but he projected the appearance of being down on his luck, almost hard up for money; he was so stingy, in fact, that he routinely took taxis instead of hiring a limousine service, though he easily could have afforded one. He created an image of himself as being trendy and liberal, but in reality he could be surprisingly conservative; he was, for instance, a devout Catholic who went to Mass every Sunday. He was a gay man who did not go out of his way to acknowledge publicly the fact that he was gay, although, to be fair, all of his friends knew his sexual preference. (In a conversation with Michael Jackson once, the two of them ended up discussing, of all subjects, children. Michael: "Do you have any kids?" Andy: "Me? I don't believe in marrying." Michael: "Really? Why not?" Andy: "I don't believe in love." . . . Michael: "You like children?" Andy: "Ahh . . . only if they're not mine.") Explaining these contradictions later in his life, Andy said: "I'd prefer to remain a mystery. I never like to give my background and, anyway, I make it all up different every time I'm asked. It's not just that it's part of my image not to tell everything, it's just that I forget what I said the day before, and I have to make it all up over again." Why did Warhol live a life so full of contradictions? Why did he foster this image of himself? Why did he feel compelled to "make it all up . . . every time I'm asked"?

Andrew Warhola was born on August 6, 1928, in Pittsburgh, Pennsylvania, to Julia and Ondrej Warhola. He was delivered at home by a doctor who never filed a birth certificate. Because of this oversight, the actual year of Warhol's birth would always be in doubt, especially since as an adult Warhol tended to lie about his age. (Even as he was filling out his medical history form in Dr. Thorbjarnarson's office, he asked Ken Leland if he should shave a few years off his age.) At the time of his birth, Andy's family lived at 73 Orr Street in Soho, a run-down working-class ghetto in Pittsburgh that overlooked the Monongahela River. In the late twenties, Pittsburgh, with a population of six hundred thousand, was one of the key industrial cities in the United States, producing the steel that would help facilitate the dramatic urbanization that the country would undergo during the next four decades. The steel mills of Pittsburgh never stopped; they ran twenty-four hours a day. Their towering chimneys pumped a never-ending stream of dense gray smoke into the air. On some days the air would be so polluted that it looked as if dark clouds were weighing down the city's horizon. So much soot fell on Pittsburgh during the night that a person often had to go out and sweep the black grime off his front porch with a broom in the morning. Between the world wars, Pittsburgh was a depressing, ugly city, almost Dickensian in its gloominess.

While industrialists like Andrew Carnegie and Henry Clay Frick had amassed fortunes in Pittsburgh that would rival any created in the United States in the twentieth century (both men died in 1919, but their families carried on with their newfound wealth), a large portion of the citizens of the city lived in abject urban squalor. The Warholas were a part of this underclass. Originally immigrants from Transylvania, Ondrej came to America in 1912, and his wife, Julia, followed nine years later. They had two sons before Andy—Paul, born in 1922, and John, born in 1925. The Warholas managed the best they could during the Great Depression, but life was difficult. The house they lived in when Andy was born didn't have an indoor bathroom; the house they moved into next had only an indoor toilet. A coal miner and a construction worker by trade, Ondrej was frequently unemployed, and it was not unusual for the family to have to get by for days at a time on soup. Finally, in 1934, the Warholas moved into a decent house on Dawson Street, for which they paid $3,200; however, because money was still tight, they had to rent out the second floor to another family just to be able to pay the mortgage. It was at this time that Andy started first grade at Holmes Elementary School, the neighborhood public school. In the school, which was attended mostly by the children of working-class laborers, Andy completed the first and second grades. Then in the third grade he suddenly had to cope with something much more serious than his humble surroundings. One day he came down with a rare disease called chorea, or St. Vitus's dance, an illness of the nervous system that under certain circumstances can prove fatal.

In the fall of 1936, Andy, who was eight, contracted rheumatic fever, a result of his living in or near unsanitary conditions. At that time a patient normally suffered from the rheumatic fever until his immune system fought it off and he recovered. Since penicillin was not yet used to treat such diseases, the body had to repel the infection by itself. However, about 10 percent of the cases of rheumatic fever worsened and turned into chorea. Andy fell into that 10 percent. The sickness caused his skin to become spotty and brought on spells in which his arms and legs shook uncontrollably. Looking back on this time of his life, Andy would refer to these episodes as his "nervous breakdowns." Soon Julia became gravely concerned about her son. On doctor's orders she put him to bed for ten weeks. During his convalescence, Andy did little besides eat—it was then that he developed a craving for chocolate, an urge he would have for the rest of his life—and read stacks and stacks of comic books and Hollywood fan magazines. Eventually he recovered enough to return to school, but on his very first day back he suffered a relapse. The doctor ordered him to bed once again. Andy would have yet another relapse before he finally got over St. Vitus's dance, and he would suffer some complications from the illness permanently. His skin would always be splotchy, his body frail, and it seemed no matter how good his diet was, he had the general appearance of being sickly and undernourished. After the ordeal with Andy's health, the Warholas' poverty fell into perspective. Andy was lucky to be as well as he was. Maybe he was even lucky to be alive.

In 1942, as if Andy's life were not difficult enough already, his father died following a brief illness. Andy was fourteen. Through the years, family and friends would speculate about the cause of Ondrej's death. While everyone agreed that it was a jaundiced liver that killed him, some friends questioned exactly why the liver was diseased in the first place. Many suggested that it was a direct result of his gallbladder being removed some years before. Others would imply that perhaps Ondrej drank excessively, the prolonged effect of which damaged his liver.

Either way, it was obvious that Ondrej's gallbladder was susceptible to disease, a hereditary trait he passed on to Andy.

What is also not in doubt is the way Andy was affected by his father's death. Andy and his mother had always been close—Andy was especially dependent on her during his bouts with St. Vitus's dance—but after the death Andy and his mother became even closer. Years later, Fred Hughes would identify the significant influences from Andy's background that determined the sort of person he turned out to be in his adulthood. One influence, according to Hughes, "was his wonderful mother, Julia, with her imagination, her whimsical sense of humor, and Old World charm, who loved nothing better than buying little things from dime stores and with whom [Andy] would converse in a combination of English and Czech." Another influence, to be sure, was the extreme poverty from which Andy came. His parents' financial struggle instilled in him a lifelong obsession with making money and an overwhelming fear that the money he made, no matter how much it was, might eventually run out.

In 1945, Andy graduated from Schenley High School. In the fall of that year, he enrolled in the Carnegie Institute of Technology, in Pittsburgh, where he studied painting and design. He graduated in 1949. He took a job in Pittsburgh, but soon Philip Pearlstein, a friend of his from college, convinced him that the two of them should move to New York City and try their luck in the art business there. So, accompanied by Pearlstein, Andy moved to Manhattan that summer. Right away, he got work as a commercial artist, a career for which he had been perfectly trained through his course work at Carnegie Tech. He even had an impressive portfolio of drawings that he was able to show to prospective employers. One of his first free-lance jobs was at *Glamour*. There, his supervisor was Tina S. Fredericks. "I greeted a pale, blotchy boy," Fredericks wrote of their first meeting, "diffident almost to the point of disappearance but somehow immediately and immensely appealing. He seemed all one color: pale chinos, pale wispy hair, pale eyes, a strange beige birthmark over the side of his face (almost like a Helen Frankenthaler wash)." Andy liked Fredericks as well. "This wonderful lady at

Glamour magazine named Tina Fredericks just said that . . . she would give me a job," he later commented. "So I went back to her, got a free-lance job, and then spent all day looking for more free-lance jobs, and did my work at night. I never did anything, except work."

From this job at *Glamour*, Andy proceeded to have an enormously successful career as a commercial artist. Throughout the fifties, he drew for almost all of the "slick" magazines, among them *Vogue*, *Charm*, *Seventeen*, and *Harper's Bazaar*. He did album covers for Columbia Records. He designed book jackets and Christmas cards for several different companies. One of his best clients was I. Miller, the shoe company. In the mid-fifties he did a series of shoe ads for Miller that were such a hit when they ran in *The New York Times* that Andy could hardly keep up with the work he started to get from other clients. During this time he was hired to draw advertising campaigns for so many retail stores—Bonwit Teller and Lord & Taylor were only two—that *Women's Wear Daily* called him "the Leonardo da Vinci of Madison Avenue." Eventually he had to hire assistants to help him keep up with his assignments. He even enlisted the services of his mother, who followed him from Pittsburgh to New York soon after he started making enough money to support them both. And he was making plenty of money too. At the height of his career as a commercial artist, Warhol was earning one hundred thousand dollars a year, a staggering sum for the fifties.

Early on, as he was beginning to become successful, Andy made a decision about his name. He would use Andy for his first name, but for his surname he would drop the "a" from Warhola, opting simply for Warhol. Tina Fredericks later insisted that Andy had reached this decision by the time she first met him in 1949. Andy himself remembered the evolution of his name differently. "Well, the reason why I dropped the 'a' is that when I was going around with a portfolio, it just happened by itself. So it just happened. There were other Warhols in the telephone book."

It was under the name Andy Warhol that in 1952 he had his first show in New York. In 1948, Truman Capote, a young Southern writer who was becoming known for his friendships with wealthy New York socialites, show business people, and other eccentric Southern writers (one was Carson McCullers), published *Other Voices, Other Rooms,* an impressionistic novella about a boy growing up in the Deep South. The jacket photograph showed a coy, youthful Capote, only twenty-four, reclining on a sofa as he looks suggestively at the reader and rests one hand on his crotch. Andy was taken with the photograph—and with Capote. Andy had always been (and would always be) attracted to young men, and he was never subtle in his pursuit of them. He mailed Capote letter after letter, each one laudatory and heartfelt. He also started calling him on the telephone at his apartment until Capote's mother, who like Julia was living with her son, told him to stop. Finally Andy did a series of drawings inspired by Capote's fiction. In turn, that series became Warhol's first public show, "Fifteen Drawings Based on the Writings of Truman Capote," which was displayed at the Hugo Gallery on Fifty-fifth Street. Capote didn't come to the show's opening; then again, he hadn't answered any of Andy's letters or calls, either. Like many other young men whom Andy would pursue through the years, Capote did not respond well to Andy's decidedly direct approach.

If the pattern of development of anyone's life can be divided into decades, Andy's can. He arrived in New York at the start of the fifties and for the whole of that decade devoted most of his creative energies to commercial art. Naturally, as he lined up one account after another, many of them lucrative—on the I. Miller account alone he made fifty thousand dollars one year—Andy found himself in the best financial position of his life so far. Not only in terms of his talent, then, but also of his gross receipts, Andy was at the pinnacle of his profession. He— and his mother, who remained with him in New York until the early seventies—could finally appreciate the comfort that money brought. For Andy, though, success as a commercial artist was not enough. He was happy with the material rewards—in late 1959 he moved into a town-house he bought on the northwest corner of Lexington Avenue and Eighty-ninth Street on the Upper East Side in Manhattan—but he wanted something else. He wanted to be an artist, not just a commercial artist, but a fine artist.

Warhol set out seriously to become that artist at the beginning of the sixties. Actually, he had started experimenting with fine arts in the late fifties, but he had not achieved the breakthrough he had hoped for. Most notably, he did a number of ink and gold leaf drawings on paper. Then in 1960 he began to paint with oil on canvas. Still, it was what he *chose* to paint that would end up being revolutionary. In America, for much of the twentieth century, the art world had been dominated by abstract expressionism. With the canvases he painted in 1960, Warhol strayed as far away from this reigning style as he could. He painted a Coca-Cola bottle, an icebox, a can of Del Monte peach halves, a "before and after" newspaper advertisement for a nose job, a television set, a Campbell's soup can, an advertisement for a hot-water heater. Warhol's images were as concrete—almost absurdly concrete—as the expressionist canvases were abstract.

He continued to paint these kinds of images on into 1961, now focusing on objects like the telephone. Then in 1962 he discovered silkscreening, a mechanical painting process that allowed him to produce an image on a canvas quickly and accurately. The process used paint, but Warhol did not have to "paint" the image by hand; instead he could use a machine. The image was reproduced through the silkscreening process itself. Warhol continued to hand-paint canvases in 1962—he did a number of variations on the Campbell's soup can and one- and two-dollar bills—but with the silkscreening process available to him he was able to produce numerous canvases in a fraction of the time it would have taken him to paint them by hand. He entered into a breathtakingly productive period of creativity during which he turned out a steady stream of iconoclastic original work. Many of the canvases dealt with Hollywood celebrities, not unlike those he had read about as a young boy—Troy Donahue, Elvis Presley, Natalie Wood, Warren Beatty, and, of course, Marilyn Monroe. In 1962, Warhol created some of his most lasting and influential paintings: *Gold Marilyn Monroe, Triple Elvis, Turquoise Marilyn, Marilyn X 100,* and *Red Elvis.* This period of euphoric creativity continued into 1963, a year that saw him produce *Double Liz, Ten Lizes, Early Colored Liz, Single Elvis, Mona Lisa, Silver Marlon,* and *Statue of Liberty.*

In 1962 Warhol also began a series of paintings that would be as disturbing as it was innovative. Titled *Death and Disaster,* the series, which he produced throughout 1962 and on into 1963, featured gruesome images of suicides, car crashes, gangster funerals, race riots, electric chairs, and assassinations. "It was Henry Geldzahler who gave me the idea to start the *Death and Disaster* series," Warhol later said. "We were having lunch one day at Serendipity on East Sixtieth Street, and he laid the *Daily News* out on the table. The headline was '129 Die in Jet.' And that's what started me on the death series—the car crashes, the disasters, the electric chairs. . . . Whenever I look back at that front page, I'm struck by the date—June 4, 1962. Six years—to the date—later, my own disaster was the front page headline, 'ARTIST SHOT.' " To cull the images for *Death and Disaster,* Warhol searched through countless files of police photographs and Associated Press stills. The pictures he found—and reproduced in chilling detail, almost always against a colorful, happy backdrop—were unnerving: a man in midair leaping from a building to his death; a dead body lying on a sidewalk; police dogs attacking black marchers in Birmingham; and car wreck after car wreck, all of them fatal. As if these images were not unsettling enough, Warhol also produced, not long after November 22, 1963, *Jackie (The Week That Was),* an assemblage of sixteen pictures of Jacqueline Kennedy taken before and after the assassination of her husband. Besides predicting the violence that would come to define the sixties, the series also perfectly realized the promise of postmodernism by breaking down the particular disaster into its individual elements.

Death and Disaster would have been an impressive enough achievement for any artist. That Warhol produced numerous other, equally important paintings at the same time is stunning. "For eighteen months in the early nineteen-sixties," Adam Gopnik would one day write in *The New Yorker,* "Andy Warhol, then a Madison Avenue fashion illustrator with a small specialty in ladies' shoes, made paintings of fading movie stars, dollar bills, and cans of condensed soup, and afterward became for a while the most influential modern artist in the world." Warhol came to be so identified with the new movement of pop art that he was soon considered the movement's principle artist, easily overshadowing other pop artists like Roy Lichtenstein and Robert Rauschenberg. In 1960, he had set out to establish himself as a fine artist. Three years later, he had.

For Warhol, both his productivity and the quality of his art slackened off in 1964, although he did produce some interesting individual pieces, among them *Self-Portrait*. But then in 1965, just at the time when galleries were showing his work and collectors were eagerly buying up his paintings, Warhol did the unexpected. At the opening of a show of his paintings that featured his cow wallpaper at Ileana Sonnabend's gallery in Paris, a venue he chose so he would be sure to get international press coverage, Warhol announced he was "retiring" as an artist. The idea that an artist would retire when he had not yet been on the art scene five years seemed bizarre, but Warhol had his reasons for doing what he did. Privately he told friends he wanted to drive up the price of his work, a good portion of which he still owned. Publicly he said he was quitting art to devote himself to filmmaking. "I was having so much fun in Paris," Warhol would say, "that I decided it was the place to make the announcement I'd been thinking about making for months: I was going to retire from painting. Art just wasn't fun for me anymore; it was people who were fascinating and I wanted to spend all of my time around them, and making movies of them."

Actually Warhol had begun to experiment with film already, shooting his first film as early as 1962. Unable to work anymore in his Lexington Avenue townhouse (he had turned a back room into a studio), Warhol rented space in an empty firehouse on East Eighty-seventh Street in 1963. There, with a 16mm movie camera he had recently acquired, he began to shoot short silent films. They had such titles as *Blow Job, Eat, Haircut, Kiss,* and *Dance Movie*. Most of the time, the film was merely one long take, or a series of long takes, of the event described in the film's title. For example, *Blow Job* is a thirty-five-minute take of a young man, shown from the waist up, who is apparently on the receiving end of oral sex, though no sexual activity is ever revealed. All the audience sees is the facial expression of the young man as the act takes place. Another exercise in voyeurism, *Kiss* is a series of fifteen shots showing fifteen couples kissing. Each shot lasts about three or four minutes. What was daring about the film was the couples featured: They are male-female, male-male, interracial. In one shot two teenagers are kissing. The camera holds tightly on their faces. Finally Warhol pulls the camera back to reveal that his subjects, both bare-chested, are in fact boys. In the end *Kiss* is powerful because the kiss becomes a metaphor for the overpowering force of erotic human contact.

In late 1963, Warhol moved into a still larger studio on East Forty-seventh Street, which his painting assistant, Gerard Malanga, named the Factory. Soon Billy Name, a friend of Warhol's who would end up living there, covered the Factory's walls and ceiling with aluminum foil, making the whole place silver. In this space Warhol continued to shoot films, now using sound. *Harlot* was the first to have a soundtrack. Among the films he made in 1964 were *Henry Geldzahler, Soap Opera, Taylor Mead's Ass, The Thirteen Most Beautiful Boys, The Thirteen Most Beautiful Women,* and *Empire.* Some of them, like *Empire*—an eight-hour film of the Empire State Building shot from the forty-fourth floor of the Time-Life Building—had even attracted press attention.

In 1965, however, he began working with a young woman who would take his filmmaking into a whole different direction. Born into wealth, instinctively stylish, arrestingly beautiful, Edie Sedgwick would one day be described by Diana Vreeland this way: "She had a little step in her walk; she was so happy with the world. She was charming. She suggested springtime and freshness. She was very clean and clear, and her hair was pulled back, almost 'Alice in Wonderland.' Freshness and proportion and a sense of the sort of rollick in her life, you know, the fun of life. She was a youthquaker, wasn't she?—one of the true personalities of the sixties." During 1965 alone, Warhol made at least a half-dozen films with Edie, among them *Beauty #2, Vinyl, Poor Little Rich Girl, Kitchen, Bitch,* and *Restaurant.* Warhol was taken with Edie's beauty and presence as soon as she made her first screen test for him at the Factory. Chuck Wein, a mutual friend, knew that Andy would be fascinated by Edie; that's why he had encouraged Andy and Edie to meet. Chuck was right, too. While Andy and Edie made film after film together, all of them unscripted, unrehearsed, inherently experimental, Warhol became an underground filmmaker worthy of the recognition he was beginning to receive. For her part, Edie became, as Andy would call her, a superstar. On-screen, she was luminous, bright, bubbly. She was always talking, it seemed—and her favorite subject was herself. In *Beauty #2*, she and Gino Piserchio have a long, disjointed, drunken conversation, the subject of which is nothing more than the minor trivialities of life; the conversation, which is absorbing, is broken up occasionally when they fall back on the bed on which they are sitting and neck. The films Warhol shot with Edie Sedgwick in 1965 are so different, so fresh, so, finally, interesting that they overshadow all of the ones he made that year without her, notably *My Hustler* and *The Life of Juanita Castro.*

As Warhol shot his films, he gathered around him a large entourage, many of whom hung out at the Factory during the day and then followed him at night to Max's Kansas City, the only place to begin the evening in the mid- to late sixties. Besides Edie, Andy made use of a huge cast of would-be actors, bored rich kids, or society dropouts, and he would call each one of them a superstar. For many, he invented names; some he encouraged to come up with superstar names on their own. During Warhol's film career, he worked with Taylor Mead, Ultra Violet, Viva, Ingrid Superstar, International Velvet, Baby Jane Holzer, Paul America, Eric Emerson, Rotten Rita, Billy Name, René Ricard, Ondine, Joe Dallesandro, Sylvia Miles, Candy Darling, Holly Woodlawn, Jackie Curtis, and Brigid Berlin, a close friend of Andy's who was the daughter of the chairman of the Hearst publishing empire. For many of his films, Warhol collaborated on the directorial duties with Paul Morrissey, a young filmmaker who, like so many of Warhol's superstars and Factory regulars, met Andy one day, fell under his influence, and found himself helping Andy create his art. It was this spirit of collaboration that also led to Andy's involvement with the Velvet Underground. The four members of the group—Lou Reed, John Cale, Sterling Morrison, and Maureen Tucker—met through Warhol, rehearsed and performed at the Factory, and sought to represent in rock and roll what Warhol was capturing in his art and films. In addition, Warhol had the idea of pairing the Velvet Underground with Nico, the alluring and provocative model-actress from West Germany. In early 1966, Warhol brought the Velvet Underground and Nico together with a live video and light show that included go-go boys dancing with bullwhips. The whole extravaganza, which Warhol called the Exploding Plastic Inevitable, was staged at a club named the Dom on St. Marks Place in New York City. By staging this happening, Warhol created what came to be known as performance art and in the process produced a piece of Americana that seemed to symbolize (at least for those who saw it) the very decade of the sixties.

In 1966 Warhol shot his underground masterpiece, *The Chelsea Girls*, which featured monologues spoken by people living at the Chelsea Hotel. When the film opened in New York in the fall, it was the first Warhol movie to be reviewed by the popular press. It was also the first Warhol production to earn a noteworthy profit. In 1967, Warhol moved the Factory into a large loft on the sixth floor of a building at 33 Union Square West. During 1967, besides producing and designing the cover for the Velvet Underground's first album, Warhol made such films as ****; *I, a Man; Lonesome Cowboys; The Loves of Ondine;* and *Nude Restaurant.* Then, in 1968, he made *Blue Movie* (originally known as *Fuck*) and *Flesh.* But after June 3, the day Valerie Solanis came into the Factory and shot Andy in the abdomen at point-blank range, Warhol stopped making films. For that matter, during his two months in the hospital he stopped doing anything at all. Nor did he do much when he was released to go home and recuperate. From late July when he left Columbus Hospital until September when he returned to work at the Factory, about all Warhol did at home was paint a few small portraits of Happy Rockefeller. He painted so little, in fact, he did not even consider it to be a breach of his retirement.

4

OVER THE YEARS, WHEN WARHOL DISCUSSED THE SHOOTING (SOMETHING HE did not do often since it upset him), he would talk about the intense pain he felt and about the fact that by taking control of the situation at the Factory immediately following the shooting Fred Hughes had probably saved his life. In time, perhaps even as a result of the shooting, Fred would be the central person in Andy's professional life. Though Hughes later insisted their relationship was never sexual, the two men became about as close as two people can get without having an affair. It was, moreover, an odd friendship. Over time they developed what can only be described as a unique business partnership: Andy knew how to get his name in the newspaper and how to create art; Fred knew how to take those two talents, neither of which necessarily would have made Andy much money, and, through properly marketing them, generate cash— lots of it. Fred and Andy were also "best" friends, although their behavior toward each other was not always friendly, especially during the last several years of Warhol's life. Finally, Andy was just enough older than Fred—fifteen years—to attempt to play the role of father figure. In the end, however, Andy's feelings for Fred could not possibly have been called fatherly.

Both men were Catholic, in many ways devoutly so. In a moment captured on film and later produced as a popular postcard image, Warhol is standing in the middle of a huge crowd outside the Vatican, about to shake the hand of Pope John Paul II. Hughes, unquestionably proud and respectful, stands beside Warhol, just slightly in the background. The picture illustrates perfectly the Warhol-Hughes partnership. Warhol was always the one out front, getting the attention and creating the photo opportunity, but Hughes was there behind him, providing guidance and encouragement. Without the other, neither could have been as successful as he was. Significantly, though, without Hughes, whose business advice was nearly flawless for two decades, Warhol never would have been able to build up the vast empire he owned at the end of his life.

Frederick Wilson Hughes was born in Dallas, Texas, on July 23, 1943, the first of the three children of Jennie Wilson and Frederick William Hughes. His father, a decorated officer in the Army Air Corps during World War II, was originally from Muncie, Indiana, where his family owned a highly profitable steel mill. When he met Jennie Wilson, who was from Houston, they fell in love; marriage was inevitable. In 1947, the Hugheses moved to Houston and bought a conservative three-bedroom house in Hyde Park, a neighborhood not far from River Oaks, the most exclusive part of the city.

Known for its Tara-esque Southern mansions and for landmarks like the River Oaks Country Club, the neighborhood had been home to some of the country's most idiosyncratic nouveaux riches. Glenn McCarthy lived in River Oaks. The inspiration for the Jett Rink character in Edna Ferber's novel *Giant* (played by James Dean in the film), McCarthy, who was intensely proud of his Irish heritage, built the Shamrock Hotel. Located a short distance south of River Oaks, it featured a décor with well over fifty different shades of green. Jean and Dominique de Menil also lived in River Oaks. Dominique was the daughter of Conrad Schlumberger, who had created one of the largest oil fortunes in the world, though he, a lifelong resident of France, had never been a real "oilman." Instead, he had invented a state-of-the-art device that could easily identify minerals, a machine oil-well diggers could use to locate oil. For years Schlumberger controlled the patent, until it was broken in 1938; even afterward, though, the Schlumberger device was preferred by oilmen worldwide. The fortune created by this device allowed the Schlumberger family to live in wealth. So Dominique, who ended up in Houston because Schlumberger opened an office there in the thirties, could well afford to live in River Oaks with her husband, Jean, and their five children—George, Philippa, François, Adelaide, and Christophe—in a house designed by Philip Johnson, no less.

As he grew up in Hyde Park in the fifties, Fred went to Woodrow Wilson Elementary School. An excellent public school, it was still not The Kinkaid School or St. John's, the city's two elite private schools that most of the River Oaks children attended. Though Fred's father came from a substantial family, he worked as a manufacturer's representative—essentially, a salesman—for several furniture companies, including Chromcraft. The job allowed the Hugheses to live a nice middle-class life, but it was a long way off from River Oaks. Even so, this didn't stop the young Fred from trying to live such a life vicariously. He became friends with the Blaffers, another wealthy Houston family, who lived near the de Menils in River Oaks. Before long, Fred was friendly with the de Menil children; he often spent the afternoon swimming in their backyard pool. Liberal in both their social beliefs and their politics (some in Texas would even call them radical), Jean and Dominique de Menil were happy to have Fred around the house. Bright, witty, charming, he was soon a kind of adopted son. Of the many reasons for this, one was paramount. From the age of seven on, Fred had an interest shared passionately by the elder de Menils: art.

When he was just seven, Fred had started taking classes at the Museum of Fine Arts in Houston. He would continue to have a strong interest in art history as he grew up. In the fall of 1957 he enrolled at St. Thomas High School, a private Catholic school. Located on a sloping wooded hill just north of River Oaks, the school was run by priests of the Order of St. Basil. Strict and demanding, the Basilians were no match for the intellectually rigorous Jesuits, who taught across town at their own school. Still, they offered Fred a well-rounded and challenging curriculum—perhaps too challenging. During his years at St. Thomas, Fred, never one to enjoy a routine, distinguished himself more for his expert social skills and his fascination with society and the arts than for his interest—or excellence—in academics.

As a result Fred chose to bypass more distinguished colleges and attend the University of St. Thomas, a small Catholic university located in Houston. He entered the school in the fall of 1961 and immediately began to focus his studies on art. With just a handful of students, the art department was unusually small; it was also heavily endowed by the de Menil family. Since the de Menils were in essence paying the department's bills, they had unique influence over how it was run. (In later years their control became so strong that the university administration had to step in to ensure some level of academic independence and integrity; in addition, the conservative administration ended up being bothered by the de Menils' decidedly liberal politics.) One of the ways the de Menils used their power was to suggest strongly that the university hire Dr. Jermayne MacAgy as chairman of the art department. Ultimately it was a brilliant appointment that proved to be especially helpful to students like Fred Hughes, who gravitated to the study of art and soon devoted all of their time (and in some cases their lives) to it.

In 1964 MacAgy, who was diabetic, died suddenly of an insulin reaction, so Dominique de Menil finished out the term for her, teaching her classes and fulfilling her curatorial duties. It was at this time that Fred became even closer to Dominique. Now older and more focused on his hopes of having a career in the field, not as an artist but more as a businessman or collector—a role similar to the one that Jean and Dominique de Menil maintained in the art world, although theirs was on a much larger scale—Fred remained an appealing figure to the de Menils, who by the mid-sixties were among the world's most avid collectors of modern and contemporary art, almost all of it bought with Dominique's Schlumberger oil money. Their collection included work by Picasso, de Kooning, Dalí, Ernst, Pollock, and Barnett Newman, in addition to an especially large collection of paintings by Mark Rothko. In acquiring their collection, the de Menils had enlisted the services of many young and eager experts. Before long, Fred Hughes seemed a perfect candidate for one of these positions. In due course he began to work for the de Menils. Without a doubt, this employment led to his growing disinterest in college, and eventually he dropped out.

One of the projects on which Fred worked was the Rothko collection, which was so large that the de Menils decided to build a small museum in which to show his paintings on a tract of land in central Houston. The Rothko Chapel would be one of the few single-artist museums in the world, and Fred was involved in all areas of its planning. Indeed, Hughes had met with Rothko in his New York apartment to discuss which paintings would be hung in the museum just a few hours before the artist killed himself. But that would come years later, in 1970, when Fred no longer worked exclusively for the de Menils. In the mid-sixties, though, Fred was hired by the de Menils to search out new young artists whose work they might want to collect. One of the artists he recommended was Andy Warhol, who was then doing work similar to Jasper Johns's and Roy Lichtenstein's but who was finally more interesting to Fred not just as an artist but as a unique personality.

Fred met Andy in 1967 under auspicious circumstances. The de Menils were hosting a benefit for the Merce Cunningham Dance Company to be held at Philip Johnson's private home—the famous Glass House—in New Canaan, Connecticut, and Fred, who was splitting his time between New York and Houston as he continued to work for the de Menils, had booked the Velvet Underground to perform at the party. The year before, he had seen them at the Dom with Nico. He had become infatuated with her after he saw *La Dolce Vita*, in which she appeared, and was impressed that she had gone on to become a part of the Warhol crowd, one of the most trendy cliques in New York in the mid-sixties. Naturally, Andy accompanied the Velvets to the party. At some point during the afternoon, Fred asked his friend Henry Geldzahler, a curator at the Metropolitan Museum and a close business associate of the de Menils, to introduce him to Andy. The rapport between Andy and Fred was instant. They went off into the house, began to talk, and spent little time socializing with anyone else. Years later, some friends would speculate that the two of them may have been physically attracted to one another at first. Andy would one day describe Fred as being, at the time of their initial meeting, "a cute kid—young and such a dandy." But Fred would vehemently deny that their relationship ever became sexual. Actually this seems to have been the case. The two were attracted to each other for mostly professional reasons. Fred admired Warhol, whose reputation was on the ascent; in fact, he liked Andy's work so much that he had already bought a small Warhol canvas for himself. He also sensed instinctively that Warhol was going to be an important artist, which was why, even though he may not have been consciously aware of it himself, he set up a situation in which he was bound to meet him. On the other hand, Andy saw in Fred a young man who was smart, hardworking, and knowledgeable about art. Fred happened to be intimately friendly with the de Menils, two of the richest and most powerful art collectors in the business. The mutual benefits of this friendship were apparent even from the beginning.

After the Cunningham fundraiser, Fred made a point to drop in on Andy one day at the Factory. Following that visit they met on several different occasions. Soon Fred expressed an interest in working for Andy, who was equally agreeable to have Fred working for him. Within months, Fred was in New York all the time because he had his first job at the Factory—sweeping floors. Always one to embrace style and elegance, Fred often played janitor while wearing one of the handsome European-cut suits that soon became his trademark in the Warhol world. In no time he had progressed from floor sweeper to Andy's general assistant. It was at this point that Fred used his influence with the de Menils to convince them to start buying Warhols. In 1968, Dominique had Andy silkscreen a portrait of herself and one of Jermayne MacAgy. They were the first two society (that is to say, noncelebrity) portraits Andy would paint. In addition to buying Warhol's art, the de Menils, on Fred's advice, put up twenty thousand dollars to help finance Andy's underground films.

Fred's access to the de Menil fortune was impressive, but Andy appreciated Fred's personal style too. He was intrigued by the fact that Fred wore business suits, for example. Whereas most of the Factory regulars dressed like beatniks or hippies or devotees to the fashion trend of the moment, Fred always looked as if he had just wandered in off

Wall Street. Fred also possessed two personality traits that Andy lacked. First, he had learned how to deal with rich people; he knew when to be in awe of their status and their power, but he also knew that one should never fawn. Second, Fred's business instincts were formidable, much more so than Andy's. Up until now, Andy had been successful; there was no question about that. One of the top-salaried commercial artists of the 1950s, he was during the sixties among a small handful of artists who commanded significant sums for canvases. Once Fred arrived at the Factory, though, Andy began to focus intensely on making money. He had always been motivated to earn money. Now he was obsessed.

From the time Fred started working for Andy in 1967 until the shooting the following year, most of Andy's energy and much of the activity at the Factory were focused on making movies. Fred did not approve of this, for one unimpeachable reason: Andy's movies didn't make money. Not many people were lining up to watch an eight-hour film of the Empire State Building. While films like *Empire* got Andy a lot of attention in the press, they did not generate cash. Moreover, those few films that did turn a profit—like *The Chelsea Girls*—didn't make much of one. Fred believed that if Andy wanted to be truly financially successful, he had to come out of "retirement" and focus on his painting. In particular, Fred wanted him to undertake two different kinds of painting projects. First, he wanted Andy to silkscreen commissioned portraits for people who were willing to pay substantial fees. Second, he felt Andy should do other series in the style of *Death and Disaster*, only this time making sure each series was commissioned by a gallery owner beforehand.

There was just one problem with this plan of action. Paul Morrissey wanted Andy to stay out of the art business and get even more involved in making films. What he hoped was that Warhol would shoot commercial films—maybe not mainstream, but at least more accessible to larger audiences. So Paul lobbied Andy to make movies while Fred tried to lure him back to painting. Then Andy was shot. In the two months that it took him to recover, Andy examined his life. How could he not? The doctors had pronounced him dead on the operating table. After such a traumatic event, he had to reevaluate what he was going to do, now that he had been given a "second" life. "Everything is such a dream to me," he said following his release from the hospital. "I don't know whether or not I'm really alive or whether I died. And having been dead once, I shouldn't feel fear. But I am afraid. I don't understand why."

Over the years, as they tried to decide if (or how) Warhol had been affected by the shooting, Warhol's friends and associates would disagree noticeably. According to Brigid Berlin, Andy did not change at all. "I think the rest of us changed and became more cautious," she said. "We started having some security at the Factory. There were so many crazies around. They were just nuts." Paul Morrissey agreed with Berlin. "He never changed at all," Morrissey said. "It was against Andy's nature to change. He was so one-track-minded and persistent in everything he did that he never really changed. One of the remarkable things was the willpower he must have had to be able to say, 'Well, a crazy girl came into my office and shot me, but I'm not going to let that bother me. I'm not going to let that change my ways.' It didn't change *any* of his ways, any of his habits. He was exactly the same." On the other hand, many friends felt that Andy had been permanently affected by the shooting. Consider this from Bianca Jagger: "The Factory had always been open to any kind of person. Suddenly it was very difficult to come in. Video cameras were installed. You were screened. [The shooting] had a very, very serious effect on [Andy's] health and on his life. It left him very frightened." And this from Taylor Mead: "Andy died when Valerie Solanis shot him. [After the shooting,] he [was] just somebody to have at your dinner table. Charming, but he [was] the ghost of a genius. Just a ghost, a walking ghost."

The shooting and its aftereffects brought Andy to one conclusion: He wanted to start making more money, significantly more than he had in the past. To this end he drastically curtailed his film production. Following a period of time during which he turned out one film after another, he made no movies at all in 1969 and 1971. In 1970, he released just one, *Trash*; in 1972, two, *Women in Revolt* and *Heat*; and in 1973, one,

L'Amour. In 1974, serving only as the producer and the creative force who lent his name to the projects, Warhol released *Frankenstein* and *Dracula.* Directed by Morrissey, the films were Warhol's two most obvious attempts at mainstream moviemaking. The investor for the films, Carlo Ponti, who was married to Sophia Loren and had financed many European movies, was an odd and complicated character. He and Warhol eventually ended up in serious conflict with one another. Paul had arranged for Ponti to put up the money needed to film both *Frankenstein* and *Dracula* on one long shooting schedule. When the two films were later released theatrically, they were extremely profitable, grossing millions. The receipts for the films, however, went not to Warhol but to Ponti, who never gave Warhol the money that was due him, or so Warhol would claim. Andy was furious. Lawyers were called in. A struggle ensued. The situation was never satisfactorily settled. Finally, in disgust, Andy gave up dealing with Ponti. It was also at this juncture in his career that he gave up on moviemaking. After the debacle with Ponti, Warhol made only one other film, *Andy Warhol's Bad,* which was released in 1977.

In 1972, at Fred's urging, Andy decided to undertake a major series in the tradition of *Death and Disaster* and produced a series of silkscreens of Mao Tse-tung—a calculated move into the international arena as well. At the same time, again at Fred's suggestion, Warhol began silkscreening commissioned portraits. After he had done the two portraits commissioned by Dominique de Menil, Warhol—and Hughes—realized that there was a demand for paintings of this kind, and because they were silkscreened they were unusually easy for Warhol to produce. Starting in the early seventies, Warhol devoted a large part of his attention to turning out commissioned portraits: of Dennis Hopper, Philip Johnson, Ethel Scull, and Nan Kempner, among many others. The portraits would remain a vital business for Warhol until the end of his life. Producing anywhere between fifty and one hundred a year, Warhol would eventually charge thirty thousand dollars for the first canvas, plus five thousand for each additional canvas. For well over a decade, Warhol made between $1 million and $2 million a year (and some years much more than that) silkscreening portraits.

Meanwhile, Fred took steps to remove Andy from the downtown bohemian world and to place him more firmly among New York's high society. One road to this end was for Andy to become a publisher and found a magazine, so in the fall of 1969 Andy started *Interview*. At first, the magazine covered the film world (it was originally subtitled "A Monthly Film Journal"), but before long it took on celebrity in general. Andy would joke that they started the magazine to make sure they got invited to all of the good parties and private movie screenings; in actuality, though, the motivation was much more substantive. The fact that Warhol was the creative force behind the ultratrendy monthly caused many people, especially the fashionable of Hollywood and New York, to view him in a different light. *Interview* made Warhol even more famous, and simply because he was famous, the rich and the celebrated wanted him to do their portraits. Founding the magazine had been a brilliant move. It made Warhol more accessible to the public, more commercial, and more recognizable. As a direct result of this, Warhol began to get offers to endorse products. In the sixties Warhol had run an advertisement in *The Village Voice* that said he would endorse any-thing—and he meant anything—for money. At that time he received few calls; now the calls came pouring in. Beginning in 1970, he lent his name and face to numerous companies and products, among them Air France, Braniff Airlines, Pioneer Electronics, Puerto Rican Rum, and *U.S. News & World Report.*

In the larger picture, Hughes affected Warhol's ability to make money in an even more fundamental way. In Europe, as of the late sixties and early seventies, Warhol had enjoyed extensive notoriety and praise by both art critics and the art establishment; it could be argued that his work was regarded much more highly there than in America. As one of his first strategic maneuvers, Hughes sought to develop actively War-hol's European market. For example, the first portraits Hughes lined up for Warhol were commissions from Europeans, specifically a number of wealthy German industrialists. Hughes also cultivated two key contacts abroad, both art dealers. Leo Castelli, the Manhattan dealer with whom Warhol worked closely, represented Warhol's work well in America, but Hughes believed that Warhol needed someone to sell his work just as aggressively in Europe. Hughes hired Thomas Ammann and Bruno Bischofberger, perhaps the two most influential art dealers in Europe, to represent Warhol's art. Beginning in the early seventies and continuing until his death, Warhol sold a steady number of paintings through these two dealers. In fact, he would become unusually close to Ammann, eventually counting him as one of his best friends and most reliable business associates.

In the handful of years Hughes had been working for Warhol, he had assumed a significant role in the Warhol business enterprise, and as a result of his advice Warhol was thriving like never before. Following the shooting, Morrissey had taken control of the film production and Hughes oversaw the art business. An unspoken battle had been waged between them about the direction Warhol's career would take. Soon, Morrissey had a lesser influence on Warhol, while Warhol seemed to value Hughes's opinion more and more. So, by the mid-seventies, with film production completely shut down and the painting business increasing dramatically, Morrissey was no longer a part of the Warhol inner circle. In time, he stopped coming to the Factory altogether. When this happened, Hughes was finally in charge. Through the years he would be helped out considerably by his "second-in-command," Vincent Fremont, a young blond Californian who had shown up at the Factory in 1971, made himself useful, and eventually found himself running the day-to-day activities of the place. Hughes was the most powerful figure within the Warhol organization besides, of course, Warhol himself.

Already, Fred and Andy had developed an unusual relationship. Neither lovers nor confidants, they were business partners, though their partnership was by no means traditional. Hughes worked for Warhol— there was never any question that Warhol made the final decision in any given situation—but Hughes could convince Warhol to do things no one else could. In 1975, for instance, Fred somehow got Andy to make a will. Death was a subject Andy avoided assiduously. If someone he knew died, Andy would say that the person had "gone shopping at Bloomingdale's." In 1971, Edie Sedgwick's apparent overdose from barbiturates had no effect on Warhol at all, or at least none that he showed to his friends and colleagues. When his mother died on November 28, 1972, she had been living in a nursing home in Pittsburgh for nineteen months; not only did Andy not attend her funeral, he didn't even tell anyone that she had died. A will was the last legal document Warhol would have wanted to draw up. After all, by writing a will he was admitting that his own death was inevitable, that death was *not* the equivalent of a shopping trip to Bloomingdale's. When Fred wrote his own will in 1975, he urged Andy to do the same. Why should I? Andy wanted to know. Because, Fred quipped, if you don't, most of your money will go to your "least favorite relative, Uncle Sammy Warhola." The argument seemed to work. Andy wrote his will.

The quality of the document, however, would underscore the scant amount of time Warhol put into thinking about life after his death. It also established who was and who was not important to him. Warhol would leave a sum of cash to Jed Johnson, with whom he was then romantically involved, and $250,000 to Fred Hughes, who was named as the estate's executor. He left no money to anyone else. Instead he directed his executor (he named Vincent Fremont as alternate executor) "to incorporate or cause to be incorporated, a corporation in accordance with and under the provisions of the New York Not-for-Profit Corporation Law, or any similar law of New York or any other state." Appointing a board of directors to be made up of Hughes, Fremont, and John Warhola, Warhol did stipulate, but in the broadest terms possible, what the corporation should do. "Such corporation shall be a foundation for the advancement of the visual arts and shall be incorporated under the name of 'THE FOUNDATION FOR VISUAL ARTS,' or of similar name (hereafter, the 'foundation'). The certificate of incorporation of the foundation shall contain any and all provisions necessary to create a corporation bequests to which are deductible for United States estate tax purposes under section 2055 of the Internal Revenue Code of 1954, as amended from time to time before my death."

5

DURING THE LAST HALF OF THE SEVENTIES, WARHOL PRODUCED A NUMBER of series. In 1976 he painted *Skulls*. The next year he did *Athletes*, a group of portraits of famous athletes; *Hammer and Sickle*, a series based on the symbol of the Soviet Union; and *Torsos*, a collection of silkscreens featuring various nude male bodies. In 1978, he produced *Oxidations*, a group of paintings he made by having Victor Hugo, a fellow artist and a friend, urinate on canvases. Rumor had it that Warhol chose Hugo to do the urinating because Hugo had an unusually large bladder, not to mention an unusually large penis, which was why, Andy slyly speculated to friends, Hugo was the lover of his friend Halston. When Hugo peed on a canvas, his urine reacted with a chemical compound that had been painted on the canvas, creating a mass of lines and squiggles. That same year, Warhol painted *Shadows*, one of his largest series. These two series—*Oxidations* and *Shadows*—would represent Warhol's only major ventures into abstract art. In 1979, Warhol did *Retrospectives*, each of whose canvases—and again there were several—used a number of images Warhol had made famous in the past as the basis of a sort of retrospective collage. That same year he also silkscreened *Reversals*.

In 1974, Warhol moved the Factory to 860 Broadway; not long after that, he bought for himself a sprawling townhouse located at 57 East

Sixty-sixth Street. He began to go to fashionable restaurants popular with the old-money Upper East Side set. He showed up at benefits and fundraisers, the mainstays of the WASP network in which he was trying to place himself. As he did this, he also wanted to surround himself with the "glamorous people"—celebrities and society figures and the girls and boys of the year. At just the time he was becoming most aware of his social life, a new club called Studio 54 opened in a former soundstage on West Fifty-fourth Street in Manhattan. Studio 54 would come to represent the entire decade of the seventies, a time of sexual liberation, overindulgence, and decadence on an order that had perhaps never been seen in America. There were a handful of public figures whose names would become synonymous with Studio 54—Bianca Jagger, Truman Capote, Liza Minnelli, Halston, as well as the club's two owners, Ian Schrager and Steve Rubell—but there was no celebrity more associated with the club than Andy Warhol.

Warhol had helped make the Dom one of the trendy spots of the sixties, yet even it could not compare to Studio 54. Music pounded through the cavernous main room, loud and thunderous. Despite the club's size, it was always crowded. Rubell often worked the door himself and adhered to a rigorous door policy that admitted, in the club's heyday, only the rich, famous, or beautiful. Drugs were prevalent, especially cocaine and marijuana, and there was a new openness about sexual activity. Almost all of the club's waiters, young men who wore nothing but silk gym shorts, were gay. In fact, Warhol regularly accompanied Rubell downtown to the gay clubs, where Rubell would offer the most attractive young men jobs at Studio 54. "I've been to an awful lot of nightclubs, and this is the best I've ever seen," Capote told *The New York Times* in April 1978. "This is the nightclub of the future. It's very democratic. Boys with boys, girls with girls, girls with boys, blacks and whites, capitalists and Marxists, Chinese with everything else—all one big mix!"

Naturally, Warhol loved the "democratic" attitude about sex. He also was intrigued by the idea that night after night a person could see in the crowd some of the most famous celebrities of the day—Diana Ross,

Elizabeth Taylor, Brooke Shields, Calvin Klein, Jerry Hall, Mick Jagger, Ryan O'Neal, and countless others. Warhol was so fascinated with the club that some weeks he went there almost every night, wandering through the crowd, giving out free copies of *Interview* and working the room. After all, Warhol never knew where his next commissioned portrait would come from, or what potential *Interview* advertiser he might meet standing on the edge of the dance floor.

Rubell and Schrager's indictment for tax evasion arguably marked the end of the decade of the seventies. "January 19, 1979—that's when the disco era ended," says William Avery, a writer and interviewer who often socialized with Warhol at Studio 54. "It was the most exciting place I've ever been to in my entire life. The place was so kinetic. Everybody would be everywhere. And when it closed an era ended. In the eighties everybody started to go to charity balls."

As would have been expected, Warhol went right along with the trend. In addition, even though he himself had not abused drugs in the seventies (during the sixties he had often used speed, but following the shooting he was forced to stop and never had a serious drug problem after that), he watched many of his friends suffer from the fallout of drug abuse. Clubs such as Studio 54 were replaced by more genteel venues like Nell's and Au Bar. Ronald Reagan was in the White House, and a spirit of entrepreneurship-at-any-price seized the country. Warhol embraced this love of capitalism. For some time, he had been interested in accumulating wealth; now he seemed almost possessed by the idea. From the beginning of the decade until the end of his life, Warhol would devote the vast majority of his time and energy—as would Fred Hughes, Vincent Fremont, and others who worked for him—to building his ever-growing empire.

Warhol started the decade by hiring a new painting assistant, Jay Shriver, a devoted young man with a flair for color and composition. Then, the following year, Warhol looked at the old Con Edison building located at 22 East 33rd Street with an eye to buying the whole building. Featuring a full basement and four floors of offices, the building would have more than enough room for the *Interview* staff, the art staff, and the additional people Warhol had working for him. In all, Warhol now had a total of thirty employees on his payroll, plus numerous other people who worked for him on a free-lance basis. As far as Warhol was concerned, the building had just one drawback: With all of its room, it still did not have a space that would be suitable for use as his studio. Even so, Fred liked the building and lobbied Warhol to buy it. Warhol put aside his fear that at nearly two million dollars it was too expensive and bought the building in August 1981. The staff began to plan to move as soon as possible. The old Con Edison building would be Warhol's fourth and final Factory.

In 1980, Warhol had painted *Diamond Dust Shoes* and *Ten Portraits of Jews of the Twentieth Century.* In 1981, he turned out five major series—*Crosses, Dollar Signs, Guns, Knives,* and *Myths.* While most of these paintings had been done at the old Factory at 860 Broadway, some were completed in the Con Edison Factory. In his new space Warhol produced several series over the next few years—*Goethes* and *Stadiums* in 1982, *Renaissance Paintings, Munchs,* and *Rorschachs* in 1984, and *Ads* in 1985—although none of these years compared to 1986. In that one year Warhol produced several substantial series, among them *Camouflages, Campbell's Soup Boxes, Frederick the Greats, Self-Portraits,* and *Cars.* During the second half of the year, he also finished his *Last Supper* paintings and a set of portraits of Lenin. Then, in the first fifty-seven days of 1987, he completed two more series, *Beethovens* and *Rado Watches,* while he started work on what looked to be one of the most ambitious series he had ever attempted, *The History of American TV.* It was as if Warhol knew subconsciously he was approaching the end of his life, and as he did he was overtaken with an all-consuming drive to create as much art as he could before he died.

During the eighties, in consultation with Fred and Vincent, Warhol invested in stocks and bonds, acquired property, and attempted to diversify his media interests—and capitalize on the name Andy Warhol—by starting up various television projects. In 1982, he produced *Andy Warhol's TV,* a cable television series that featured short personality profiles of celebrities like Diana Vreeland and David Hockney. Four years later, he produced *Andy Warhol's Fifteen Minutes*, a series that ran on MTV. He continued to oversee the growth of *Interview* (in 1986 it had a circulation of 180,000, with an annual advertising-page total of 1,177—impressive numbers for a magazine of its kind) even as he published two books, *POPism* (1980) and *America* (1985). At the same time, he appeared in and directed rock videos, signed with the Ford agency to model, and, besides making several commercials, did some guest spots on television shows. Warhol particularly enjoyed his appearance as a guest star on *The Love Boat* in 1985. He was even thinking about getting back into filmmaking, going so far as to buy the film rights to Tama Janowitz's collection of short stories about the Manhattan art world, *Slaves of New York.*

Now in the fourth decade of his career, Warhol began to feel, so he said, as if he were running out of ideas. To help fuel his creative impulse, he became friends with younger artists who were at the beginning of their careers. In particular, he grew close to Keith Haring, Kenny Scharf, Jean-Michel Basquiat, and Francesco Clemente. With Basquiat and Clemente, he even collaborated on a number of paintings.

There may have been another reason why Warhol was making a concerted effort to form friendships with other artists. Despite his fame and success, in many ways Warhol, who was approaching sixty, was a lonely and unhappy man. He seemed unusually discontent with his personal life. In the seventies he had had his only successful serious relationship. One day in the mid-sixties, Jed Johnson, blond with delicate features, made a delivery to the Factory. While he was there, he and Andy struck up a conversation. In no time, Jed and Andy were friends; soon after that, they had become lovers. Jed helped Andy furnish the townhouse on East Sixty-sixth Street when the two of them lived there together, and Andy helped Jed start his own lucrative interior decorating business. But Jed and Andy's relationship ended in 1980. Andy was extremely difficult to live with; he could be so overpowering and possessive that, according to friends, sometimes Jed felt trapped and stifled emotionally. To Andy, the breakup was painful. For the longest time, he wouldn't discuss Jed; he would even go out of his way to avoid him in public. In time, Andy recovered enough to think about becoming involved with someone else. After Jed, he had a relationship with a Paramount Pictures executive in his thirties who was an odd character in his own right. Then Andy had a crush on a boy who was young enough to be his grandson.

They met in the late summer of 1985 at a charity ball in Newport, Rhode Island. Sam Bolton was nineteen; Andy was about to turn fifty-seven. The thirty-eight-year age difference didn't seem to matter much to either of them. They struck up a conversation, and before they knew it they had talked for five hours. Sam was enthralled with Warhol, who had always been one of his heroes; indeed, it had been a dream of Sam's not only to meet Warhol but to work for him. From Andy's perspective, Sam was just the kind of young man he found attractive: blond, rich, boyishly pretty. In their long, free-flowing conversation, Andy did most of the questioning. Sam was amazed that Andy Warhol wanted to know about *his* personal life. So he went on at length, telling Andy what it was like to be raised in Newport the son of Brownie Worburton, a woman who, through her own wealthy mother, was a fixture in East Coast society. Andy made a point of meeting up with Sam the next day. When he did, Sam told him about his dream of working for him. It just so happened, Andy told Sam, that Fred was looking for an assistant.

By September, Sam had moved to New York to start his new job, a position that required him to handle Fred's correspondence and type his letters. To Sam's surprise, Andy hardly said a word to him during those first weeks at the Factory. When they did talk, their conversation consisted more or less of Andy shouting at Sam for forgetting to do something. Then, in October, Andy asked Sam if he would like to go with him that night to a gallery where a show of his was opening. Sam agreed. Later, at the gallery, Andy came up to Sam and started talking to him. "So," Andy said, "are you going to be my favorite?" At the end of the night, Andy had the taxi drop Sam off at Sam's apartment. As Sam got out of the taxi, Andy handed him a hundred-dollar bill. "Take this," Andy said. "Why are you giving me money?" Sam asked. "I *work* for you." Then he rushed inside without taking the money.

Not long afterward, Andy asked Sam to another event—and soon another. Slowly, during the fall of 1985, the two of them began to spend more and more time together. As they got to know each other, Sam understood that, even though he was wealthy and famous, Andy wasn't happy. On rare occasions Andy would talk about Jed. Once, as Andy was opening his wallet, a picture of Jed fell out; Sam thought it was surprising that Andy would be guilty of so sentimental a gesture as keeping the picture of a former boyfriend in his wallet.

Most recently, Andy had had a three-year involvement with Jon Gould, the Paramount executive, who seemed much less interested in Andy than Andy was in him. Theirs had been a turbulent relationship that may in fact have never been physical. Still, Andy must have been deeply taken with Jon; otherwise, why would he have lavished so many gifts—clothes, money, jewelry—on him? Even so, in March 1985, Jon left New York, where he had divided his time between Andy's townhouse and his own Upper West Side apartment, to move to Los Angeles. There, with money he made from selling off some of the expensive gifts Andy had given him, he bought a house in Beverly Hills. Between March and September, Andy and Jon saw each other occasionally, but in September Jon broke off the relationship completely. It was at this time that Sam arrived on the scene at the Factory.

By the end of 1985, Andy and Sam saw each other almost every night. Soon Sam would go to the Factory on Saturdays to help Andy with his painting. Sam also began to schedule the bookings for the commissioned portraits, line up makeup artists, and serve as Andy's photography assistant on the day of the shoot. Finally Andy tried to make his and Sam's friendship more than just platonic. This is how Bolton would describe the sexual tension that became a factor in their relationship: "I didn't want to have a romance. But Andy did. He used to put his hand on my leg and hold hands all the time. I *thought* about having sex with Andy. I remember once in a taxi he did something funny but it was nothing. I never felt uncomfortable with Andy. He was always gentlemanly. But if I had said that I wanted to have an affair I'm sure Andy would have done it. I know it."

By the summer of 1986 Andy was so lonely for companionship that he suggested Sam leave his apartment and move into the townhouse. "Oh, I think you should come here and live with me," Andy would tell Sam late at night when they talked on the telephone. "I can take care of you." Sam would dodge the question or change the subject altogether. "What's wrong?" Andy would ask. "You don't love me anymore?" Soon Sam began to realize that he had no other friend whom he saw as regularly as Andy. By the early fall of 1986, Sam concluded that he wanted to start seeing other people. But when he went out on an occasional night with a friend, Andy would become so jealous that he'd call Sam to check up on him. Finally Sam began lying to Andy about what he was doing. When he started doing this, Andy was sure Sam was having an affair.

Then, later in the fall of 1986, Andy and Sam had a falling out. "I can't stand you," Sam yelled at Andy at one point as they fought on the telephone. "I want you out of my life. I want to end all this." Within the next day or so, Sam complained to Fred, who told Andy that he was much too involved in Sam's private life. Andy got the message. Andy and Sam didn't speak to each other for almost two months. Then, one day, Andy invited him to a party—for no reason, really—and Sam decided to accept the invitation. In time, they were even talking on the telephone again late at night. In retrospect, Sam would be happy that he and Andy made up when they did because it was not too long after that that Andy checked into New York Hospital.

6

IN THE SUMMER OF 1986, ANDY DID NOT APPEAR TO BE A MAN WHO WAS nearing the end of his career; at fifty-eight, he could have lived for another twenty years. At this point in his career, no matter what his motivations, Warhol was astonishingly prolific. Nor was he churning out mediocre work. Some of the canvases—*Self-Portraits* and *Last Suppers*, for instance—were as challenging and innovative as his work from the early sixties. Besides the painting, Warhol was also making significant strides in other areas of his professional life. Vincent was producing—and planning to produce—more television. Andy was confident that he had made excellent investments in stocks, bonds, and real estate. And he was always adding to his hoard of collectibles.

Of all the various aspects of his professional life, only one area caused him concern, and unfortunately it was one that could not be overlooked. For some time now, Andy was having trouble with Fred. The friction between the two of them had started about five years earlier. For fifteen years they had been close friends as well as business associates. If Andy was invited to a dinner or a party, he would always bring Fred along. Even after a long day of work at the Factory they would talk on the phone at night. Andy made no major decision without consulting Fred first. Theirs had been a creative, fruitful partnership for much longer than most partnerships last; yet the closeness they shared, the intensity with which they did business, and the sheer amount of time they had spent together for a decade and a half doubtless contributed to the tension that began to build up between them.

There was, however, another, more fundamental reason for the rift.

For years Fred had stayed out of the spotlight for the good of the Warhol enterprise. He had marketed Andy brilliantly, but as Andy thrived Fred grew tired of his thankless—and often frustrating and demeaning—job, one that may have brought him plenty of money yet no fame or recognition. It was not unusual, friends report, for Fred to be told by a hostess that if Andy could not attend a function, Fred was not invited to come alone.

At first, the strain in their relationship caused them simply to spend less time together. If Andy was going out at night, he merely neglected to include Fred. Meanwhile, Fred began to work harder at developing friendships he made on his own and not through Andy. Over time, he counted among his friends people like Mick Jagger, Jerry Hall, Whitney Tower Jr., Paloma Picasso, and—his closest friend of all—Diana Vreeland.

It was almost to be expected that as Fred worked at creating a more identifiable image for himself Andy became bothered—maybe even threatened—by Fred's independence. In due course, the coolness that had settled over Fred and Andy's relationship turned ugly. They started to have disagreements over business matters and their personal lives. Soon the disagreements became fights. From the early to the mid-eighties, Fred and Andy's relationship deteriorated so drastically that their open dislike for one another was apparent to everyone in the Warhol inner circle.

Andy coped with "the Fred problem"—he had not yet given up on trying to reconcile their differences, though as time passed and their disagreements worsened he started to lose faith that they could—by focusing his attention on his productivity as an artist and on the pursuit of other friendships. By 1986, Andy and Paige Powell had become so close that when he was not out with Sam, he was either with Paige or talking to her on the telephone. Certainly Paige was the most successful advertising director *Interview* had ever had; it seemed that almost every month she was bringing in another major advertising account. Through her contacts in the business world, Paige had also gotten Andy some commissions for work. It was Paige, for example, who was instrumental in convincing Absolut vodka to hire Andy to paint canvases featuring their product, which they then used in an advertising campaign.

Beyond this, Paige had a plan for Andy. She wanted big businesses to commission Warhol to produce corporate art. Andy had been thrilled by Paige's efforts. Not surprisingly, Fred had been threatened by them (or so Paige believed), which was another source of conflict between Fred and Andy and one of the main reasons why Fred developed a strong distaste for Paige. Andy had always pursued the connection between art and commerce, and now Paige seemed to be forging a way for him to exploit that connection, much to Fred's displeasure.

Paige and Andy also had a weekly ritual in what Andy referred to as their "blind dates." One of Paige's best friends was Tama Janowitz, who in the mid-eighties was publishing stories in *The New Yorker* that would make up *Slaves of New York.* Andy grew fond of Tama right away, and before long the three of them were going on a blind date once a week. Only they didn't date each other; they had to find dates for one another. Andy would get a date for Tama, Tama would get one for Paige, and Paige would get one for Andy; the next week they would all shift. On no two nights could anyone bring the same date; and no one could disclose whom he or she had lined up for someone until all six people met at a restaurant. These were Andy's rules. Tama and Paige followed them, even though, as they would later admit, it was sometimes difficult to arrange a date for Andy (it had to be a man, of course) if the date found out he was going to be with Andy Warhol.

Though Andy loved these blind dates with Tama and Paige, a night out to dinner with another friend in late August 1986 disturbed him in ways he could not even discuss. For near the end of this particular evening a seemingly minor event took place that caused Warhol, who was extremely superstitious, to question more consciously the prospects for the rest of his life.

As always, it was crowded at the Odeon on the night in August 1986 that Andy and his party were having dinner at a large table over by the window. Andy was with four casual friends, among them Bernard Jennings and Frank Andrews. Andy had known Frank for about a year and a half—in fact, Bernard had introduced the two of them—and during that time Andy and Frank had often seen each other socially, going out to dinner and then on some nights stopping by a gay bar afterward. They normally went to Rounds, a hustler bar located in the East Fifties, or Cowboys, "a sleazier version of Rounds," as Andrews would remember it. Andy didn't go to gay bars with many friends, but there was another reason why he spent time with Frank. A psychic by profession, Frank was famous for having a client list that included people like John Lennon, Yoko Ono, Perry Ellis, Princess Grace, Madonna, Francesco Scavullo, and the Begum Aga Khan. Actually, it had been Frank's involvement with Lennon and Ono that had led Bernard to introduce him to Andy. Frank owned a set of sixteen lithographs taken by Lennon called *Bag One.* The set had been autographed by Lennon and given to Frank by Ono as a birthday present. Bernard knew that Andy would want to own them, so he proposed that Frank give them to Andy in exchange for a portrait of Frank by Warhol. It would be an even swap. Like Andy, Frank agreed to the deal.

It was this business arrangement that had first brought Andy and Frank together back in late 1984, but because of various commitments Andy did not get around to taking the Polaroids he needed to do Frank's portrait until late March 1986. Finally, in June, Andy was finished with the portrait and they made the trade. Andy and Frank saw each other once or twice between then and this night in August at the Odeon.

In all the time Andy had known Frank Andrews, he had never had a tarot card reading. He was too scared, he told Frank; he didn't want to know if something bad was going to happen. And Frank did have a way of knowing if something bad was going to happen. He had foreseen, for example, the death of Princess Grace. And he had seen John Lennon's death at the hand of a fanatical fan as well. The only fact Frank had gotten wrong was the timing: The shooting took place five years earlier than he'd thought.

Since Andy had never asked for a reading, Frank did not presume to suggest one, especially to someone as superstitious as Andy. But that night at the Odeon, Frank was inexplicably moved to take out a deck of tarot cards from his coat pocket. Then, without looking at the cards, he flipped through the deck until he settled on one card in particular. Slipping it from the deck, he signed it, "To Andy, Love, Frank." Then he slid the card facedown across the top of the table to Andy who picked the card up slowly. It was the Death card. Andy hid the card in his coat pocket without ever saying a word.

In September, Andy got on with his life. He worked at the Factory during the day and went out at night, just as he had done for years. On the night of the thirteenth, he went to see Elton John perform at Madison Square Garden. While he was there, he was approached by a girl who asked him for his autograph. As always, he happily obliged. What struck Andy about the girl, though, was the fact that her boyfriend had thanked him more than once for giving her the autograph. "She's so lucky," Andy told Pat Hackett the next morning. "It's so nice to have someone care about you." No doubt Andy was thinking about boyfriends that night because Jon Gould had been on his mind lately. In Los Angeles Jon had become extremely ill. Andy had heard rumors that Jon had come down with AIDS—full-blown AIDS—something Jon himself would not confirm. The disease had become so bad, Andy was told, that Jon could die at any time. In fact, he did die only four days later, on September 17. When Fred pulled Andy aside at the Factory and told him about Jon's death, Andy didn't do or say anything.

In early November Warhol enjoyed the successful opening of two shows of his work in the same week. On Monday, November 3, the Dia art foundation, an organization originally founded (and funded) by Philippa de Menil, presented his *Hand-Painted Images 1960–62;* four days later, Larry Gagosian opened a show of *Oxidations*—"the piss paintings," as Warhol called them. Following years of being ignored by the art press, many of whom believed Warhol had not done any serious work since the sixties, both shows were prominently—and favorably—reviewed.

December passed quietly, but early in January 1987 Warhol had yet another opening—this time of his sewn photographs, at the Robert

Miller Gallery. The opening was so well attended that Warhol signed autographs until he was exhausted. Again, the show was well reviewed.

Twelve days later, Andy, Fred, and Christopher Makos, a photographer who was a friend of Andy's, flew to Paris on their way to a show of Warhol's *Last Supper* series that was opening in Milan. They stayed in Paris for three days, then flew on to Milan on the twenty-first. Hundreds were expected for Warhol's appearance at the opening; thousands showed up—maybe as many as ten thousand. Indeed, the trip would have been an overwhelming success if it had not been for one ominous development. At the beginning of his stay in Milan, Warhol felt a pain in his right side—a pain that worsened quickly. Andy told everyone that he was probably coming down with the flu, yet he had to know that the cause of his problem was really his gallbladder. By the morning of the twenty-third, he didn't even feel like getting out of bed; he sent for cold medication to help him sleep but instead it kept him awake. The next morning, in pain and tired from lack of sleep, he was anxious to get out of Milan, so he and Chris boarded a plane for New York, leaving Fred behind to do some business.

On the seemingly endless flight to New York, Warhol was so ill he was barely able to sit up in his seat. "And on the plane a milestone happened—I was in *The International Herald Tribune* and I didn't even bother to clip the article," Warhol would tell Pat Hackett. "I just—didn't care." On the ground in New York he was no better. He even forgot to get a receipt from the limousine driver for the ride from the airport to his house—a seventy-dollar fare. As he told Pat, "I really wasn't feeling well."

Over the next few days, as mysteriously as it had appeared, the pain went away, and Warhol got back to work. He had to. February looked to be a busy month.

Andy still had not recovered completely from his trip to Milan—he was tired, worn out, and occasionally in a bad mood—when in early February Ingrid Superstar, one of Warhol's superstars from the sixties, went missing in upstate New York, where she had been living for several years.

Andy had not remained close to any of his superstars in the seventies or the eighties. Occasionally he saw Viva or Ultra Violet at an event in the city; if she was in New York, Nico would drop by the Factory, although Andy didn't necessarily look forward to seeing her because she always asked him for money to buy drugs. He had no patience for people he considered to be wasting their lives, and he now regarded many of his friends from the sixties in just this way. However, out of all of the superstars, he still had good feelings for Ingrid. So he read with more than passing interest the article in the *New York Post* headlined WARHOL STAR VANISHES. Ingrid had gone out for a pack of cigarettes, the article said, and no one had seen her since. "Brigid never told me they called about her," Andy told Pat Hackett in their diary session for February 4. "I would've cared that *Ingrid* was missing." The disappearance of Ingrid Superstar was an odd, unsettling omen.

The next night Andy had made plans with Sam and a few other friends to have dinner at Nippon and then see *Outrageous Fortune,* Bette Midler's new comedy. The dinner was pleasant and relaxing, but as they were leaving the restaurant Warhol felt a sharp, penetrating pain in his right side, precisely in the area of his gallbladder. "I got scared and said I couldn't go and they dropped me off," Warhol told Hackett the next morning. "I was trying to think positively and mind-over-matter and when I got to my front door it was like a miracle, it suddenly went away. It was completely gone. And then I wished I'd hung on for a few minutes because then I wouldn't have had to tell anybody something was wrong."

For the next week or so, Warhol resumed his usual schedule. He was still spending time with Paige, who made working at the Factory bearable for Andy even though he and Fred had reached the point where they fought openly over nearly every sort of dealing they had to have with one another. "Fred would get into these vicious cat fights with Andy in Fred's office," Sam Bolton remembers. "They fought a lot over *Interview.* Fred wanted to get rid of Christopher Makos's column because it was too gay. It was nothing but muscle boys, Fred said." Fred also wanted to fire Gael Love, *Interview*'s editor, and Andy didn't. Fred wanted to use someone besides Richard Bernstein to create the covers, and Andy didn't. In fact, Fred wanted to change the direction of the magazine, and Andy didn't.

Nor was Andy particularly happy with the way Fred had been conducting his private life. Fred was drinking a lot lately. From the stories Andy had heard, Fred was having more and more trouble controlling himself. One night at Nell's Fred had gotten drunk, dropped his pants, and climbed up on top of his table in the middle of the crowded club. He had to write a letter to Nell apologizing for his behavior before he felt comfortable enough to go back. Andy was told that on another night Fred had gotten drunk at Area, unzipped his pants, and stood in a public hallway with his penis hanging out until he was asked to leave. Andy had reached the point of exasperation with Fred where he didn't know what to do. They were like an old married couple: All they did was fight, but neither one could force himself to make the first move to end the partnership.

On February 12, 1987, Andy hosted a Valentine's Day dinner for thirty of his friends. The guest list included Mariel Hemingway, Michel Roux, Victor Love, Heather Watts, Kenny Scharf, Richard Johnson, and Denton Cox, whom Andy often saw socially but whom he had not visited professionally since May 1984. That night, as he normally did, Andy chatted at length with Doc Cox (the nickname he had given him). In their conversation Andy never brought up his health. "I've been bad—I've been eating chocolate and butter" was the closest he came.

The next day, Friday the thirteenth, Andy went to work at the Factory. During the day his right side started to hurt, especially when he began to work out with his personal trainer. Indeed, the trainer called off the exercise session, saying they would resume on Monday. At one point in the afternoon, Brigid stopped by Andy's studio and ate either a cake (as Andy remembered the incident) or a box of chocolates (as she remembered it) and announced that she was leaving for a week to go to a fat farm in London. Andy didn't believe her, but he didn't make an issue of it, nor would he join in her binge. "I've got a bad pain," he said, and Brigid knew exactly what he was talking about. She had had her own gallbladder removed years ago and had told Andy over and over to have his taken care of.

Not much else happened on Friday the thirteenth. Besides his encounter with Brigid, Andy's day involved a lunch at the Factory for the new president of Henri Bendel's and work on a commissioned portrait in the afternoon. That evening, Andy had dinner at eight o'clock with friends at Castellano's—Andy ate manicotti—and later went to a birthday party for Barry Tubb at Raoul's. Andy got home at a little after one o'clock in the morning.

"A really short day," Andy told Pat Hackett for his diary entry on Saturday, February 14. "Nothing much happened. I went shopping, did errands, came home, talked on the phone. . . . Yeah, that's all. Really. It was a short day."

The entry wasn't even remotely accurate.

When Andy woke up on Saturday morning, the pain in his right side had gotten considerably worse. Andy decided not to call Denton Cox, even though he had seen him only two nights before at the Valentine's Day party. Instead he talked to Karen Burke, his dermatologist. He had been seeing her for some time now to get collagen injections to help fill in the wrinkles that had begun to creep into his face; he happened to have an appointment with her this Saturday. Andy described the severe pain he was feeling in his right side—he was sure, he said, that the manicotti he had eaten for dinner the night before had aggravated his gallbladder condition—and asked Dr. Burke to prescribe some Demerol. Burke said she would give him Tylenol with codeine instead, but first she wanted him to go to Dr. Clement Barone for a sonogram of his right side. Andy went, although he also took two Demerol he happened to have with him. After Barone did the sonogram, he called Burke with the results: Warhol's gallbladder was enlarged because it contained two stones. Burke prescribed the Tylenol, then stressed to Andy that he should call Cox. Andy took the Tylenol and went to bed. He did not call Cox.

On Sunday Andy stayed in bed all day, watching television and talking with friends on the telephone. He didn't even bother to go to Mass, the first time he had missed church in months. He just wanted to rest all day so that he might feel better by Monday. But on Monday morning Andy was feeling even worse. He called the Factory and canceled his appointments for the day; he also canceled his exercise sessions for the entire week. Then Ken Leland, his new "bodyguard," arrived and the two of them took a taxi to the Chiropractic Healing Arts Center on the Upper West Side, where Dr. Linda Li practiced. Andy had been going to Dr. Li for shiatsu massage. Today he was having pain on his right side; she dug into that area with her fingertips and the balls of her hands in an effort to break up the pain. But at some point during the massage another pain, a *new* pain, shot through the right part of Andy's abdomen, up his right side, and down his right shoulder. It was not a dull, aching pain, like the one he had been having, but a sharp, acute one. Disoriented and hurting, Andy left Linda Li's and went to the Factory, where he saw Julian Schnabel and learned that Brigid had not shown up for work. Apparently she *had* gone to the fat farm in London after all.

On Monday night, Andy was feeling so bad that he stayed in bed, took enough medication to help him go to sleep, and slept through the night until the next morning. When he woke up, he felt no better. He wanted to stay in bed all day, but the Ford agency had scheduled him to appear as a model in a fashion show that afternoon at the Tunnel, a club that had recently opened. He and Miles Davis were supposed to model a new line of clothes by Aarston Valaja and Koshin Satoh, the Japanese designers. So, after stopping by the Factory, where, as he recorded in his diary, he "worked hard," he went to the Tunnel with Stuart Pivar. An enormous building near the West Side docks, the club was extremely cold. "Andy stood in a cold dressing room for hours, waiting to model," Pivar later told a journalist. "He was in terrible pain. You could see it on his face." Andy didn't talk about it, though; he just wanted to get out on the catwalk and model. Finally the fashion show began. Andy hated the clothes, because they were all "alligator, fur, and lace," but he enjoyed the modeling and hammed it up. In the show's finale, he and Miles Davis strutted down the catwalk together, with Andy following after Miles holding up the tails of Miles's long coat. The crowd loved it. The audience was still applauding when Andy darted offstage and frantically approached Stuart, who was standing in the wings. "Stuart, help," Andy said, his voice now brittle with pain and fear. "Get me out of here. I feel like I'm gonna die."

That night, Andy was in such pain that he canceled his dinner plans and went to bed. Eventually the telephone stopped ringing and he fell asleep. "But," he would report to his diary, "I woke up at 6:30 and I couldn't get back to sleep, so I took some Valium and a Seconal and two aspirin, and I was sleeping so heavily that I didn't wake up when PH called at nine. And when I didn't answer she got scared because that had never happened before, so she called on the other line and Aurora"—she and her twin sister, Nena, were Andy's housekeepers—"answered in the kitchen, and PH made her come up to my bedroom and shake me but I wish she had just let me sleep."

Awake now, Andy had to confront the fact that the pain in his right side had still not gone away. Sick and frustrated, he finally called Cox. That same morning Cox had gotten a call from Karen Burke, who had spoken with Andy on Monday night only to learn that his condition had not improved. She told Andy to telephone Cox but had contacted Cox herself on Wednesday morning to make sure he was aware of Andy's illness. As a result Cox knew some of the details, though he had Andy describe his condition to him anyway. Cox instructed Andy to come in at once. With Leland as his escort, Andy got to Cox's office, located around the corner from Sotheby's on Seventy-second Street, in the early afternoon. Following a brief discussion, Cox gave Andy a complete physical examination—which included a rectal exam, an EKG, and a comprehensive blood workup—and a systems analysis. When he was finished, Cox wrote the following in Warhol's chart: "RUQ [right upper quadrant] pain up to the right clavicle. Pain remains in RUQ. No tenderness to patient pressure. Temperature to 100 degrees three weeks ago. Went down to normal. Temperature to 100 degrees on February

15 and since in the PM. Temperature 98.6 in the morning, 100 degrees in the PM. No appetite. Bowel movements with enemas for four years, rarely spontaneously. Last spontaneous bowel movement four days ago. Enema with results yesterday. The stool was brown." Besides the gall-bladder condition, Andy was also somewhat dehydrated and under-weight, Cox noted, weighing just 128 pounds. But Cox did not have the option of trying to increase Warhol's weight. His gallbladder was now so inflamed and swollen that it had to be treated at once.

Following the physical, Cox took Andy into his office and told him what, on some level at least, Andy knew already: Andy had an infected gallbladder—a result of the two gallstones—and needed to have it removed immediately.

"Denny," Andy said, "I'm not afraid of death. But I will not go into the hospital. You *must* help me. You're the only one who can—the only one I can trust. I will do anything else you say."

"You must have an operation," Cox said sternly. "There is no way to cure you without an operation."

Cox prescribed 500-milligram Augmentin capsules to be taken every four hours—an extremely powerful form of antibiotic therapy—and put Warhol on a clear liquid diet. "Since you won't go into the hospital," Cox continued, "I want you to see Dr. Thorbjarnarson."

"I will do anything you say," Andy reiterated, "except I won't go to the hospital."

While Andy was sitting in Cox's office, Cox picked up the telephone and called Dr. Bjorn Thorbjarnarson. Cox told him he wanted him to see a patient of his immediately if possible, which Thorbjarnarson agreed to do.

Still accompanied by Leland, Andy went from Cox's office to Thorbjar-narson's. He had with him a copy of his 1968 records from Columbus Hospital (by then defunct), which Cox had supplied, as well as a copy of the sonogram of his gallbladder, which Dr. Barone's office had sent to Cox. In Thorbjarnarson's office, Andy was met by a secretary, who filled out Andy's data sheet for him. She did not seem to doubt him when, giving her the year of his birth, he took ten years off his age. Andy next went to Thorbjarnarson's inner office and, once he had performed his own physical examination of Andy and studied the Barone sonogram, Thorbjarnarson told Andy he agreed with Cox. The gallbladder was infected, probably severely; it needed to be taken out right away. But wasn't there *any* alternative means of treatment other than surgery? Andy wanted to know. No, Thorbjarnarson said; surgery was the only solution.

Even with the opinion of one of the world's leading experts on gastrointestinal surgery, Andy refused to check into the hospital. As soon as he knew Andy's position, Thorbjarnarson called Cox. "I have told Mr. Warhol that this is what is wrong with him," Thorbjarnarson said, "but he refuses to go into the hospital." Taking the phone from Thorbjarnarson, Andy listened to Cox, who suggested that Andy not only see Dr. Michael Schmerin the next day for a third opinion but also have a second sonogram. Andy said he would take both of Cox's suggestions, as long as he didn't have to go into a hospital. Cox had Andy give the phone back to Thorbjarnarson. Speaking briefly, Cox and Thorbjarnarson agreed that there was nothing else they could do. When Warhol left the office, Thorbjarnarson assumed, judging from the extent to which he seemed to have made up his mind, that he would never hear from Andy again.

After his visit to Thorbjarnarson, Andy went home, started taking the antibiotics Cox prescribed, and put himself on the liquid diet. That night he had trouble sleeping, so around two o'clock in the morning he called Paige Powell. Earlier in the day, Paige had thought it was unusual that Andy hadn't shown up for a scheduled luncheon at the Factory. She had had an instinctive feeling that Andy was very sick. On a hunch she'd called Cox's office. When Paige asked the receptionist if Andy was there, the woman told her that he had been but had left several hours ago. Now, as Paige and Andy talked on the phone, every time she brought up his health Andy changed the subject. Still, Paige could tell that he wasn't well. He was breathing heavily, sometimes almost gasping for breath, and more than once he mentioned that he was eating Jell-O while they spoke.

The next morning, Cox called Andy at about nine o'clock to make sure he was going to see Dr. Schmerin and have a second sonogram. Andy reassured him that he was. At Dr. Schmerin's, Andy went through a procedure with which he was becoming familiar: conversation, examination, diagnosis. As both Thorbjarnarson and Cox had done, Schmerin told Andy that he needed to have his infected gallbladder removed—the sooner the better. Andy then went back to Cox, who performed another physical, told him the diagnosis remained the same, and sent him for the second sonogram.

That afternoon, when Cox got the results of the sonogram, he was alarmed: Andy's condition was significantly worse, because one of the stones now was lodged up in the neck of the gallbladder. While Linda Li would later insist that she had performed only a "gentle abdominal manipulation" on Andy, Cox believed that, gentle or not, the manipulation had shoved one of the stones deep into the gallbladder's neck. This was possible because Andy's abdominal wall was unusually thin, due to the hernia that resulted from his shooting and subsequent surgery. Cox called Andy at home and told him the bad news. No matter how many rounds of antibiotics he took, no matter how many different forms of alternative medicines he tried, Andy had no choice but to have the gallbladder removed. What's more, if he did not, the gallbladder would eventually rupture—perhaps very soon—and spill poisonous infection throughout his abdominal region. "I told him of the absolute imperativeness of his being admitted to the hospital and that surgery was emergent, needed, and necessary," Cox later said. "The gallbladder was enlarging rapidly and thickening and in danger of bursting." If that happened, Andy would be in extreme danger of dying, possibly even before an ambulance could rush him to a hospital. Though he was now in a life-threatening situation, Andy still would not agree to check into the hospital. He wanted to think about his dilemma one more night.

Why was Warhol doing this? What paralyzing fear could have forced him to delay taking care of a problem that had been in existence since at least April 1973? Why would he insist to one friend after another that if he checked into a hospital he would never come out alive?

7

MONDAY, JUNE 3, 1968, WAS AN UNBEARABLY HOT DAY IN NEW YORK CITY, much hotter than it usually was so early in the summer. Outside, the heavy air was thick with heat. Just moving from place to place in the city was exhausting, almost not worth the effort. Over the last several years, Andy had never been in a hurry to get to the Factory in the morning since nothing really started happening there until the afternoon. Today, because of the sweltering heat, he had an even better reason to waste away the morning at his house, where he was certainly a lot cooler than he would have been in the un-air-conditioned Factory. Andy spent a good part of the morning talking on the telephone to Fred, who was upset because the night before, as he was walking home from Max's Kansas City, he had been mugged by three black teenage boys in front of his apartment building on East Sixteenth Street, just across from the Factory on Union Square West. They had stolen his wallet and a watch that his grandmother had given to him, which could never be replaced. Still, it was out of character for Fred, always one to look on life's bright side, to be as depressed as he was this morning. He hadn't even gone into the Factory yet, and it was already well past mid-morning. Andy couldn't remember the last time Fred had not been at the Factory by nine, no matter how late he had been out the night before. So Andy tried to cheer him up.

Next he spoke with Ultra Violet, who filled him in on the gossip about the shooting of *Midnight Cowboy*, the John Schlesinger film in which she and Viva had been given small parts. Ultra also talked about Valerie Solanis, a woman Andy had met for the first time a year ago, right around the time he was filming *The Chelsea Girls*. Solanis had called the Factory one day to tell Andy about a film script she'd written entitled *Up Your Ass*. Intrigued by the title, Andy asked Valerie to bring him the script. It was not until later that he learned Solanis was a radical feminist who had established an organization called the Society for Cutting Up Men (SCUM). The organization even had a manifesto, which Solanis herself had written. Andy flipped through the script for *Up Your Ass*. At once he saw that it was too pornographic for him to shoot. In fact, the script was so lurid that as Valerie watched him glance through it he was trying to decide whether she was an undercover police officer who somehow was trying to entrap him.

That first day, Andy kept *Up Your Ass*. Then, over the next few days, he must have lost it, for he couldn't locate it when Valerie called sometime later to ask for the script back. Finally he told her that someone must have thrown it away. Furious, Valerie accused Andy of lying to her so he could steal the story and use it himself. Before long, she started calling up and asking Andy for money to pay her rent at the Chelsea Hotel. To give her some money, Andy cast her in a small part in *I, a Man*; she received twenty-five dollars for her work. Eventually, Valerie stopped bothering him about the script, and Andy decided that the saga of *Up Your Ass* had ended.

By the spring of 1968, Andy had all but forgotten about Solanis. Lately, though, Valerie had started calling the Factory again. Now Ultra told Andy she was concerned about Valerie and this new round of phone calls. Andy should read what she said in her SCUM manifesto, Ultra said. "Here's something about men," Ultra said, reading from the manifesto. " 'The male's by his very nature a leech, an emotional parasite, and, therefore, isn't ethically entitled to both live and prosper.' " Maybe she was nuts. Shouldn't Andy be at least a little worried? Ultra wanted to know. Andy didn't comment; instead he just laughed.

After his morning on the telephone in his cool, dark bedroom, Andy finally dressed for the day in black jeans, a black T-shirt, and black boots. He ate a quick lunch and left his house to run some errands. He stopped by to see Sy Litvinoff, an attorney. He picked up a renewal for a prescription of Obetrol at his doctor's office. He browsed in Bloomingdale's for a few minutes. The last stop he made was in the East Fifties at the home of his friend Miles White, a fashion designer. Miles wasn't home, so Andy hailed a taxi to the Factory.

He got out of the cab on Union Square—it was now four-fifteen—and saw Jed coming down the street carrying an armful of fluorescent lightbulbs. At the same time, Andy saw Valerie Solanis, who, though he did not know it, had come by the Factory at around two-thirty, had been told by Paul Morrissey that Andy was not in, and had decided to wait outside the building on the sidewalk until he showed up. Andy and Valerie and Jed took the elevator together to the sixth floor. As they rode up, Andy looked Valerie over and noticed that there was something odd about her this afternoon. Even though it was oppressively hot, she was dressed in pants, a turtleneck sweater, and a heavy winter coat. She also carried a brown paper bag in one hand. But neither the outfit nor the paper bag was what Andy decided was truly out of character for Valerie. It was this: Today Valerie had on lipstick and eye makeup. It was as if she had made herself up for a special occasion, like having her picture taken.

Upstairs, when the three of them stepped out of the elevator into the Factory, Andy saw that Mario Amaya, a well-known art critic and an old friend, had stopped by for a visit. Amaya was standing on the other side of the Factory's main room between two large desks. As Andy started across the room toward Mario, he remembered that he had had a meeting scheduled with him to talk about an upcoming retrospective of his work in London. Andy also saw that Fred had finally come in; he was sitting at his desk doing paperwork. At the other of the two large desks, Paul was sitting nonchalantly, talking on the telephone. Even with all of the windows wide open, the temperature in the Factory was still insufferably hot. It didn't help matters that today there was no wind at all, not even a breeze.

No sooner had Andy reached the two desks than Paul handed him the telephone receiver. "It's Viva," he said, then got up to go to the bathroom down the hall. Jed headed for Andy's office to start changing the lightbulbs. Meanwhile, Valerie had followed Andy over to the desks. As she stood there, Fred looked up from his work long enough to acknowledge Valerie's presence with a snide remark. "You still writing those dirty books?" he said. Valerie didn't bother to answer, and Fred returned to his work. On the phone Andy listened to Viva ramble on endlessly about having her hair colored for her part in *Midnight Cowboy*. Actually, he wasn't listening very carefully—only about as much as he normally did when he was on the phone with someone like Viva. Mostly he just said "Yeah" and "Ummm" and "Oh" while Viva went on and on with her story. Finally, so bored that he didn't even want to pretend to listen, Andy motioned for Fred to pick up the telephone and take over the conversation.

It was at the precise moment that Fred was lifting his receiver and Andy was lowering his to its cradle that Andy heard a sharp *pop*. On the other end of the line, Viva thought that someone had started fooling around with one of the bullwhips left over from the Exploding Plastic Inevitable. Fred thought that the Communists—the American Communist party rented space two floors above the Factory—had finally had their offices bombed. Mario Amaya thought that they were being shot at by snipers, a problem in New York that summer. Andy wasn't so naive. He knew where the *pop* came from. He whirled around to look at Valerie, who was pointing a gun—a .32-caliber revolver—at the ceiling. Then, as Andy stood there watching her, Valerie lowered her arm until she was pointing the barrel of the revolver right at him.

"No! No, Valerie!" Andy shouted. "Don't do it!"

It did no good. Valerie pulled the trigger again. *Pop*. The second bullet either grazed him or missed him completely. Even so, Andy dropped to the floor and started to crawl toward the desks. Before he reached it, Valerie rushed closer and stood right over him. Now, at point-blank range, she fired the gun again. *Pop.* This time she didn't miss. While Valerie stood above him, Andy felt, as he would later remember, "horrible, horrible pain, like a cherry bomb exploding inside me." The bullet had entered on the right side of his body and come out on the left side of his back. In between, it had zigzagged through the midsection of his torso, tearing into six major organs—the esophagus, the liver, the spleen, the stomach, and both lungs. On the wooden floor of the Factory, Andy writhed in pain, blood gushing from his wounds.

It would be hard to determine whether or not Valerie thought Andy was dead. If she had intended to kill him, she must have believed that she *had*, because she next turned her attention to the other people in the Factory. When she looked up from Andy, the first person she saw was Mario Amaya, who had dropped to the floor. Valerie fired at him—*pop*—but missed. Then she fired again—*pop*. Fortunately for Mario, her aim was not very good, and the bullet only nicked his hip. He wasn't even aware that he had been hit when he got up from the floor, rushed to the back of the main room, and disappeared through a set of double doors. In the hallway he met up with Paul, coming from the bathroom, who had no idea of what was going on. "Valerie shot Andy!" Mario said, barely able to control his emotions. "She shot Andy!" Shocked, Paul ran to the projection room, where he could look out into the main room and see what was happening. In the meantime, Mario held the doors shut to keep Valerie from coming after him.

By now, Jed was also hiding—in Andy's office. He had slammed the door and, because the doorknob was broken, pressed his weight against the door to keep Valerie from entering the office. Jed was lucky. After Mario ran out of the room, Valerie went over to the office door, but she couldn't budge it. Standing in the office, Jed watched while the broken knob turned around and around.

Finally, Valerie remembered Fred, who had left his desk to go stand near the elevator. Slowly she walked up to Fred and pointed the gun at him. When she did, Fred said sternly in his most authoritative voice, "*Please!* Don't shoot me! Just leave!" Valerie seemed startled by his tone of voice. Disoriented, she pushed the button for the elevator; then she turned her attention back to Fred, once again pointing the gun at him. She seemed to freeze. Valerie had Fred dead in her sights. If she pulled the trigger, she could not have missed. She probably could have killed him with one shot. But something kept her from pulling the trigger. Finally the elevator arrived and the doors slid open. "There's the elevator!" Fred said, his voice clear and bold. "Just *take* it!" And for reasons that would never be clear to anyone, least of all Fred, Valerie turned, walked into the empty elevator, and pushed the button for the first floor. As she was leaving, Fred noticed that she was still carrying a paper bag. Later, he learned that in the bag Valerie had a second revolver and a Kotex.

Suddenly the room was quiet. Fred rushed over to Andy, who was lying on the floor in a pool of blood. He kneeled down and started to give Andy mouth-to-mouth resuscitation, but Andy made him stop because it hurt too much. So Fred scrambled to his feet, grabbed the telephone, and called for an ambulance. As he did, Paul and Mario emerged from the back hallway and went over to Andy, who was in such pain that he had started to laugh. Viva had listened to the whole episode on the other end of the telephone; now she called back to see why Andy had stopped talking to her. Jed answered the phone. Almost shouting, he told Viva, "Andy's been shot."

In the darkroom, Billy Name had heard the shots. He ran into the main room of the Factory. When he got to Andy's side, he couldn't believe what he saw. Andy's entire midsection was covered in blood as the puddle in which he lay grew larger. Andy was still laughing, but he was starting to lose consciousness. One of the last images he remembered of the Factory that day was Billy Name hovering over him. At first, he thought Billy was laughing too. Then he realized that Billy wasn't laughing at all. He was crying.

To those at the Factory, it seemed like the ambulance would never arrive. As they waited, all they could do was watch Andy while he lay on the floor and bled. Finally, when the ambulance got there at 4:35, the two attendants did not bring up a stretcher on which to carry Andy out; they had, of all things, a wheelchair. The attendants weren't even so sure they should bother rushing Andy to the hospital: He didn't look like he was going to make it. Still, they lifted him up off the floor and sat him in the wheelchair. "I thought that the pain I'd felt lying on the floor was the worst you could ever feel," Andy later said, "but now that I was in a sitting position, I knew it wasn't." With him propped up in the chair, the attendants took Andy down as his entourage followed after. It was not until they had all reached the street that Mario finally realized he had been shot. When he did, he got in the ambulance with Andy. Abruptly the ambulance lunged forward. Then the driver looked back at Mario and said, "If we sound the siren, it'll cost five dollars extra." To this, Mario replied, "Go ahead and sound it. Leo Castelli will pay."

The ambulance took Andy to Columbus Hospital, located on Nineteenth Street near Third Avenue. At 4:45 the ambulance arrived at the emergency room entrance and Andy was taken directly into the operating room. A team of doctors, headed by Giuseppe Rossi, examined him. His pulse was faint, his vital signs failing. Mario, who had been wheeled into the same operating room as Andy, heard the doctors talking. "Forget it," one doctor said. "No chance," another one added. At last, Mario spoke up. "Don't you know who this is?" he blurted out. "It's Andy Warhol! He's famous. And he's rich. He can afford to pay for an operation. For Christ's sake, do something!"

Finally the doctors decided to operate on him even though at 4:51, only six minutes after he had arrived at the hospital, Andy was pronounced "clinically dead." Rossi cut open Andy's chest and started to massage his heart. When he got a heartbeat, he and four other doctors began the operation. It lasted more than five hours. During that time, they removed his spleen, cut off the bottom part of his right lung, and tried to repair the damage the bullet had done to his vital organs. When they closed him up, Andy's best odds of survival were fifty-fifty. Sometime later, Rossi wrote up his diagnosis. "This patient was brought to the emergency room via ambulance and at the time of admission was without blood pressure and heartbeat," Rossi stated. "He had a gunshot

wound entering the left chest at the midaxillary line at the ninth interspace and exiting in the right chest, midaxillary line at the fourth
interspace. He was in deep shock and there was profuse bleeding from
the right chest wound. . . . The patient was immediately intubated and
via a venous cutdown a large amount of Ringer's lactate solution was
injected with no visible effects on blood pressure and other vital signs.
He was taken to the operating room and exploration of the right chest,
left chest and abdomen was carried out with control of bleeding and
evacuation of blood volume."

Around seven o'clock, while Andy was lying on the operating table,
Valerie Solanis walked up to a rookie police officer named William
Shemalix in Times Square and turned herself in. "I'm a flower child,"
she told the officer, handing him her gun. "The police are looking for
me. They want me. He had too much control over my life." Shemalix
arrested Solanis and took her to the 13th Precinct, where the police
released Fred and Jed, who, up until the time Valerie confessed, actually
had been suspects in the shooting. "I have a lot of very involved reasons,"
Solanis told the police. "Read my manifesto, and it will tell you what
I am."

The next day, as Andy was lying in his bed, he could hear a television
set playing off in the distance. Through his haze of morphine and other
painkillers, he could only make out a word here and there while the
announcer was talking: "Kennedy . . . assassin . . . shot." At first, in this
dreamlike state, Andy thought that for some reason he was reliving the
assassination of President Kennedy. Then he noticed that the nurses
around him were crying. It was at this point he realized that there had
been a second Kennedy assassination—that Robert Kennedy had been
shot.

In its way the Warhol shooting was just another instance in a national
pattern of violence in 1968 that also included the murder of Martin
Luther King, Jr. On June 4, six years to the day after the New York
Daily News ran the banner headline 129 DIE IN JET—the inspiration for his
Death and Disaster series—the same newspaper put Warhol himself on its

cover. ACTRESS SHOOTS ANDY WARHOL, the headline read. (The late edition would offer Solanis's correction: "I'm a writer, not an actress.") The *New York Post* rivaled the *Daily News* with its own front-page headline, ANDY WARHOL FIGHTS FOR LIFE. But the next day the Kennedy story took the front pages away from Warhol, a fact Andy deeply regretted. After all, what were the odds of Andy's shooting being overshadowed by another Kennedy assassination?

Andy stayed in the hospital for two months. Early on, he was visited by few people other than his mother and Jed. Eventually he started calling friends from his hospital room. One of the first he contacted was David Bourdon. "For days after the operation, his existence teetered between survival and the void," Bourdon would one day say. "I called the hospital every morning to inquire whether he had made it through the night. A couple of weeks later, when he telephoned me from his hospital bed, I was so startled and overcome with joy that I collapsed in a fit of choking sobs, and it was he who had to comfort me. In a voice that sounded weaker than ripping facial tissue, he lamented that the attempted assassination had not been recorded on film. 'If only she had done it while the camera was on!' "

8

ON THE MORNING OF FRIDAY, FEBRUARY 20, 1987, ANDY WARHOL FINALLY decided that he had no choice but to have his gallbladder taken out. He called Denton Cox and told him he was ready to go into the hospital. Relieved, Cox instructed Andy to proceed to New York Hospital and check in. Cox would call Thorbjarnarson. The surgery would take place on Saturday morning; Thorbjarnarson felt Warhol needed to be rehydrated before he could be operated on. Saturday was not a preferred day for surgery—hospitals are always short-staffed on weekends—but Andy didn't have any choice. If they waited the weekend, the gallbladder might rupture.

While Cox was taking care of the medical arrangements, Andy disposed of his own last-minute business. He called Stuart Pivar and told him that he would not be able to fulfill a commitment he had made to serve as a model that day at the New York Academy of Art, on whose board of directors Stuart served. (A couple of years back, Stuart had even talked Andy into joining the board, the only art board on which Warhol served.) When Stuart found out why Andy was canceling, he told him he would send his limousine over to pick him up, so at least Andy wouldn't have to take a taxi to the hospital.

While Andy waited for the limousine to arrive, he started rummaging through his jewelry and money, stuffing as many valuables and as much cash into his safe as it would hold. When Ken Leland reported for work at ten o'clock, Andy had him wait downstairs while he continued to hide his belongings wherever he could put them—in drawers, in closets, under his mattress. In the middle of all of this frantic activity, Paige Powell called to ask if Andy was going to make it to the Factory for his lunch with the Fendi sisters. Andy told her he wouldn't be able to. She asked him why, but he wouldn't tell her. With this, Paige said that she would send up some *Interviews* for him to sign instead. "How about the ballet tickets?" Paige asked Andy—she had a pair for Sunday night. "Don't cancel," Andy said, before he hung up the telephone.

Around this time, Sam also called. Fred, whom Andy had finally apprised of his condition, had told Sam that Andy was going into the hospital, so Sam called to wish Andy luck. He also mentioned that he was going to visit his father in New Hampshire for the weekend. When the limousine arrived, Ken shouted up to Andy to tell him that the car was waiting outside. Andy was still rushing from room to room, hiding valuables. Eventually Andy had hidden away as much of his jewelry and money as he could, so he was ready to go. At the front door on his way out, Nena and Aurora said goodbye, which was unusual since they never told Andy goodbye when he was leaving for the day. This morning, of course, was different: Andy was going into the hospital.

Outside, as he descended the steps, Andy made the comment to Ken that once the weather had warmed up he was going to get the broken gate fixed.

They got to the hospital around eleven. After being put through various admission procedures, Andy finally checked into his room at three-fifteen in the afternoon. During the first hour in his room, Andy changed into his pajamas, but because he was cold he wore his black leather jacket in bed. Andy was annoyed that the television in his room did not have a good picture; he was barely able to make out what was happening on *Divorce Court*. At one point, Andy told Ken to go downstairs to a newsstand and buy him the *New York Post*, the *Daily News*, *TV Guide*, and the *National Enquirer*.

Hospital personnel stopped by. A nurse connected Andy to an IV drip; an intern stayed long enough to examine him; and Thorbjarnarson came in, along with another doctor, Michael Canning, to see how Andy was feeling.

"Are you feeling worse?" Thorbjarnarson asked after he had examined the right side of Andy's abdomen.

"Yes," Andy said.

"You have decided what recommendations to follow?" Thorbjarnarson asked.

"Yes," Andy answered.

"We are planning to do surgery on you tomorrow morning?"

"Yes," Andy replied.

An hour or so later, at six o'clock, Denton Cox arrived in Andy's room and, combining a physical examination with a chat, ended up staying for forty-five minutes. In general, Andy's condition had not changed since Cox had seen him in his office the day before. From all indications, Andy appeared to be ready for surgery the next morning. As Cox was leaving, he ran into Vincent Fremont, who was coming to visit Andy. When Cox saw Vincent, he reminded him of a conversation they had had on the telephone earlier in the day. Because Andy was going in for major surgery, Cox had wanted Vincent to arrange for Andy to have a private-duty nurse around the clock, starting at eight o'clock on Saturday morning. The hospital did not supply such nurses but referred the patient to a registry service that arranged for the nurses' employment. The patient hired the nurses and paid them directly; they then reimbursed the registry a small percentage of their wages as a commission. In their short exchange, Vincent told Cox not to worry about the private-duty nurse. He had already taken care of the situation.

After Vincent left, little else happened for the rest of the night. Doctors and nurses came and went. At some time, Andy called Paige and asked her to run some errands for him on Saturday. He still didn't mention that he was in the hospital.

Andy was awakened early on the morning of the twenty-first. After being prepped in his room, at eight o'clock he was taken down on a gurney to the waiting area outside the operating room. He remained there for forty-five minutes. During that time, various nurses and doctors, among them Thorbjarnarson, stopped by to see how he was doing now that the sedative he had been given was in full effect. Then at eight forty-five he was wheeled into the operating room—room K—where the anesthesiologist, Michael T. Tjeuw, placed the mask over his mouth and turned on the gas. Andy went under right away. Starting at nine o'clock and continuing for the next three hours and ten minutes, Thorbjarnarson, along with Paul Halebian and Michael Canning, the two doctors who were assisting him, operated on Andy. First, Thorbjarnarson, with the help of Halebian, took out Andy's gallbladder, which they determined was gangrenous as soon as they saw it. At the rate the gallbladder was deteriorating, it would be only a matter of time before it ruptured, causing peritonitis to set up in Andy's abdominal region so quickly that in all probability he would have died before he could be treated.

Once he had removed the gallbladder, taking care not to rupture the organ himself, Thorbjarnarson repaired Warhol's hernia, though he had not originally planned to. Since the shooting in 1968, Warhol had had a hernia so severe that he had to wear a girdle to give him the support his stomach muscles would have provided, had they been healthy. Repairing the nineteen-year-old hernia was another complicated procedure, but hernia surgery was one of Thorbjarnarson's specialties. Like the gallbladder removal, the hernia repair was completed without any problems.

At twelve-ten, Andy was taken into the recovery room, where Thorbjarnarson checked on him more than once. Canning also catheterized him. At three-forty, Warhol was well enough to be taken back up to his room. There, he was met by the private-duty nurse Vincent had lined up, Ellen McDonald. Andy had been in his room for only fifteen or twenty minutes when Denton Cox visited him. At the time Cox arrived, Andy was conscious and coherent. He was glad to see Cox—and obviously relieved to have made it through the operation without any complications. Cox told Andy that everything had gone well. Thorbjarnarson had removed the gallbladder "without spillage," as Cox put it, and, much to Cox's surprise, Thorbjarnarson had also repaired Andy's "monumental hernia." "You won't have to wear that binder anymore," Cox told Andy. "That's great," Andy said. "The next time, I'll come to the hospital for a facelift."

In fact, Andy complained about nothing except for some pain he was experiencing in the area of the incision. He had been given a small dosage of morphine in the recovery room, so Cox told the nurse to give him another modest dose, this time six milligrams. Cox encouraged Andy to do the required breathing and coughing exercises and showed him how to do leg exercises; then he performed a brief physical examination. From all indications, Andy was in excellent condition, especially for a fifty-eight-year-old man who had just endured a major three-hour operation. In particular, Cox listened to Andy's lungs, which were clear, and his heart, which was strong. Andy's heartbeat was absolutely normal, and had been throughout the operation. This was in itself remarkable since many patients often experience irregular heartbeats during surgery. Finally Cox glanced over the doctor's orders, which had been written by Halebian: "150 cc of lactated Ringer's solution per hour. Weighed daily.

Vitals every four hours. House officer called if not voided by 6." Andy would be able to urinate on his own because the catheter had been removed when he was taken out of the recovery room.

Cox left at four-fifteen. Andy rested in bed under the care of Nurse McDonald, but since he was doing so well the services he required were minimal. At seven, Thorbjarnarson came by. "He was bright," Thorbjarnarson would remember. "He was alert. He was interested in the surgery. He was interested in knowing whether there had been any spread of infection when I told him that he had had a gangrenous gallbladder. I told him, 'No, it had not perforated.' I saw no problem with his breathing. He had with me a normal conversation. . . . The nasogastric tube was in place. He looked to me like one of the healthier patients that I have seen postoperatively." On Warhol's chart Thorbjarnarson wrote: "2/21/87. 7:00 PM. Doing well." After that, he left.

For the next hour, Nurse McDonald continued to look after Warhol. Then, at eight o'clock, Min Cho, McDonald's replacement, came on duty to begin her twelve-hour overnight shift.

9

MIN CHO HAD WORKED AT NEW YORK HOSPITAL FOR WELL OVER A DECADE, during which she had served as both a staff and a private-duty nurse (she had handled at least one thousand private-duty cases). However, she had grown tired of living in New York, and in November 1986 she moved to Apopka, Florida, a suburb of Orlando. There, she intended to work as a private-duty nurse in the homes of individual patients. Though Orlando was going through an enormous economic boom, Min Cho was not able to find the work she hoped for. By early February 1987 she was beginning to have serious financial problems. If her circumstances didn't improve at once, she would have to return to New York. In the mid-eighties hospitals in New York City were experiencing severe shortages of nurses. Medical headhunters searched through cities both in the United States and abroad to find nurses who could be lured to relocate to New York. Since Min Cho's circumstances in Orlando were not improving, in February she flew back to New York City. She arrived near the end of the week of the ninth, registered at the Avalon agency to begin working as a private-duty nurse as soon as possible (she hoped she could get jobs at New York Hospital, the only medical institution with which she was affiliated), and, beginning on the fourteenth, worked every day for seven days in a row. She did not really want to work on Saturday the twenty-first. "I usually don't work Saturday," as Min Cho put it. "Every Saturday I don't want to work. And then Avalon called me, they have emergency and we need nurse, would you come." Min Cho received the call from Avalon early on Saturday to go to New York Hospital that night and, probably for no other reason than that she needed the money, she took the assignment. Happy to find someone on such short notice, the agency worker told her to report to room 1204 in the Baker Pavilion at eight o'clock. Her patient, the agency worker also told her, was a Mr. Robert.

It was when she came on duty at eight o'clock that Min Cho learned from Nurse McDonald that she was not going to be working for a Mr. Robert but for Andy Warhol. In addition, McDonald briefed her on Warhol's condition. "She told me he had a cholecystectomy and he had gangrene gallbladder that they removed," Min Cho later said. "[Nurse McDonald] gave me all vital signs that she took, is everything OK, and she told me he voided and he was in recovery room and he returned to the floor. And she said that he wanted not to disturb, he doesn't want any visitors, no disturbance, he like to be quiet and sleep." After McDonald left, Min Cho walked down the hallway to the nurses' station to pick up Warhol's doctor's orders. The orders did not call for any special treatment, merely the sort any postoperative patient would receive. Later, experts would question Warhol's doctors' decision to give him the antibiotic cefoxitin since Warhol had a history of being allergic to penicillin (a parent drug to cefoxitin), as he had told Nurse Cannon before he went into surgery. (There was some question whether Warhol *was* allergic to penicillin since Cox had given him Augmentin, which contains a form of penicillin, without any adverse effects.) Regardless of whether or not he should have, Warhol took the cefoxitin. When Min Cho returned to room 1204 from the nurses' station, she and Warhol had a brief conversation in which he told her that he was feeling some discomfort in the area of the surgery. Min Cho followed doctor's orders and gave Warhol ten milligrams of morphine, a standard dosage for this situation. Then Warhol was ready to go to sleep. "He say," Min Cho recalled, " 'I want to sleep.' He told me not to disturb him. He doesn't want me disturb him. Anybody come, don't let him come. I say, 'I already got the report from the day nurse. I know about it.' " Before he went to sleep, Min Cho took his vital signs. He had a blood pressure of 120 over 70, a pulse of 86, a respiration rate of 20, and a temperature of 37.3 Celsius (99.1 Fahrenheit). She also wrote the following informa-tion on Warhol's chart: "Abdomen: wound dressing dry and intact. Abdominal binder on. I.V. runs well. Sump tube to wall suction intact. Draining 300 cc greenish color. Replaced. He had morphine for abdom-inal pain. Relieved."

Between eight and ten Andy mostly slept, although he did keep the television set playing. At ten o'clock, a staff doctor stopped by and asked Min Cho how Warhol was doing. Min Cho said he was doing fine. She then checked his vital signs, she later said. They were unchanged. At some time between ten and midnight, Andy must have awakened, for Min Cho would help him with two different activities. She assisted him as he sat up and did his deep-breathing exercises. Closer to ten o'clock than eleven, Andy also placed some telephone calls. For about fifteen minutes, he had Min Cho dial a series of numbers for him, but he was not able to find anyone at home. Soon he told Min Cho why he was trying to locate one of his friends: He couldn't remember his home telephone number. With this, Min Cho went down to the nurses' station and got Andy's home number off his chart. When Min Cho dialed the number, one of Andy's housekeepers answered, and she and Andy had a brief conversation; he told her that he had made it through the surgery and that he was doing all right. Finally Andy hung up the telephone and lay back in his bed. Again he started to doze on and off. Around midnight, Min Cho got a telephone call at the nurses' station from Michael Canning, one of the team of doctors assigned to Warhol. Canning also wanted to know how Warhol was doing. Again, Min Cho said he was doing fine. Canning asked if Warhol had voided, and Min Cho said he had. "Good," Canning said. Once she got off the telephone, Min Cho returned to Warhol's room.

Between midnight and two o'clock, little happened. A staff nurse stuck her head in the room on two separate occasions just to make sure that Warhol was in stable condition. At one point Min Cho returned to the nurses' station to pick up the valuables Warhol had brought with him to the hospital. It was an assortment Warhol usually carried: a camera, a tape recorder, and about three hundred dollars in cash. Then at two o'clock in the morning Min Cho took Warhol's vital signs again. They were still the same.

"Do you have pain?" Min Cho asked Andy while he was awake.

"No," he said.

"Do you want pain shot?" she asked anyway.

"No," Andy answered. Following this short exchange, Warhol seemed ready to go to sleep for the night. Min Cho figured this out, she said later, because for the first time that evening Warhol himself turned off the television set. Every other time Min Cho had turned the set off—and she had more than once—Andy had turned it right back on.

From two o'clock in the morning on, Andy seemed to be sleeping soundly. Min Cho claims she sat in a chair in his room the whole time, watching him intently. Through the years people would question whether Min Cho did in fact stay in Warhol's room. Did she ever wander down the hall? If she did stay in the room the whole night, except for when she went to the nurses' station, was she paying attention to her patient? Did she doze off? Or could she (as evidence indicates) have become so wrapped up in reading her Bible that she lost track of what was happening around her?

According to Min Cho, she first noticed something odd at four-thirty. "He was pale. But anyway, I like to make sure, so I took pulse. Then I like to make sure that I look at the carotid pulse." He had a pulse, so Min Cho felt somewhat relieved. It was probably then that she went to the nurses' station to pick up Warhol's morning medication. At four forty-five, she claims, she took his pulse again. "I took, then I took apically. By 'apically' means you do with a stethoscope." Now Warhol's pulse was weaker. "So I shake him and he didn't respond. So I ran out to—first the nurse I saw was Maggie, so I brought into the room. Then I start CPR." By five o'clock, according to Min Cho, it became clear to her that Warhol was not going to respond to CPR, and the cardiac arrest team was called in.

Over the years, when she had to describe the sequence of events that led up to the cardiac arrest team being called, Min Cho would be vague and hesitant. In actual fact, Min Cho's version of the story does not seem accurate. As evidence suggests, there is a more likely scenario.

Sometime around five o'clock in the morning (it could have been as late as five forty-five), Min Cho glanced up from her Bible to realize, by observing the way he was (or was not) breathing or the color of his skin or simply his general state, that something was wrong with Andy Warhol. Something was terribly wrong.

Getting up from her chair, she took his pulse. There was none. All she could think to do was run for help. So, frantic, Min Cho rushed out of room 1204 and ran to the nurses' station, where the first nurse she encountered was Maggie Smith. "Maggie, help me," Min Cho said, clearly frightened. "I think I'm in trouble. He doesn't respond."

Smith dropped what she was doing and rushed down the hall with Min Cho into Warhol's room. In the room, she found Andy lying in his bed—stiff, cold, motionless. From the way he looked to Smith, he already may have been dead. Smith and Min Cho shook him. He did not respond. Instantly Smith could tell that Min Cho was absolutely right:

She, no, *they* were in trouble. If Andy Warhol wasn't dead, he was dying, right there in a private room on the twelfth floor of New York Hospital. "Call code team," Min Cho said to Smith, meaning the cardiac arrest team. Smith ran out of the room as Min Cho began artificial respiration. When she returned, Smith brought a code team cart with her. While Smith and Min Cho were placing a board under Andy, another nurse, Anesia Pereira, who had seen Smith get the cart, came dashing into the room. Having helped position Andy, Min Cho started to give Andy chest compressions. With sure, direct force, she jammed the palms of her hands down into Andy's chest over and over. Suddenly Smith looked at Pereira. "Go call the code team," Smith said.

"I thought you called them already," Min Cho said.

"No, I didn't," Smith said, now performing CPR on Warhol. Pereira ran out of the room.

No sooner had Pereira left, it seemed, than she came back. She had called the code team; an announcement had gone out over the hospital's public address system. The team would be in Warhol's room within moments. Almost immediately, members of the code team hurried into the room. First, there was Leslie Vensel, the doctor in charge of the team; then came a pavilion manager, or area supervisor. Next came two more doctors, both men; two residents; additional nurses. In all, the code team would contain some ten people, each with a different duty; the team had rehearsed so often that each member knew exactly what he or she was supposed to do. To begin with, an EKG had to be connected to Warhol to monitor his heartbeat, or lack of one. Immediately the pavilion manager, Nurse Smith, Min Cho, and one of the doctors connected Warhol to an EKG machine. When the machine was finally turned on, much to everyone's surprise, Warhol had a heartbeat. He was not dead after all. The senior staff members, those who knew all too well who Andy Warhol was even if Min Cho didn't, were particularly relieved. The doctors and nurses stopped their CPR and stood back to watch Warhol. There was a palpable sense of relief in the room as the monitoring tape inched its way out of the EKG machine, dutifully recording the fact that Warhol's heart was beating. It continued to beat for well over a minute. Then, suddenly and inexplicably, the line on the machine went flat.

Now the code team flew into action again. The anesthesiologist inserted a tube down Warhol's throat—not an easy procedure to perform since Warhol's body had become stiff from the imminent onset of rigor mortis; the doctor had to force the tube down Warhol's windpipe. While the anesthesiologist worked with the tube, which would pump oxygen into Warhol's body, members of the code team carried out other prescribed emergency treatment. A lidocaine drip with 5 percent dextrose was infused into Warhol. In all, during the rescue attempt, three bags of lidocaine would be fed into his body. In addition, other bags, most of them containing medication to help resuscitate the heart, were connected to Warhol through IV drips. Soon Warhol had as many as seven different IV drips attached through needles to his body. At some point Min Cho began to manipulate an ambu bag that covered Warhol's mouth. In addition, blood gases were drawn, and, in a drastic effort to force the heart to start pumping, a defibrillator machine was connected to Warhol and Warhol's heart was shocked with an electrical current. The efforts of the code team paid off. Warhol's heart started beating.

As they had before, the code team, which had grown to a dozen or more people, stood and watched the tape emerge from the EKG machine. The room was still enough that they could hear the beep of the machine. As much as thirty minutes had passed since the team first came into Warhol's room. But this second reprieve, like the first, was short-lived. Again Warhol's heart stopped beating and the line on the EKG machine went flat.

Once more the code team set to work. More blood gases were taken. Warhol's heart was defibrillated. At some point a pacemaker was inserted. Ultimately the team got a heartbeat a third time, but almost as soon as it started it stopped. Despite this, the code team pressed on. Drugs, manual manipulation, electronic manipulation—the team used every possible remedy available to them. In reality, Warhol was probably dead—or dangerously near death—when the code team had arrived to begin with. The odds of his being revived were extremely small since so much time had passed from the moment he went into cardiac arrest until the moment the code team got to him. At any rate, his physiological state had now become so dire that the code team's resuscitation efforts were pointless. The team carried on until six-thirty, when Dr. Vensel told everyone to stop. The team had been trying to revive Warhol for about an hour. They had gotten three different heartbeats, though none was strong. The last hardly qualified as a heartbeat. Even if they had somehow revived him, he had had so little oxygen to his brain for so long that he no doubt had sustained massive cerebral damage. At six thirty-one on the morning of the twenty-second, Dr. Vensel pronounced Andy Warhol dead.

Suddenly it was over. The hospital room, which had been the site of so much activity for the last hour, was now quiet. Some of the code team began to leave, dejected that they had not been able to save their patient. The senior members of the team had another real concern: How were they going to release to the public the news that Andy Warhol had died in New York Hospital following routine gallbladder surgery from what appeared to have been a heart attack?

There was an explanation. A large percentage of fatal heart attacks occur between the hours of four and eight o'clock in the morning, when the body experiences a natural adrenaline surge. That's why so many people die of heart failure in their sleep. But most people are at home in bed when it happens, not in one of the largest hospitals in the country with their own private-duty nurse sitting a few feet away. If Min Cho had been able to determine that Warhol was having a heart attack within a minute or so of when the cardiac arrest had actually started, would the code team have been able to revive him and save his life? Yes, Cox would later say, because Warhol was in overall good health. He had no severe heart disease, only a slight narrowing of the arteries normal for a man his age. In fact, he did not at all fit the profile of someone likely to have a heart attack. So maybe the reason for his attack was no more complicated than this: Because of the extreme pathological fear Warhol had experienced as a result of having to check into a hospital, his general adrenaline output had increased substantially. When the natural adrenaline surge started around four o'clock, the rush was so powerful that it threw his system into cardiac arrest.

After Warhol was pronounced dead, someone removed the endotracheal tube from his throat, and the assortment of IVs was disconnected from his body. After that, Min Cho was told that it was her responsibility to clean the body, then the room. Carefully she sponged down Andy's body—his arms, his legs, his torso, his face. There was a lot of blood that had to be washed off. As she cleaned the body, Min Cho felt a numbing sadness come over her; it was always unsettling when a patient died, especially under circumstances such as these. Once she was finished with the body, she moved on to the room. She gathered up two garbage bags full of soiled material before she was done. At last, well past eight o'clock, the time her shift should have ended, Min Cho was able to leave. One of the nurses offered to go out to breakfast with her to try to make her feel better, but Min Cho just wanted to go home. When she left, the body of Andy Warhol was still lying in the bed in room 1204. Until the ambulance came to take him to the morgue, he would be in the room all alone. There were no colleagues, no family, no friends. Of course, there had been no family or friends in the room with him that night while he was asleep because Andy had wanted it that way. Still, would it have made a difference if someone close to him—Vincent Fremont or Paige Powell or his brother John—had been in the room this first night after surgery? Would someone who cared about Andy have kept a more fervent vigil? Was there anything that could have been done differently that would have prevented him from dying?

1 0

AT TEN-THIRTY IN THE MORNING ON FEBRUARY 23, 1987, DR. BEVERLY LEFFERS performed an autopsy on the body of Andy Warhol in the presence of Dr. Elliot Gross, chief medical examiner of the City of New York, Dr. Michael Ferenc, junior medical examiner, and Dr. Daniel Alonzo, of New York Hospital. The procedure took between three and four hours. Noting that Warhol was five feet six inches tall, weighed an estimated 140 pounds, and had a "general appearance consistent with the stated age of 58 years," Leffers observed in her report that "there is balding across the top of the head where there is in place"—even then, during the autopsy—"a hairpiece which is white on the top and white mixed with brown in the back." She concluded her external examination, which revealed nothing untoward, by describing the body in general. "When the body is reviewed there is nasogastric tube in place. There are gauze bandages over the needle puncture holes on the right lateral neck and on the right supraclavicular region. There is adhesive tape present covering both of these gauze bandages. There are gauze bandages over the drain with adhesive tape present. There are gauze bandages and adhesive tape over the needle puncture holes on the left inguinal region." Then Leffers turned her attention to Warhol's internal organs. The heart was not dilated and had "no visible scars or infarcts" although the "coronary arteries contain multiple yellow atherosclerotic plaques causing up to 30% narrowing." Besides the heart, every other internal organ—the liver, the pancreas, the kidneys, the brain, and so on—was for the most part unremarkable, except for the lungs. "The lungs are densely adherent to the chestwall bilaterally," Leffers wrote. "The left lung weighs 740 grams and the right lung weighs 730 grams. The trachea and bronchi as well as the larynx contain abundant, frothy, pinkish fluid. The lungs are congested, atelectatic and edematous. The cut surface exudes frothy fluid. . . . The lungs show no evidence of consolidation." During the entire autopsy, only the weight of the lungs concerned Leffers. Normally a lung weighs about three hundred grams, with the left lung weighing slightly more than the right. Warhol's lungs weighed more than twice as much as they should have. Since this was a serious irregularity (which still could have been explained by the enormous amount of various liquids that had been pumped into his body during the cardiac arrest), Leffers wrote, under the phrase "Cause for Death," "PENDING FUR-THER STUDY." She would have to examine the evidence more closely and interview hospital personnel before she could reach a final decision about the cause of Warhol's death.

On April 14, after an extensive investigation, Leffers offered her opinion. According to Leffers, Warhol died as a result of "cardiac arrhythmia of undetermined origin following surgical removal of the gall bladder and repair of an abdominal incisional hernia under general anesthesia. . . . Examination of available records and our interviews [with the involved parties] indicate that the cardiopulmonary arrest occurred an indeterminate but significant time prior to notification of a 'cardiac code' and initiation of cardiopulmonary resuscitation. . . . Notes and recordings in Mr. Warhol's chart do not adequately reflect his clinical status during the morning hours prior to 5:45 a.m. when the cardiac code was called."

The next day, Elliot Gross released his own statement concerning the cause of Warhol's death. Also calling the immediate cause of death "a cardiac arrhythmia of undetermined origin," Gross went on to say that "in the absence of significant anatomical or toxicologic findings, the cause of death is, therefore, a disturbance of the heart rhythm." Gross could not establish any suspicious reason for the failure of the heart. He did, however, make one serious allegation. Because Warhol's "cardiopulmonary arrest occurred an indeterminate but significant time prior to notification of a 'cardiac code' and initiation of resuscitation" and because "notes and recordings in Mr. Warhol's chart do not adequately reflect his clinical status during the morning hours prior to 5:45 a.m.," Gross was forced to conclude that Warhol's death "warrants investigation by the office of the District Attorney." Eventually, on July 30, 1987, following his own investigation, Robert Morgenthau, district attorney of the County of New York, issued a report in which he stated the findings of his office. First, Morgenthau reiterated the fact that "tests [had] failed to disclose the cause of [Warhol's] fatal arrhythmia. . . . As a consequence, [the medical examiner's] investigation failed to disclose any evidence that Warhol's death was a homicide." As for Min Cho, her "notes, to the extent that they exist . . . do not reveal evidence of criminal liability." Because of this, Morgenthau concluded that "there is insufficient evidence of criminal liability to indicate a grand jury investigation of Andrew Warhol's death."

While the district attorney decided that no one was criminally liable for the death, the New York State Department of Health, which also investigated the case, concluded that the care Warhol received from New York Hospital was severely lacking. In a report issued in March 1987, the department cited the facts that no one on the hospital staff had given Warhol "a complete history and physical examination," which should have included (but did not) a rectal examination and "a stool examination for occult blood"; that his doctors ignored his allergy to penicillin in prescribing cefoxitin; that the hospital staff did not "provide this post-operative patient with proper drainage" ("the wall suction to drain the nasogastric (NGT) was not functioning"); and that the "medical and nursing staff [did not] insure fluid intake and output were properly recorded as ordered by the physician on 2/21/87." The report noted that "an intravenous intake of 5250 cc of fluid and a documented output of 915 cc indicated overhydration during a period of less than 24 hours after the start of surgery"—another possible reason the lungs were so heavy. As for Min Cho, the report charged that she "failed to provide clear and specific nursing notes to determine the condition of the patient, the nursing care given, the time and dosages medications were administered, or details of the treatment provided." What's more, she "failed to confer with physicians immediately when patient condition started to deteriorate in the early morning of 2/22/87" and did not keep "nursing notes [that were] informative or descriptive of the nursing care given." Min Cho did not adequately document Warhol's vital signs, his "nasogastric tube therapy," and his fluid intake and output. "The physician ordered strict INTAKE and OUTPUT," the report revealed. "Yet, the only entry of urine output was made at 6:45 PM. From then on, the notes by Nurse MC made no mention of whether or not the patient voided during the next nine hours." Finally Min Cho, who dated all of her entries "2/21/87" even though many citations should have been dated the twenty-second, "failed to describe the patient's pulse rate, rhythm, frequency, force, and regularity." As a result of this report, the department concluded that "the active medical staff of the hospital did not assure the maintenance of the proper quality of all medication and treatment provided to [the] patient."

At New York Hospital, two separate internal investigations into the conduct of Min Cho found fault with her treatment of Warhol. As a result a "Stop Work" order was issued by the hospital against Min Cho. On the day of Warhol's death, Anne Alexis Coté of New York Hospital interviewed Min Cho on the telephone. In a memorandum, which she marked "Privileged and Confidential," Coté reported that Min Cho stated to her that "at 5:00 AM . . . the patient still looked pale," that his pulse was so weak that "she decided to wake the patient," but that "he did not respond." Min Cho called Maggie Smith "and started CPR herself." The cardiac team "came around 5:50 AM and worked on the patient until 6:31 AM." Finally Coté revealed: "I asked Ms. Cho why she wrote two sets of nurse's notes. She indicated that she decided to write more detail after the summary note. She said she wrote her first note at 5:00 AM and finished the notes after Warhol arrested."

The following day, Karen Kirschner, the director of medical and surgical nursing, interviewed Min Cho at the hospital in the presence of Virginia Sanders, night nursing supervisor. In a memorandum (also marked "Privileged and Confidential") addressed to Kathleen Burke, another hospital administrator, Kirschner disclosed her impressions of that meeting. To explain why she had not kept adequate records but then dummied up notes following Warhol's death, Min Cho said: "For the first night post-op and this is a famous person so someone might read notes, I better write more notes." In fact, most of the notes on Warhol's chart written by Min Cho were done, according to Kirschner, "after the patient expired." When Nurse Sanders suggested to Min Cho that Warhol needed to be "moved and vigorously nursed," Min Cho merely said, "Yes." Finally Kirschner observed that "Min Cho talked about how upsetting the situation is, i.e., she asks herself if there was anything she could have done differently, but indicated by a shrug of her shoulder that she had not found an answer to this." So Kirschner told Min Cho the "Stop Work" order would remain in effect. "I sorry you're not pleased with my care" was Min Cho's answer just before she left. "She," Kirschner stated, "did not seem to have any insight . . . that her documentation did not reflect the care she claimed she gave him nor that she gave him less than satisfactory post-operative care, nor the significance of her observations at 4:30 AM nor that she should have reported anything at that time."

On March 13, 1987, a Ms. Evans at New York Hospital put in a call to Claire Luppi at the Avalon Agency. During their brief conversation, Evans conveyed to Luppi information regarding Min Cho that caused Luppi to write a brief note on Min Cho's employment chart at Avalon. "We received a call barring Ms. Cho from New York Hospital," Luppi recalled, adding that part of the notation she placed on Min Cho's chart contained the phrase "Not up to clinical standards."

11

THE INVESTIGATIONS AND REPORTS WOULD COME IN THE WEEKS AND months following Warhol's death, but on the morning of February 22 the news was spread by a barrage of telephone calls. At six forty-five, Dr. Halebian, still at New York Hospital, called Denton Cox and woke him from a sound sleep. "I have terrible news," Halebian said. "Mr. Warhol is dead."

Cox was so devastated he could barely speak. "Oh, my God!" he finally said. "What happened?"

"Cardiac arrest," Halebian said.

"But why?" Cox asked.

"We don't know," Halebian answered. "I'm so sorry."

When Cox asked how the death had occurred, Halebian said that Warhol had been discovered by nurses after he was already in cardiac arrest. The code team had been called in, a resuscitation effort was attempted, but Warhol had died. Cox told Halebian that he would call Fred Hughes, whom Warhol had listed on his hospital admission papers as his next of kin.

Before he tried Fred, though, Cox called Thorbjarnarson. Like Cox, Thorbjarnarson was asleep. As soon as Cox told him what had happened, Thorbjarnarson later recalled, "I expressed my surprise and amazement and anguish and said I would be in." Once he and Thorbjarnarson hung up, Cox called Fred. Hughes too was asleep.

"Fred, I've got some terrible news," Cox said. "Andy has died."

"But how?" Fred asked.

"Cardiac arrest," Cox replied.

"How?"

"We just don't know." There was a pause. "I just want you to know, Fred, that I am devastated by this," Cox said. "And I'll do all that I can do to help you and the family."

To this end, Cox called John Warhola and spoke with him and his wife, Margaret.

"How did it happen?" John wanted to know.

"Cardiac arrest," Cox said. "We don't know why."

By late morning, the news of Warhol's death had been announced on the Cable News Network. In Exeter, New Hampshire, Sam Bolton's father saw the story on CNN, so he went to the upstairs bedroom where Sam was still asleep and woke him. "Sam, Andy Warhol died," Sam's father said. At first, Sam couldn't believe it, so he got out of bed and started calling friends in New York until he found someone who could tell him whether the story was true. Meanwhile, Tama Janowitz, who was in Princeton, where she was teaching at the university, got a call from a friend who told her Andy was dead. Immediately Tama called Paige, who, like Sam, did not believe the news when she first heard it.

Paige called Andy's house, where Fred, who by now had taken a taxi from his house to Andy's, answered the phone.

"Andy—" Paige blurted out angrily.

"This isn't Andy," Fred said, cutting Paige off. "This is Fred."

At that moment Paige knew Andy was dead because Fred never went to Andy's house. "What are you doing at Andy's house?" she asked him.

"Because Andy is dead," Fred said.

Suddenly Paige broke down; she was crying hysterically.

"Stop crying!" Fred shouted. "You've got to come over here and help me. I need you. My friend David Whitney is here, but I need the two of you. I'm dependent on the two of you."

Unable to control herself, Paige hung up. She was still upset when Stuart Pivar called her sometime later.

"Why haven't I heard from Andy this morning?" Stuart asked her.

"Andy's dead," Paige said, and again began to cry.

. . .

At eleven o'clock, back at Andy's house, Fred got another in what was becoming a never-ending string of telephone calls. This one was from John Warhola.

"We're coming up," he said. "What happened?" Fred told him that all he knew was that Andy had died in the hospital. "Well, we're coming up," John said again.

"Don't bother even coming to the house," Fred said. "We're putting a padlock on it."

Now Fred waited for the arrival of the one person he hoped might be able to help him make it through all of the personal and business dealings he would have to endure in the coming days and weeks. Earlier in the morning, after he had received the call from Denton Cox, Fred knew that he was going to need an attorney. For years Andy had used the law firm of Paul Weiss for all of his legal work. Lately, he had been dealing with one lawyer in particular at the firm, Robert Montgomery. Since Montgomery was out of the country at the moment, Fred knew he would not be able to call on him. Actually, Fred was not even sure he wanted to continue to use Paul Weiss. Regardless of what Andy felt about the firm, Fred had not been pleased with its service for some time now. Instead he decided that he would contact a lawyer he had been friends with for the last two or three years, a former South Bronx assistant district attorney whose relentless, no-holds-barred style had made him one of the most talked-about lawyers in the city and a familiar face in the New York social scene. His contacts cut across all cultural barriers. He was probably one of the few attorneys in Manhattan who could count among his friends Robert De Niro, Tom Wolfe, most high-ranking police officials in all five boroughs, *and* mob lawyer Bruce Cutler. For all of these reasons—and more—Fred called Ed Hayes, who seemed like the perfect partner now that Andy was dead.

DISASTER

1

IT WAS A PEACEFUL, FRIGID WINTER MORNING IN BELLPORT, ONE IN THE string of quaint, affluent small towns situated on the southern shore of Long Island halfway between Manhattan and the Hamptons. The view from the town dock spans a narrow bay across which lies Ho-Hum Beach, a slender piece of Fire Island that is actually owned by the town of Bellport. In the summer, the trees of Bellport, mostly sycamores and maples, give the town a cool green feel. In the winter, though, with all the trees bare, the landscape is raw but not without a stark elegance.

Ed Hayes bought his house in Bellport in 1984. From the back porch of his Cape Cod–style home he could look down onto the town dock, to its rows of sailboats and small yachts, and beyond, across the bay to Fire Island. The house was so picturesque and charming, so much like the home he had always wanted, that he left his apartment in the city and made the trip out to Bellport almost every weekend, even during the winter and fall. As a result, while it may have been the dead of winter, on the third weekend in February in 1987, Ed Hayes was at home in the country with his wife, who was then pregnant with their first child.

Statuesque, ash-blond, classically beautiful, Susan Gilder Hayes had been a high-fashion model for years before she married. During her career, she had done print work and fashion shows for all the major designers and magazines in New York, Paris, Milan, and Tokyo. Because of this, her friends included fellow models such as Jerry Hall, Iman, and Pat Cleveland. In 1982 Susie met Eddie at a party in New York given by the designer Willi Smith. Toukie Smith, Willi's sister, knew Ed and

Susie and made the introduction. As it happened, another mutual friend had already arranged for Ed and Susie to go on a blind date just two weeks later. "So you're supposed to be the girl of my dreams," Eddie said to Susie.

"Yeah, they tell me I'm gonna like you," she said. "I'm probably gonna hate you."

In fact, she didn't hate him. Boyishly handsome and immaculately dressed, Eddie projected himself in such a way that from the start Susie found herself intrigued by what she called "his quirky nature." In short, Eddie was a blend of contradictions. He had clearly worked hard at developing the tough-guy persona that had made him extremely successful, yet at the same time he could be profoundly caring of other people's feelings. He was macho and virile, but he could also be soft, vulnerable. He had the reputation of being a playboy, yet on that very first night at Willi Smith's party Susie suspected that what he wanted more than anything else was to settle down, marry, and have children—several children.

To a large extent, the course of Ed Hayes's life changed the night he met Susie Gilder. Soon Hayes, the perennial bachelor, was dating only Susie. They fought the whole first year, and, according to Gilder, "the second year was not so hot, either." Even so, after two years Ed and Susie were discussing marriage. The wedding finally took place on May 31, 1986, in the Mary Immaculate Catholic Church in Bellport. Among the guests were Robert De Niro, Harvey Keitel, Ed Marinaro, Lorraine Bracco, Tom Wolfe, Taki, Geraldo Rivera, Bruce Cutler, Michael Daly, Cheryl Tiegs, Anthony Peck, Toukie Smith (the maid of honor), and a large contingent from the New York City Police Department. ("There were no gangsters there," Hayes later said, "because of all the cops.") Afterward, the guests convened at Hayes's Bellport house for a reception on the back lawn. As with so much of Hayes's biography, there was a storybook quality to the whole affair, a suggestion that, above all else, this man somehow led a charmed life.

. . .

Years later, Tom Wolfe would say that the events of February 22, 1987, transpired the way they did because, it being Sunday, Paul Weiss was not open and Ed Hayes was. For that matter, Ed Hayes—the one-man law firm—was always open. If someone is booked for murder in the middle of the night, he can't wait for normal business hours to contact his lawyer. So Hayes kept both of his home numbers listed in the telephone book.

Fred Hughes and Ed Hayes had been friends for some time. They had met in the city at a party given by Taki, the gossip columnist. "I remember the meeting clearly," Taki would write. "I looked at Fred, who had just met Eddie, and told him to take the counselor's card. 'With the horrible things you and Warhol are up to, you'll need him,' I said. 'He can reduce a murder charge to jaywalking' was the way I put it." Ed liked Fred. He admired his worldly and entertaining nature. He respected the social position Fred had achieved by associating himself with some of the most influential people in New York, Los Angeles, and Europe. And he appreciated the fact that, if he wanted to, Fred could be witty and congenial—a true gentleman. Indeed, when he was "on," no one could be more wry, more outright funny than Fred. At the same time, Fred liked Ed, though for more complicated reasons. An aficionado of fashion, Fred was impressed by Ed's wardrobe, most of which had been made for him personally by Vincent Nicolosi in New York and Anderson and Sheppard in London. What's more, Fred liked Ed's tough, no-bullshit style, which allowed him to get things done—and done quickly. But there was something else. A personal tension had developed between the two men, one whose origin was complicated and mostly unspoken—but it was there.

On the morning of the twenty-second, Fred called Ed shortly after seven o'clock, startling him from a deep sleep.

"Hello," Hayes said in his flat, clipped voice. Even in conversation, he often sounded as if he were cross-examining a hostile witness.

"Hello, Ed. It's Fred Hughes." Fred's tone was cool and emotionless—without a trace of sadness or grief. "Andy Warhol died last night."

Waking up, Ed focused on what Fred was saying. "I'd like for you to come into the city and help me."

"Fred, this is not my area of expertise in the law," Ed said. "Don't you know someone in this area? Why don't you let me find someone who can help you?" Ed looked over at Susie, who had also been awakened by the telephone. She was now two months pregnant, and the pregnancy had not been easy. "My wife is pregnant. She'd be very uncomfortable if I left her."

"But you have to," Fred said. "Eddie, you're my friend. I want you to come in and take charge of the situation."

Hayes thought quickly. In his career he had been a homicide prosecutor in the South Bronx, perhaps the most violent district in the entire city; after that he had made a lot of money as a criminal attorney defending the very sort of criminals he had been prosecuting. In the process he had established a name for himself. He was invited to the chic parties. He was regularly mentioned in the gossip columns. He socialized with millionaires and movie stars. There was no doubt that Ed Hayes played the part of the celebrity lawyer—and he played it well. One of his best friends in the city was Tom Wolfe, who used him as the basis for Tommy Killian, the crafty prosecutor-turned-lawyer in *The Bonfire of the Vanities*. Wolfe even dedicated the book to him—to "Counselor Eddie Hayes, who walked among the flames, pointing at the lurid lights." Still, in his entire career Ed Hayes had never handled the sort of high-profile case with which his name would be instantly identified—the way, for example, his friend Bruce Cutler had become associated with mob boss John Gotti.

"Ed, you have to do this for me," Fred said. "As a friend."

"Okay. I'll be in."

"Good," Fred said. "Get a car to bring you in, and make sure it has a phone in it so you can call me on the road."

Hayes hung up the phone and looked over at his wife.

"Who was that?" she asked.

"Fred Hughes. Andy Warhol died. Fred wants me to come in."

"Do you have to?"

"Yeah," Ed Hayes said. "I have to."

In the backseat of the limousine, Hayes spent the entire ride to Manhattan on the car phone. One of the first people he called was his brother, Steven Hayes, who was also an attorney. Ed and Steve had been unusually close their whole lives. As quiet and reserved as Ed was flamboyant and outgoing, Steve, an expert in contracts, specialized in entertainment law. In his career he had represented some of the most successful acts in the music business, among them Diana Ross, the Rolling Stones, Bruce Springsteen, Gloria Estefan, and Paul Simon. Ed and Steve talked briefly. Steve suggested that Ed call Frank Harvey, a Manhattan estate attorney who worked exclusively in the surrogate's court, the wing of the court system that handles estates. He also agreed to drive in to Manhattan from his home in Garden City, Long Island, to be of whatever help to his brother he could.

Hayes called Harvey and asked him to come to Warhol's townhouse later that day. Hayes also contacted Jack McCann and Ronnie Marsenison, two New York City Police Department first-grade detectives who moonlighted as private investigators, and arranged for them to meet him there as well. Then he made a number of phone calls to other lawyers who had experience in estate law. Since Hayes had done little estate work, he needed to determine as quickly as possible what exactly would be required of him if he actually ended up being the attorney for the Warhol estate.

Hughes had called Hayes not because of his experience in estate law, but because he knew he needed an attorney who would fight for him, who could tackle any situation that came along, and—this was vital— who could not be intimidated. After all, Hughes, more than anyone except Warhol himself, was aware of the extent of Warhol's holdings; he knew the last kind of lawyer he needed was a paper-pushing estate attorney. Hughes wanted someone who could walk into a bad situation—one as highly charged as a murder scene, for example—and take control of it in a direct and uncompromising manner.

As it turned out, Ed Hayes had been doing this—finding a way to deal with a bad situation—for most of his life. The first child of Edward and Jean Hayes, Eddie was born on November 3, 1947, in Jackson Heights, Queens, a middle-class neighborhood made up mostly of Irish Catholics. It was a neighborhood in which, as Jean Hayes remembers, "everyone went to church every day, and if someone's husband came home staggering up the street the women, my mother included, used to say, 'Oh, he's not drunk. He was gassed in the First World War.' Nobody ever said that somebody was drunk. I remember growing up thinking there were an awful lot of people gassed in the First World War."

Ed's father was a hard worker—early on in his marriage he even held down two jobs—but every night when he came home Jean could see that he had been drinking. He hadn't had just one or two cocktails, either; he was drunk. Edward's drinking did not improve after Steven was born in 1949, and as the years passed the Hayeses' domestic situation became progressively worse. Before too long, Jean understood just how bad it was. "When the children were babies, their father was okay with them," she says. "But when the boys got older he became very violent with them. And anything could set him off. We could be sitting at the dinner table and Eddie could use the wrong fork and that would set him off. It was just a horror story. He hit. He never slapped. He hit. If I jumped in, he hit harder. So I just stood there and prayed that he would finish fast, and he usually did."

Jean Hayes realized she was trapped; after all, as she says, "no Catholic gets divorced." Also, like many women of her generation, she simply did not see that she had any options available to her. So Jean stayed with her husband; she had no choice, she concluded, but to get by from one day to the next. The family moved to Charlottesville, Virginia, when the company Edward worked for, Sperry Rand, transferred him; the Hayeses' third child, Barbara, was born there on November 13, 1956.

After living in Virginia for three years, the Hayeses moved back to New York, this time to Smithtown, Long Island. Around this time, Jean Hayes began to plan for her two boys' future. She had decided that her boys would attend the University of Virginia in Charlottesville. So they could afford it, she would take money to put aside for their tuition from her husband's wallet when he came home drunk at night. She aimed only to pay for each of her sons' freshman year; she was sure that the boys would somehow make it the rest of the way on their own. She also decided that, after Virginia, she wanted her sons to go to graduate school at Columbia University. Finally she knew what she wanted them to be, too: lawyers.

Oddly enough, Jean's boys followed her plan precisely. In 1965, Eddie entered the University of Virginia. His mother paid for his first year, and through scholarships and money made from part-time jobs, Ed paid for the remainder himself. In the fall of 1969, he entered law school at Columbia University. Steve followed one year after him at both Virginia and Columbia. It was not until they graduated from law school that their lives diverged appreciably. Steve went into private practice; unsure about whether he could fit into the nine-to-five work world, Eddie decided he wanted a job with the district attorney's office in the South Bronx. He wanted to do "what's right"—and at the beginning of his career at least, that meant going after murderers.

Jean Hayes has a favorite of all the stories from Eddie's childhood, one that, to her, reveals a key personality trait. When the Hayeses were living in Smithtown, Eddie had a job busing tables and doing odd jobs at a local restaurant owned by a woman named Dottie Payne. Between studying and football practice, he had limited time to work at the restaurant. "Dottie Payne had a great scheme," Jean Hayes says. "She used to pay Ed according to what he did. In other words, if he worked harder than he was supposed to in an hour, he got paid for it. He loved it. She offered him an incentive to work harder. And boy, did he work harder! Once Dottie Payne said to me that if he kept on working as hard as he was, he was going to break her."

2

THE LIMOUSINE PULLED UP IN FRONT OF ANDY WARHOL'S SIX-STORY FED-
eral-period brick townhouse at 57 East Sixty-sixth Street around eleven
o'clock. Naturally Ed Hayes had never been inside the house before;
some of Andy's closest friends, most notably Brigid Berlin, had never
been invited inside the house. In fact, Hayes had met Warhol on only
a handful of occasions, usually at parties. The first time he encountered
Warhol, Ed was trying to squeeze by him in a crowded room when Andy
reached down inconspicuously and pinched Ed on the butt. Ed looked
back over his shoulder at Andy, who just smiled. Perhaps it was this
incident that caused Warhol, after meeting Hayes one night at a party,
to describe him to Pat Hackett as a defense lawyer who "wear[s] funny
clothes and jump[s] around and makes things 'kooky.' Sort of forties
clothes, really crewcut, about twenty-nine." And what did Hayes say to
Warhol that night at the party? "I can get ya outta anything."

Over the last few years, as he became friends with Fred Hughes, Ed
had not been friendly with Andy, though more than once Fred had tried
to convince Ed to represent Warhol. Fred had grown displeased with the
representation Andy was receiving at Paul Weiss. Some lawyers and staff
members at the firm often treated Fred with disrespect. They made him
come to their offices to do business and then had him wait until Andy's
attorney was available—to Fred, an indication that the firm did not value
Warhol's business. What's more, Fred believed that, because of his style
and personality, Ed was simply the better lawyer for Andy.

Ed was certainly flattered, yet he resisted Fred's overtures. Warhol
had a penchant for bartering his own art for services and property, which

he was supposed to report on his income tax return but never did, as well as a tendency to secrete money generated from European art sales in a Swiss bank account. Through his contacts in the art world, Hayes had heard rumors about Andy's business affairs. He didn't want to represent someone who habitually—and knowingly—skirted the law, perhaps even broke it. Flirt with the person, yes—but not represent him. Ed Hayes had a saying by which he ran his legal practice: "Anything I'm willing to do for myself I'd do for a client, but I won't do *anything* for a client." Hayes had a single overriding reason why he would not take such risks. Throughout much of his adult life, he had one ultimate career goal: to run for public office—mayor, governor, maybe something even more ambitious.

Hayes rang the doorbell. Fred answered wearing a dark business suit. "I'm glad you're here," Fred said as he showed Ed into the large entryway. "I can't do this by myself."

"Let's go somewhere where we can be alone," Ed said. There were not many people in the house—only three or four besides Fred. Even so, the two men went off to a room by themselves.

From talking to his various legal contacts, Hayes knew that the first document he needed to see was Warhol's will. Fred handed him a copy that Andy had asked him to keep at his house. Quickly Hayes read it over. Considering Warhol's wealth and the status he had achieved in his profession, it was an unusually simple document. Fred was to be the executor with Vincent Fremont serving as the alternate executor. Hayes and Hughes would soon learn that sometime after 1980 Andy had gone into his attorney's office and revised the original will he had made in the mid-seventies. Dated March 11, 1982, the new will was essentially the same as the original except for one key difference: Andy had written out Jed Johnson. Now, the only people to whom Andy left any cash were his brothers and Fred, each of whom would receive $250,000. The remainder of Warhol's estate was to be liquidated in order to fund a foundation for the arts.

Once Hayes had ascertained that Hughes was going to be the central person involved in Warhol's estate, he turned his attention to more

practical matters. Fred was alert and completely in control of his emotions—indeed, Ed thought it was odd that Fred showed so little evidence of being upset—but he was understandably apprehensive about
what was going to be required of him as executor. Ed told Fred that the
house and the Factory had to be secured. He felt there was a good
possibility that someone—a disgruntled employee, a deranged fan—
might try to do something as crazy as what Valerie Solanis had done.
The two logical places for an incident to occur were Andy's townhouse
and the Factory. Since Fred had been so closely associated with Warhol
for so many years, he would be the most likely target of any bizarre act.

To get a feel for the place, Ed took a tour of the house alone. As he
walked from room to room, he could hardly believe what he saw.
Warhol used the townhouse less as a place to live than as a warehouse
in which to store the enormous amount of merchandise he had been
buying for years. Only a few rooms—the kitchen, a couple of sitting
rooms, and the two maids' rooms—were set up in a way that was
functional. Most of the other rooms were jammed with boxes, with stray
pieces of furniture and canvases, with crates and cartons and baskets and
shopping bags. Even the staircases had packages piled up on the steps
and landings.

Andy's bedroom contained the large Federal-period four-poster canopy bed, an oversized antique chifforobe, and a large-screen color television that was positioned so that Andy could watch it as he lay in bed.
Every flat surface in the room was covered with jewelry, watches, money,
trinkets. In addition, Andy liked to toss valuables—cash and jewelry—
on the top of the bed's canopy. Clothes, books, magazines, and cowboy
boots were strewn everywhere—on the floor, on chairs, wherever he
could find an empty spot to toss something. Warhol may have projected
the image of being in control to his friends and colleagues, but many
who knew him would have been shocked if they had seen how he lived.
Ed Hayes was.

When Ed finished his tour, he met with Fred again to go over the moves
they needed to make. First they had to secure the premises; to this end,

Ed had arranged for Jack McCann, his former colleague and a security expert, to stop by the townhouse that day. If Fred approved, Ed would immediately have guards stationed twenty-four hours a day at both the townhouse and the Factory. Ed expected that as the story of Warhol's death was picked up by the newspapers and television, fans and curiosity seekers would be coming by those two locations. Once they were secured, Ed and Fred could proceed to the legal work. The will had to be filed in surrogate's court as soon as possible. Since it was the single document that established the fact that Hughes was the one—and for now the only—decision maker involved with the estate, the will needed to be filed at once, so that anyone concerned with Warhol's business dealings would know that he was going to have to deal with Fred.

Once Fred approved Ed's plan of action, they began to discuss Warhol's burial. Fred assumed that the Warhola family would want the funeral to take place in Pittsburgh; he was more than willing to comply with their wishes. Sometime later, he would hold a memorial service for Warhol in New York. Since the two men were in agreement, they could proceed with the business at hand. Fred spent time with Vincent Fremont and then John and Paul Warhola, who had flown in from Pittsburgh in the afternoon and come directly to the townhouse. As Fred had suspected, they wanted to bury Warhol alongside their mother in the family plot in Pittsburgh. Meanwhile, Ed Hayes met with Steve Hayes, Jack McCann, and Frank Harvey, all of whom gave him advice on what he would have to do in the coming days. With Fred's approval, Ed went ahead and arranged for McCann to provide security immediately.

As Ed spoke with various people, Fred rummaged through the house. He opened boxes and bags, dug in closets, and sorted through room after room of what he was beginning to realize was a mind-boggling trove of collectibles, a staggering fortune in itself. Fred had known, of course, that Andy had been buying impulsively for years; but because he had rarely been invited to Andy's house he had no idea of the extent of his compulsion. At the end of that first day, Ed and Fred left the house. "Fred was extremely affected by the situation," Ed Hayes later recalled of that day, "but not in an emotional way by his relationship with Andy.

He was very concerned that he was the executor. There was no grief. I never saw the guy cry. I never saw him show any grief whatsoever." Instead, Fred seemed consumed with the daunting job that lay ahead of him, and more than a little worried about the role he would take in the management of Warhol's estate. It would be the job of a lifetime, a job that would define his own biography, and he knew he wanted to live up to the undertaking—not to mention to make some money along the way if he could.

On Monday, February 23, Hughes and Hayes met at the Factory. When Hayes toured this building, he saw that he would need the same sort of security detail here that was being put in place at the house—skilled, professional watchmen working around the clock. He noticed that the parts of the building where Warhol worked—and he had used relatively little space in the huge complex—were as cluttered and messy as his house, maybe even worse. Warhol's workspace was littered with half-painted canvases, buckets, pails, brushes, and the mops he sometimes used to apply paint to canvases. What surprised Hayes most, however, was the condition of Warhol's tiny office near the end of the main hallway on the first floor. Hayes tried to open the door, but he could barely get it to budge. When he did pry the door wide enough to reach in and turn on the light, he could just peek in to see that the room was jammed full of boxes, cartons, and bags. Obviously, for some time now, Warhol had merely come to the door, cracked it open, and tossed whatever box or bag he had at the moment onto the pile.

On the other hand, Fred's office could not have been any more different. Located on the second floor, with a small balcony that over-looked the main lobby, it was an idiosyncratic blend of styles and periods, as individual in tone and spirit as Hughes himself. The center-piece of the room was a large rectangular antique desk; sitting around the room were matching antique chairs. On one of the walls, which were painted a soft shade of red, hung an enormous Renaissance painting featuring Frederick, King of Denmark. Near the painting a small television sat on a cart. Stuck in conspicuous spots around the room were several small signs with sayings printed on them: SHIT OR GET OFF THE POT, one read. NO FAVOR GOES UNPUNISHED, read another.

It was in this office that Hughes and Hayes continued to discuss their future plans. On that day, Monday, they would have Frank Harvey go to the surrogate's court and get temporary letters of administration, the first document they would need to conduct business. Later in the week, Harvey would also begin to probate the will. There was, though, a larger problem that needed to be dealt with at once. In various areas in the Factory, especially in the basement and the space that he had used for his studio, Warhol had stored countless canvases. There were also a number of canvases on the fourth, fifth, and sixth floors of his town-house, many in one small back room on the fifth floor; the majority of these canvases, unstretched and merely rolled up, were from the sixties, the period of his work that had consistently brought the highest prices through the years. Almost all of his unsold canvases from the seventies and the eighties—a staggering amount of artwork, as it turned out—were stored in the Factory. Hughes and Hayes decided to gather up all the work, properly stretch and package it, and transport it to a storage space in an art warehouse in Queens.

During that first week, Hughes had several Factory employees prepare Warhol's work to be shipped out. The image of the packing of the paintings for the move would leave a memorable impression on the many people who saw it. "It was like the fall of Kuwait," recalls an employee and confidant of Warhol's. "Tons of paintings were heading out of that place," says a friend of Warhol's who stopped by the Factory soon after his death. William Avery, an acquaintance of Warhol's from Studio 54, remembered that "the staircase and the landing were completely covered with boxes. There were other things too—furniture and statues. It was total chaos."

Through the years, Warhol insiders would allege that a lot of Warhol's art and valuables disappeared at this time. Some would even speculate about who might have ended up with Warhol's belongings. "I am sure Fred took a lot of things out of the house after Warhol died," says Sam Bolton, who continued to work for Hughes following Warhol's death. "I can understand why Fred would have taken some things from the house, after all of those years of working with Andy. In Andy's bedroom there were watches all over the place. There was jewelry. When they opened the safe, Fred told me this, there was so much jewelry and money, it fell out onto the floor." Fred later maintained that whatever he ended up with was either his to begin with or a gift from Andy.

Along these lines, Jack McCann, the man who provided security, would make the following observation: "Is it possible [that people could have taken things]? Yes, it's possible. Fred wouldn't have been challenged. Hayes never removed anything from the premises. [Other people] were sometimes there without Hayes, but I don't recall Hayes being there without them. There were times when [Fred] would take something and not leave a detailed description of it."

During this first week, it became clear to Hayes that Hughes wanted him to start working officially as the estate's attorney. When they discussed an appropriate fee, Hayes made Hughes a proposition. Since he did not know exactly how many hours he would have to spend on the job—already he suspected that the case would be fairly complicated—Hayes suggested to Hughes that he pay him a flat fee of 2.5 percent of the value of the estate at closing. If the estate were worth somewhere between $10 million and $15 million, which for legal purposes was the value placed on it in papers filed in surrogate's court not long after Warhol's death, Hayes would pick up—at most—$375,000. Hughes accepted Hayes's proposal. In a retainer agreement dated February 23, 1987, the two men signed a deal solidifying their arrangement. "As attorney for the Estate," Hayes wrote in the letter, which Hughes countersigned, "I shall probate the Will, assist you in collecting the assets of the Estate, review all claims against the Estate, negotiate those claims on your behalf as Executor, establish a foundation as required by the Will, transfer assets to the legatees named in the Will, prepare all Estate tax returns and all Fiduciary income tax returns, attend to the proper accounting of all Estate transactions and, in general, assist you in all the normal activities of Estate administration." For this, Hayes would be paid "two and a half percent of the gross taxable estate." The money would be paid in thirds: one third after the will was admitted to probate, one third after the estate tax return had been filed, and one third after the estate was closed out.

At some point during March, Hughes realized that the estate was going to be worth more than he had anticipated, so he asked Hayes if he would agree to a reduction of the percentage he was going to receive as a fee. Hayes agreed, and the men set down the terms of their new agreement in a second retainer letter. "Supplementing our agreement of February 23, 1987," Hayes wrote, "and taking into consideration the fact that the Estate is larger than originally thought, I agree to your request to reduce the attorney's fees due to me to two percent of the gross taxable estate. All other terms of our agreement of February 23, 1987 remain in effect."

The negotiations and the renegotiations would come later. First, Andy Warhol had to be buried.

Warhol was scheduled to be buried in St. John the Baptist Byzantine Cemetery, just outside of Pittsburgh, on February 26, 1987. John and Paul Warhola had the body transported from New York, following the autopsy on Monday, to the Thomas P. Kunsak Funeral Home in Pittsburgh, where a wake was held that Wednesday. When the mourners passed the open coffin, they saw Warhol dressed in a simple black cashmere suit, a paisley tie, one of his platinum wigs, and sunglasses. He held in his hands, which lay clasped together on his chest, a black prayer book and a single red rose. Those who came to pay their respects at the wake were mainly family members and family friends from Pittsburgh.

Again, at the funeral on Thursday, there were no movie stars, no art world celebrities, no socialites from New York or Europe. There was only a small contingent of Factory employees. Fred had informed anyone who asked about the funeral that the Warhola family wanted only family members to attend. In reality, the family had never made such a request, and more than one person at the wake and the funeral remarked on the small showing of Warhol's friends and associates. Apparently

Hughes exercised tight control over who was permitted to attend because, according to Sam Bolton, Fred was afraid "the crazies" would show up and "freak out Andy's family."

Fred actually drew up a list, bought each person a ticket on the same flight to Pittsburgh, and then made sure that only those people with tickets went. Among the Factory crowd who were allowed to go were Paige Powell, Pat Hackett, Sam Bolton, Jay Shriver, Vincent Fremont, Shelley Fremont, Brigid Berlin (she had flown back from London), and, naturally, Fred, who was accompanied by Ed Hayes. Most of the Factory attendees watched from the sidewalk outside the Holy Ghost Byzantine Catholic Church in the bitter February cold as the hearse pulled up and pallbearers carried the casket into the church. "[That's when] it all finally became real," says Bolton, who along with the rest of his friends and colleagues followed the casket into the simple, modest church and sat in one of the back pews.

An all-male choir sang a hymn before Monsignor Peter Tay delivered a brief eulogy. "The whole world will remember Andy," said Tay, who had never met Warhol. "While he said everybody would be famous for fifteen minutes, his own fame spanned three decades. Andy never knocked anyone. He had a deep, loving trust in God. This man will reach to the steps of the very throne of God." In closing, Tay added an odd and unsettling observation. "Though it seems at times that he wandered far from his church, we do not judge him. Jesus forgave the thief on his right. He did not forgive the thief on his left. It means there is always hope, but it also means nobody should take salvation too much for granted."

At the end of the service, the mourners filed out of the church, got into cars, and followed the hearse from the church to the cemetery in Bethel, a Pittsburgh suburb not too far away. There, they gathered in a small chapel for another brief ceremony. Afterward, they left the chapel and, on this cold, gray winter day, walked behind the hearse as it crept up a hill to the plot next to Warhol's mother. Standing around the grave, they watched while the casket was positioned to be lowered into the ground and while Monsignor Tay sprinkled holy water on the coffin as he said a short prayer. Before the casket was lowered, Paige Powell came forward and threw a handful of *Interviews* and a bottle of Estée Lauder perfume into the open grave. (Estée Lauder had been a strong supporter of the magazine.) Finally, overcome by grief, Paige broke down weeping, as did Pat Hackett and Brigid Berlin. Some people feared Brigid would become hysterical; she, like Pat and Paige, simply could not believe Andy was dead. Not far from the grave, three cemetery workmen waited for the service to conclude so they could lower the coffin into the ground, cover it with dirt, and get on with their day.

When the service was over, the Warhola family hosted a luncheon at a restaurant called the Mona Lisa. It was the kind of event Warhol himself would have loved to laugh about with Pat on the telephone. Then, after the lunch, which did not last long, the group from the Factory headed for the airport to make their flight back to New York.

3

THE MEMORIAL SERVICE THAT WAS HELD AT ST. PATRICK'S CATHEDRAL IN New York City on April 1, 1987, could not have been more different from the Pittsburgh funeral. Coordinated by Fred Hughes, it was a study in elegance on a large scale. The church, grand and historic, was beautifully decorated with sprays of white flowers hung on the end of each pew; the ceremony was simple and dignified. The service confirmed beyond any doubt that by the end of his life Andy Warhol had become an integral part of the New York social establishment. The guest list, which was put together primarily by Hughes, included some of the most prominent names in the business, art, fashion, and entertainment communities as well as Warhol associates from various eras. A horde of onlookers lined the sidewalk to watch the invited arrive for the Mass:

Halston, Liza Minnelli, Calvin and Kelly Klein, Steve Rubell, Ian Schrager, Fran Lebowitz, Roy Lichtenstein, Claes Oldenburg, Richard Serra, Leroy Neiman, Jean-Michel Basquiat, Jamie Wyeth, David Hockney, Julian Schnabel, Keith Haring, Kenny Scharf, Leo Castelli, Tom Wolfe, Terry Southern, Bianca Jagger, Viva, Ultra Violet, Billy Name, George Plimpton, Anne Bass, Dominique de Menil, São Schlumberger, Consuelo Crespi, Ahmet Ertegun, Lynn Wyatt, Mary McFadden, Sylvia Miles, Don Johnson, Patti D'Arbanville, Philip Niarchos, Lou Reed, John Cale, Ric Ocasek, Grace Jones, Swifty Lazar, Richard Gere, Peter Allen, Francesco Scavullo, Robert Mapplethorpe, Andree Putnam, Philip Johnson, Paloma Picasso, Henry Geldzahler, Susan Blond, Jerry Zipkin, John Waters, Nell Campbell, Ann Magnuson, Régine, Timothy Leary, Debbie Harry, Raquel Welch, Jed Johnson, Gerard Malanga, Monique van Vooren, Stuart Pivar, Paige Powell, Vincent Fremont, Jay Shriver, Sam Bolton, Pat Hackett, Ed and Susan Hayes, Brendan Gill, Bob Colacello, Baby Jane Holzer, Catherine Guinness, Paul Morrissey, Claus von Bulow, and Denton Cox. It was the ultimate guest roster. No one in St. Patrick's Cathedral would have been more impressed by the names on the list than Andy Warhol himself.

The church was packed—all the seats were taken, and people stood at the sides and the back of the auditorium—when the service began with a prelude of music, which included a selection from *The Magic Flute* by Mozart. Father Anthony Dalla Villa read from the Mass for the Dead: "Lord God, Almighty Father, you have made the cross for us a sign of strength and marked us as yours in the sacrament of the resurrection. Now that you have freed our brother Andy Warhol from this mortal life, make him one with your saints in heaven." After the Mass, Brigid Berlin read from the Book of Wisdom: "But the souls of the just are in God's hands and torment shall not touch them. In the eyes of foolish men they seemed to be dead; their departure was reckoned as defeat, and their going from us as disaster. But they are at peace, for though in the sight of men they may be punished, they are assured hope of immortality; and after a little chastisement they will receive great blessings, because God has tested them and found them worthy to be his."

Berlin was followed by three speakers. John Richardson talked about Warhol's commitment to spirituality, observing that Andy was a regular worshiper in church on Sunday. Yoko Ono noted that "so many people's lives were touched by Andy in a very personal way." Finally Nicholas Love, an actor whom Hughes had insisted be a part of the ceremony even though he was not close to Warhol, read a quote about dying that Warhol had once given to a reporter. "When I die I don't want to leave any leftovers," Warhol had said. "I'd like to disappear. People wouldn't say 'He died today,' they'd say 'He disappeared.' But I do like the idea of people turning into dust or sand, and it would be very glamorous to be reincarnated as a big ring on Elizabeth Taylor's finger."

Once the service was over, a number of the mourners—about four hundred—proceeded from St. Patrick's to a luncheon at Billy Rose's old Diamond Horseshoe nightclub located in the basement of the Century Plaza Hotel, which was now owned by Rubell and Schrager. For the luncheon, the basement had been spray-painted silver, in honor of Warhol's Silver Factory. But the party that took place just was not the same as it would have been if Warhol had been there too, standing in a corner, talking to whoever stopped by, often watching the room in silence—and missing nothing.

In the wake of the memorial service, which was covered extensively in the New York, the national, and the international press, Hughes and Hayes had to get back to conducting the actual business of settling the estate. First they turned to the will once again. Though the will had been executed by Frank Harvey on February 23, the decree was not admitted until April 1. With the will now executed and admitted, Hughes could begin the payment process for the three people whom Warhol had indicated he wanted to receive money: $250,000 each to himself and John and Paul Warhola. In the weeks following Warhol's death, as the terms of the will became known to members of the inner circle, the

Warhola brothers had let Hughes and Hayes know that they were not at all happy with the amount they were going to inherit from their brother, who, they believed, was extremely wealthy when he died. In fact, they were considering challenging the will in court. The brothers had expressed their discontent as early as the week of the funeral. Indeed, at that time Hayes had made more than one attempt to have them sign release forms, but they would not comply.

With this conflict still unresolved, Hughes and Hayes began the process of setting up "a foundation for the advancement of the visual arts." On this point Warhol had commented further in his will: "Without limiting the generality of the foregoing, the certificate of incorporation . . . shall specifically state that the foundation is organized and operated exclusively for charitable purposes; no part of the net earnings shall inure to the benefit of any private stockholder or individual; no part of its activities shall consist of carrying on propaganda, or otherwise attempting, to influence legislation; it shall not participate in, or intervene in . . . any political campaign on behalf of any candidate for public office; and its directors shall be prohibited from engaging in any act . . . that would prevent any bequest to the foundation from qualifying as a deduction for my estate under section 2055 of the Internal Revenue Code, as amended." To fund this foundation, Warhol gave "the balance of my residuary estate." To maintain its status as a charitable organization, the foundation had to give away on a yearly basis a mere 5 percent of the value of "the balance of [the] estate."

In his will Warhol had stipulated that the foundation's board of directors was to be made up of Hughes, Fremont, and John Warhola. Hughes then had to make two key decisions: He needed to name the foundation and to provide the organization with a statement of purpose. Hughes decided to call the corporation the Andy Warhol Foundation for the Visual Arts. At the same time, he wrote the foundation's statement of purpose. It read: "The Andy Warhol Foundation for the Visual Arts supports and awards grants to both cultural institutions and organizations (as well as to park and landmark preservation) in the United States and abroad. The term 'visual arts' is generally defined to include the plastic arts—painting, sculpture, printmaking, photography, film, video, decorative arts, art publishing, etc.—and those aspects of the performing arts (dance, theatre, music) which may incorporate the plastic arts. The Foundation does not accept donations but encourages donations to the programs that it plans to support." With this in place, all that remained was for Hughes and Hayes to file the proper corporation papers, which they did on May 26, 1987. It was a simple enough act—and one, of course, that Warhol had demanded in his will. In the end, however, it would be an event Hughes probably would have liked to avoid. For through the Warhol foundation Hughes would be introduced to a world—the foundation world—that bore no resemblance to any world—art, business, high society, or otherwise—to which he had been exposed in the past. Along the way Hughes would meet a cast of characters—lawyers, board members, foundation administrators—that would make him wish for the days when all he had to worry about were "the crazies" that somehow found their way into Warhol's inner circle.

For the people who were working in the Factory in early 1987, it was interesting to watch the way Fred Hughes changed as a result of Warhol's death. For two decades, the nature of their relationship positioned Fred behind the scenes as a sort of silent strategist. Then Warhol died, and the entire focus of the Warhol legacy, at least in the area of business, shifted to Fred. "You could see a change in Fred," Sam Bolton recalls. "He was so mopey the last year Andy was alive. He had no interest in anything. He and Andy were really fighting a lot too. But after Andy died, though I'm sure he was sad, he was also excited in a way. He was really up and in a good mood." In many ways, Andy's death presented Fred with the opportunity to resolve situations he and Andy had been fighting about for years. Curiously, the main area on which Fred focused his attention in the six months after Warhol died was *Interview.* In a move that angered many people close to Warhol, Fred immediately took Warhol's name off the masthead. In response to the criticism he received, Fred quickly pointed out, "Well, after all, Andy *is* dead."

The first person to feel the fallout of Fred's actions was Richard

Bernstein, who had been friends with Warhol for twenty years and who had created over 180 *Interview* covers. Immediately following Warhol's death, Fred told Bernstein that "we are going to take care of you" because "you are family." Fred's last words to Bernstein were "Don't worry." Within weeks, though, Fred, who had come to dislike Bernstein's covers, let it be known to the staff that Bernstein would not be creating covers in the future. "All those years Fred was in the shadow of this man," Bernstein says. "So all of the relationships that he had with people were because of Andy. This was the first time he could throw some weight around and have some wind in his sails and do things himself. The rest is history."

Fred also disliked Gael Love, who had been the magazine's editor-in-chief for a while. Some of the most heated fights Fred and Andy had had in the last year or so of Andy's life were over whether Andy should fire Love, whom Fred privately referred to as "Gael Hate." Andy refused; then again, Andy never fired anybody. But on August 27, 1987, the day Love checked into the hospital to have minor surgery, Fred fired her. He later claimed a group of *Interview* staff members had come to him to complain about Love's abilities as an editor. Still, he never actually told Love she had been fired. No one told her. On her first day back at work, Love tried the door to her office, only to discover that the lock had been changed. A witness to the scene remembers, "She freaked out."

Hughes replaced Love with Shelley Wanger, a former editor at *The New York Review of Books* who was then an articles editor at *House & Garden.* Critics of Hughes's decision believed that he had not selected the most appropriate editor to put out the kind of hip publication that had earned *Interview* its reputation and readership. They speculated that Hughes had hired Wanger not for her professional experience but because she was the daughter of Joan Bennett, the actress, and Walter Wanger, the Hollywood producer, as well as the companion of David Mortimer, the grandson of Averell Harriman. This was not surprising; for years Hughes had hired employees because of their family backgrounds or for their social contacts.

. . .

Warhol and his Brillo box sculptures, 1964.

A Pop party—(*from left*) Tom Wesselmann, Roy Lichtenstein, James Rosenquist, Warhol, and Claes Oldenburg—at the Factory in April 1964.

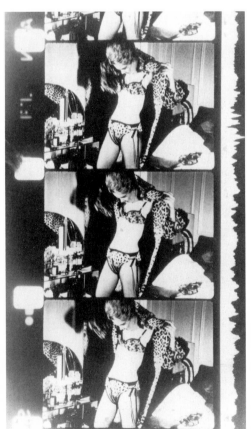

A filmstrip of Edie Sedgwick in *Poor Little Rich Girl*, 1965.

Valerie Solanis *(center)* being booked for the shooting of Andy Warhol at the 13th Precinct, June 3, 1968.

Warhol with his longtime art dealer and friend, Leo Castelli, at the Whitney Museum, 1979.

Warhol patron and the
mentor of Fred Hughes,
Dominique de Menil.

Warhol and the man
behind Warhol,
Fred Hughes.

Hughes and Paloma Picasso, one of his many high-society friends, 1975.

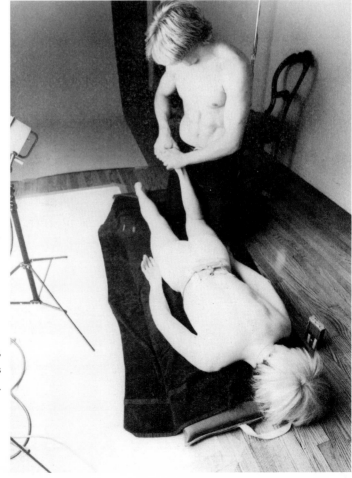

Warhol, in wig and girdle, at the hands of his masseur, 1983.

Now a famous postcard: Warhol meets Pope John Paul II at the Vatican in 1983. As usual, Hughes is at the artist's right hand.

Warhol with his shopping partner, Stuart Pivar.

Paige Powell (*right*), *Interview* advertising manager and Warhol confidante, with Benjamin Liu, one of Warhol's "walkers."

Warhol and writer Tama Janowitz on one of their "blind dates."

Warhol with Dolly Parton and Sam Bolton, Warhol's last would-be boyfriend.

Warhol standing before his version of *The Last Supper*, at his last gallery show in Milan, January 1987.

Warhol's pallbearers and
gravesite.

Warhol's brothers,
Paul (*left*) and
John Warhola.

Halston and Liza Minnelli on
April 1, 1987, the day of
Warhol's memorial service at
St. Patrick's Cathedral, where
Yoko Ono was a speaker.

Dr. Denton Cox, the artist's
longtime physician.

Objects from the 1988 estate auction at Sotheby's (*clockwise from upper left*): Fiesta Ware and cookie jars; jewelry; fine art and antique furniture photographed in Warhol's townhouse; Sotheby's warehouse before the sale.

A London pop singer, paddle in hand, inspects a bust of Napoleon on the first day of
the ten-day auction.

Edward and Susan Gilder Hayes
on their wedding day in 1986.

The godfathers: Fred Hughes and attorney Bruce Cutler at the christening of the
Hayeses' first child in 1987.

Hughes, confined to a wheelchair,
surrounded by friends (*from top*)
Nina Tower, Whitney Tower, Jr.,
and Barbara Allen, 1991.

Friends and dandies
(*from left*): Ed Hayes,
illustrator Richard
Merkin, and writer
Tom Wolfe.

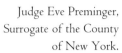

Judge Eve Preminger,
Surrogate of the County
of New York.

Archibald L. Gillies,
president of the Andy
Warhol Foundation for
the Visual Arts.

Hayes delivering his own opening argument at the trial that would determine the authentic value of the Warhol estate, 1993.

Surrogate's Court, January 1994: Robert Jossen, Hayes's attorney, delivers his closing statement. At the lawyers' table (*from right*): the estate and Foundation legal team, including chief counsel Beth Jacob (*second from right*) and Assistant Attorney General David Samuels (*leaning over table*); Hayes and his legal team. Seated behind Hayes is Jeffrey Hoffeld, art authority and Hayes's star witness. In the spectators' seats at the far end sit Tom Wolfe and Susan Gilder Hayes.

Hughes and Hayes worked together day after day throughout 1987. Hughes had become so reliant on Hayes that he had, in essence, forced Hayes to give up his law practice so he could devote all of his time and energy to the estate and the foundation. Hayes even relocated his law offices to the Factory. But despite what some Factory employees thought about Hayes—they complained about his aggressive, sometimes intimidating manner, a style completely unlike Andy's—Hayes and Hughes had had a good year. They had gotten through the funeral without any serious problems. They had put on a memorial service for Warhol that highlighted his importance not only as a fine artist but also as a celebrity and, by extension, as an American cultural figure. And they had started the extensive legal work that was going to be necessary to liquidate the estate and set up the Andy Warhol Foundation for the Visual Arts. Finally, at the end of the year, Hughes and Hayes pulled off yet another major success.

For years, Warhol would call Pat Hackett on the telephone each morning and dictate to her what had happened to him the day before. Warhol had thought about publishing this diary while he was alive—he had been approached about the project by at least one agent—but he had never pursued a deal. In the fall of 1987, Hughes and Hayes decided that the time would never be better to sell the diaries. Hughes hired Lynn Nesbit, the most powerful literary agent at International Creative Management at the time, to serve as agent for the book. In a spirited auction that ended in early December—before it, publishers were permitted only a brief, confidential "viewing" of the pages—Nesbit sold the American rights to *The Andy Warhol Diaries* to Warner Books for $1.2 million. Hackett was to edit the manuscript in exchange for a fee of some 40 percent of the proceeds. In addition, over the coming months, ICM sold off the foreign rights to the book for another million dollars. Of the twenty thousand diary pages available to Hackett, Warner Books decided that it would print only about a thousand—still an enormous amount of material to be published by a celebrity known more for his art and his own publicity than for his writing. The publication of the diaries would further promote Warhol as a cultural figure, and, even though Hackett would be paid a large percentage of the advance, a significant portion of the $2.2 million would go into the estate to help finance the foundation.

Despite all of these successes, this period of time had not been free of conflict. Most of the troubles centered around the fact that a lot of the Factory workers found Ed Hayes's presence increasingly intrusive and unacceptable; they simply could not abide his abrasive style and his security men. Since Warhol had never worked closely with an attorney, they bridled at the fact that Hayes had become a fixture at the Factory. There was little doubt, though, that Hughes and Hayes made a good team. They seemed to like and respect each other—and they certainly got things done. But what no one could know at the time, what no one except Hughes and Hayes would realize for a good while, was that there was a potentially disastrous tension forming between the two of them. More and more, Fred was feeling a growing attraction to Ed, or so Ed thought.

Throughout his youth and adulthood, Fred had always been in conflict about his sexuality. Whereas Andy had been exclusively homosexual (even if during significant periods of his life he had little if any sexual activity with partners), Fred had made an effort to live his life as a heterosexual, although no one who knew him well doubted his homosexual tendencies. The problems with his sexuality had started during his teenage years, when his father, a war hero who had received numerous medals of honor, became disgusted by what he perceived to be Fred's effeminate ways and, as a result, began to castigate him. The conflict with his father pushed him even closer to the de Menils, who were always supporting and accepting of Fred. During the sixties Fred focused more on developing his career than on forming relationships. Then, in the seventies, a decade in which he dated several different women, he married Marina Schiano, an executive in the fashion industry who through the years has been close to Giorgio Sant'Angelo, Calvin Klein, and Yves Saint Laurent. The Hugheses' marriage ended in divorce after only two years. Following the divorce, Fred dated other women, most notably Sara Giles, an editor at *Vanity Fair*, but many people who knew Fred believed he was not happy in his life, in large part because he wanted to be involved with men, not women. Though he would say he was heterosexual, he also admitted to having had homosexual encounters—after he had downed "enough gin and tonics." As late as 1993, Hughes himself seemed to identify this conflict in his personality when he told journalist and Warhol associate Bob Colacello, on the subject of what he wanted to have put on his grave: "I thought of a tombstone that says, on one side, HE WAS, and on the other side, HE WASN'T. Because that was always the question, Bob, wasn't it?" To many of his friends and colleagues, the situation was not quite so mysterious.

Throughout their friendship, Ed believed on some level that Fred was sexually attracted to him. "I knew he was in love with me," Hayes contends. "I said, 'Fred, I'm just too old to change. I'm not like that. I love you, you're my friend.' " Though Ed was famously heterosexual, he was also socially liberal in such a way that Fred may have felt comfortable enough to become unusually close to Ed.

Victor Bockris, a friend and biographer of Warhol's, observed the relationship between Hughes and Hayes. "Fred is very romantic," Bockris says. "Andy was an extremely romantic person, like Fred is a romantic person. Fred would have loved the image [of Hayes]—the character, the physical image, the way Ed dressed. To me it made sense. [It explained] their great togetherness. And I did feel there was a closeness. That's what I saw when I saw them together. There's no question that Fred had enormous admiration for Ed, so I can see him falling for him on a certain level."

At first, this did not present too much of a problem. As he had examined the contents of the estate more closely, Ed was beginning to see that he had enormous possibilities here. If Ed had ever been up front about one thing it was this: He saw no reason why someone should apologize for making money. It was an essential element in the public character Hayes had created for himself—a character that in many ways grew right out of the eighties, a decade when an unabashed thirst for money was celebrated. Of course, Warhol himself loved money as much as anyone, as did Fred Hughes.

. . .

On October 24, 1987, Susan Hayes gave birth to a baby girl, Avery Gilder Hayes. Six weeks later, on the occasion of Avery's christening, three men served as the baby's godfathers: Bruce Cutler and Michael Daly, two longtime friends of the Hayeses', and Fred Hughes. Critics of Hayes would contend that naming Hughes as a godfather to his daughter was merely a cynical move to position himself more firmly in the Warhol world. Hayes disagrees. "I really cared for the guy," he says. And this seems to be true. Ultimately, though, whatever Hayes felt for Hughes would not be enough.

4

FOR THE WEEK AND A HALF IN THE SPRING OF 1988 WHEN THE AUCTION OF the Andy Warhol Collection took place, Sotheby's was considered one of *the* places to be seen in New York. Even in death, Warhol had a way of bestowing trendiness. Here and there in the crowd were friends of Warhol's or Factory regulars or maybe even a superstar or two. There were Ultra and Viva and Paige and Stuart and Paloma and Bianca, all looking through Andy's belongings for something to buy.

In a sense the Sotheby's auction was inevitable. After all, Warhol had so much crammed into his townhouse, how else were Hughes and Hayes going to get rid of it? For a while Paige Powell had tried to convince a corporate sponsor to buy the collection to use as the basis for setting up a Warhol museum or gallery, but she could not find a company willing to invest the money. When she failed, Hughes and Hayes decided to sell off all of Warhol's collectibles—and the sooner the better; they couldn't put the townhouse on the market until all the merchandise was cleared out. With an auction, they would realize the added benefits of not having to pay someone to appraise the collection and of not having to incur any shipping and storage expenses. So, in the fall of 1987, the two men had approached both Christie's and Sotheby's; of the two auction houses, Sotheby's gave them the better financial deal. As they began to look through the collection, the Sotheby's staff had a hunch that would later be confirmed: The Warhol collectible collection, which ultimately contained ten thousand items, would be the largest single collection sold at Sotheby's since its founding in 1744.

The auction began on April 23. Over the next ten days, sixty thousand people would go through Sotheby's simply to look at the collection or, in many cases, to buy items from more than 3,400 lots. Initially Sotheby's believed that the auction would raise somewhere between $10 million and $15 million, but as the auction catalogues went on sale— thirteen thousand priced at $95 each—it became apparent that the total figure could climb much higher. The catalogues were selling so fast that before long the entire printing was sold out. On display were paintings by, among other artists, Salvador Dalí, Norman Rockwell, Maxfield Parrish, Man Ray, Jasper Johns, Roy Lichtenstein, Marcel Duchamp, and Cy Twombly. There was a Rolls-Royce, a group of pedestals (Warhol's last collecting interest), and a sampling of Warhol's personal effects, such as his books and memorabilia. Then there were all those "masterpieces": Navajo blanket rugs, Navajo pottery, Indian jewelry, Puiforcat silver, Wedgewood art deco pottery, art deco furniture, Fiesta Ware, Swatch watches, rare pieces of furniture like a pair of Legrain console tables and a Ruhlman armchair, vast quantities of jewelry representing several different styles and periods (Salvador Dalí ear clips, a gold Patek Philippe wristwatch, a plastic Fred Flintstone wristwatch, a Cartier brooch, a Seaman Schepps bracelet, to name just a few), and the list went on. Among the lots, though, the ones that generated the most press attention were those that contained Warhol's cookie jar collection. Through the years, Warhol had slowly built up his collection by buying one cookie jar after another at flea markets and junk sales, usually for a modest price—five or ten dollars apiece. Of the ten days of the auction, surely the oddest was the Sunday Warhol's collection of cookie jars went on sale.

They had come from Florida and Paris and Halifax, Nova Scotia—a throng of people, maybe as many as ten thousand, who had jammed into Sotheby's enormous five-story building on the corner of York Avenue and Seventy-second Street, only a short walk up from New York Hospital. There were so many people that the Sotheby's security staff had to shut the doors and turn away potential customers, a rarity in the auction business. Some of the thousands had come to buy a specific item—an article of jewelry or a particular antique—but many had shown up in hopes of purchasing anything that had belonged to Andy. As it turned out, a number of these memorabilia seekers had planned on buying one of the lots of cookie jars. After all, the jars were colorful and different, they had belonged to Warhol, and they were moderately priced, at least by Sotheby's standards. In the catalogue, the highest any of the thirty-five lots was predicted to bring was $250, and the lowest was $75—less than the cost of the catalogue itself.

The first lot of cookie jars went on sale. In the front of the room, at the large podium, John Marion, a genial man in his early fifties who was the head auctioneer for the entire sale, called out the lot number, and the bidding began. In the crowded auction room, which had been set up with chairs to hold as many spectators as possible, one and then another bid came up from the audience until the going price had climbed through the hundreds and over a thousand dollars. A palpable sense of astonishment came over the audience. When the gavel came down, the cookie jars in the lot had sold for the amazing sum of $1,980. The room buzzed as the spectators whispered to each other in disbelief. Even Marion, who had seen almost everything in the auction business over the years, seemed surprised.

I know I was. I was in the audience at Sotheby's that afternoon. Like so many people, I had been aware of the public image that Warhol had created. I had seen him in the newspapers. I had seen him in the Pontiac commercial, the one in which he had stood silently staring at the camera for the full thirty seconds, holding in his arms Brigid Berlin's pug. Unfortunately, I had missed Warhol's appearance on *The Love Boat*, but I had imagined that in content and style it probably rivaled the Pontiac commercial. Despite such examples of the way he had built his public persona over the years, a persona in which he almost always appeared detached, even superficial, I was drawn to Warhol because of the body of work he had created, work that I believed was anything but superficial. More than any other artist, he had, as Ezra Pound said a writer must do, anchored the abstraction. I came to Sotheby's that Sunday to see the spectacle of Warhol's belongings, to try and learn something about him as an artist and, yes, maybe even to buy one of those lots of cookie jars. But not for several thousand dollars.

The second lot went for an equally outrageous price; so did the third and the fourth. As the lots sold, it became clear that almost all of them were being bought by one man. Who was crazy enough to pay so much money for a bunch of relatively worthless cookie jars? His name was Gedalio Grinberg, we would find out later, when the story was inevitably picked up by the press. The president of the North American Watch Company, Grinberg later told *The New York Times* that he was a friend of Warhol's who was planning to have his company make a Warhol watch. Some extraordinary motive must have been driving him. Out of the thirty-five lots of cookie jars that were sold that Sunday at Sotheby's, Grinberg bought all but four.

One lot Grinberg lost was bought by Stuart Pivar, who paid $11,550 for it because it contained a National Silver mammy. "Andy always said if you are going to own a cookie jar you have to have a Silver mammy," Stuart said following the sale. Grinberg also lost the other lot that had a National Silver mammy in it. That lot, made up of only two jars, sold for $23,100, the record price paid for a lot of cookie jars sold at auction. The man who bought the record-breaking lot, Jim Judelson, an executive from New York, said he paid that much because his friend "wanted that set of cookie jars very much." At the end of the bidding, Warhol's collection of cookie jars had fetched $247,830.

When the ten-day Sotheby's auction was finally over, it had generated

$25.3 million, almost twice the amount Sotheby's had predicted it would raise. Of the 3,436 lots, only 78 remained unsold. The most expensive item in the auction was a Cy Twombly painting that went for $990,000. In the end, the auction was an unqualified success. It had raised an astonishing sum of money; it had been the focus of extensive media coverage, all of it positive; and it had established Warhol as one of the most avid collectors of his generation.

In the months following Warhol's death, many people, even some who knew him well, were shocked when it became apparent exactly what he had owned. Warhol had put together a substantial portfolio of investments. He owned the townhouse on Lexington Avenue that Fred had been renting since 1974; the townhouse at 57 East Sixty-sixth Street; a compound, made up of five buildings on nineteen acres, in Montauk, Long Island, which he owned with Paul Morrissey; and the Factory, actually three separate properties known collectively as the Old Con Edison Building. In addition, he owned pieces of investment property—a forty-acre parcel of land near Aspen, Colorado; a cooperative building at 3 Hanover Square in Manhattan; and two rental buildings on Great Jones and Bowery on the Lower East Side of Manhattan. Warhol owned stock in numerous companies, including Boeing, General Motors, IBM, Reliance Group Holdings, the Signet Banking Group, Wellcome Farmers Group, Inc., Great American Management Investment, LIN Broadcasting Co., Sage Analytics International, and Shearson Daily Dividend. He also held bonds of the New York State Power Authority and the Port Authority of New York and New Jersey. He had $1 million in cash in various bank accounts in New York, plus just over $4.5 million in life insurance policies. In a Keogh plan, he had accumulated $104,514; in different retirement accounts he had another three-quarters of a million dollars. Finally, though they would never appear as part of the formal estate accounting, Warhol was widely rumored among his employees to have bank accounts in Switzerland that, at the time of his death, may have contained as much as several million dollars in cash.

These were the assets that Hughes and Hayes expected to liquidate without too many complications, but Warhol had other—more
unique—assets that would have to be disposed of on an individual basis.
There was *Interview* magazine, which at the time of Warhol's death had
both a good circulation and a sound advertising base. Warhol also
owned the film rights to Tama Janowitz's *Slaves of New York*, which was
already in development. Then there was the name Andy Warhol, which
could be licensed and marketed, and finally, the single largest asset of the
estate, Warhol's own work, which included his films, video and television projects, paintings, drawings, prints, and photographs. While
Hughes and Hayes had started liquidating Warhol's nonart assets, they
would have to deal with Warhol's own artwork in a special way, for it
was like no other asset in the estate, perhaps like no other asset in any
other estate in this century, except for Picasso's.

By now, Hughes had grown so dependent on Hayes—who had become
rather expert as a self-educated estate attorney—that the two men
renegotiated their retainer agreement one more time. "In the last six
months," Hughes wrote to Hayes in June 1988, "[you and I] have both
gained a greater appreciation of the amount of work, time and effort that
an estate of this size and complexity involves. For all intents and
purposes, you have had to give up your law practice in order to properly
advise the Estate. Although I have not required you to account for the
hours spent on the Estate, I recognize that you are now devoting
substantially all of your time to Estate matters. I have asked you to
relocate your office to 22 East 33rd Street so that you can be on constant
call for Estate activities and you have done so. You have had to retain
a staff of other attorneys to be able to attend to the wide variety of legal
questions that have arisen. Further, you have had to participate, under
my direction, in a number of complicated matters in, for instance,
publishing and licensing, to prudently increase the value of the Estate.
The inventory and management of the art assets is much more demanding than originally contemplated." Because of these developments,
Hughes wanted to tell Hayes he now "agreed that the attorney's fees in

this estate shall be computed on the same basis as, and in an amount equal to, an Executor's Commission." Hughes then established a new payout schedule: One fourth of Hayes's fee would be paid by January 15, 1988, one half by October 15, 1988, and three fourths by January 15, 1989. The rest would be paid when the estate was closed out.

Later, on December 12, 1988, the payout schedule was modified yet again. The October 15, 1988 deadline was extended to January 15, 1989. The payment for the last 25 percent "will be made beginning October 1, 1989 through January 30, 1990, as funds are available." As before, both Hughes and Hayes signed the letter of agreement, making this the fourth agreement concerning Hayes's payment the two men had reached.

In the late summer of 1988, Fred took a hiking trip to Costa Rica with some friends, among them Sara Giles and Tim Hunt, a curator at the Factory. As they were hiking through the forest, one of Fred's legs gave way and he fell to the ground. When he tried to stand up, he couldn't. He had not tripped; his knee had not buckled. His leg simply had ceased functioning.

When he returned to New York, Fred went to see his doctor, who confirmed his worst fears. Some years back, Fred had been diagnosed as having multiple sclerosis, the degenerative muscular disease that causes the muscles in the body to harden and, as a result, to lose their ability to function. The disease had remained in remission until now. Slowly it would render the muscles in Fred's body useless, unless—against the odds—it slipped back into remission. More likely, Fred was doomed to a life of steadily failing health.

Through the years, doctors have debated what exactly causes a person to develop multiple sclerosis. The gene that produces the disease is probably present at birth, yet some other factor will trigger the disease into action. There are two probable catalysts that could have caused Fred's disease to become active. One was his years of heavy drinking; alcohol abuse has been known to activate latent multiple sclerosis. The other possible cause was stress. Though most of the decisions Fred had made during 1987 and 1988 had been good ones, he still frequently found himself under a level of tension he had never before experienced. This stress was no doubt the reason he was sometimes grumpy and short-tempered, but it may have also ended up creating a medical condition that ultimately would be severely debilitating, perhaps even life-threatening. As Fred's physical condition deteriorated, more than one of his friends would note how ironic it would be if the tragedy of Andy's death held in it the beginnings of Fred's demise as well.

In September, Fred was hospitalized because of complications caused by the disease. It was soon after this hospital visit that Fred concluded he needed help with some of the day-to-day administrative duties relating to the foundation. He could handle the estate, but over the past year the responsibilities associated with running the foundation had grown significantly. Hughes decided to hire an administrator who would essentially oversee the foundation's daily activities. Hughes would still be on the board of directors; he would remain the chairman of the board, a position he had held since the foundation was created; and he would continue to make all of the important decisions involving the foundation's business dealings. Hughes envisioned the position as a glorified secretary, someone who seemed to have power within the foundation but who merely enacted the decisions Hughes and the board would make.

Hughes discussed whom he could hire for the job with Paige Powell. It was an odd move since Fred and Paige had often clashed through the years. Paige said that the one person she knew on the foundation circuit was Linda Gillies, the director of the Vincent Astor Foundation. Fred was impressed if for no other reason than because the Vincent Astor Foundation was affiliated with Brooke Astor, the prominent New York social figure. Fred instructed Paige to visit the offices of the Astor foundation. Paige learned that Gillies ran the foundation with a modest staff on what amounted to a shoestring budget. Paige told Gillies that she liked her management style; it was wonderful that so much of the foundation's money went to charities and not to the administration of the foundation. In response, Linda told Paige that she needed to meet her husband, Arch. So Paige set up a lunch with Fred and Arch.

The lunch took place at a small Italian restaurant down the street from the Factory. Paige joined Fred and Arch for the lunch. After exchanging a few idle pleasantries, the three of them got down to business.

"I have to tell you right off," Gillies said, "I don't know anything about art."

"It's not really important that you know about art," Hughes said. "I don't know anything about running a foundation. I want your expertise about running a foundation."

Gillies perked up: This was his world. "You have to put together a board," he said. "You have to have meetings. You have to have a person who can take the minutes. You have to have a really nice social lunch for board members—if you're bringing in outside people."

Hughes seemed to be taking in what Gillies was saying. They ate for a while and chatted leisurely. That is, Hughes and Gillies talked; Paige mostly listened. Finally, Hughes got back around to the subject at hand. "It's great the way your wife runs the Astor foundation with such a small staff," Hughes said. "The quality of what she does is just remarkable. That's why I wanted to speak with you."

"You have to streamline the overhead of the operations," Gillies said in response. "It's very easy to do—to keep the operating costs down. You can do it with a minimum staff and low overhead."

That's all Hughes needed to hear. By the end of the lunch, he had offered Gillies a position at the foundation as a consultant. Arch would begin work on a trial basis. They agreed on a consulting fee in the days following the lunch, and in the early fall of 1988 Arch Gillies began his new job.

Archibald L. Gillies was born on March 29, 1934, in New York City into a solid middle-class family. Despite his father's humble financial situation, Gillies attended Choate Academy, where he graduated in the early fifties. From there, he went on to Princeton University, graduating in 1956. As a middle-class student in two student bodies made up of the children of the wealthy and socially connected, Gillies learned to make his way in environments defined by privilege and money. In 1956 he started working for Nelson A. Rockefeller, first on the financial side of Rockefeller's operations, then on the political side. By serving on Rockefeller's various political campaigns, Gillies became fascinated with politics. Eventually he himself flirted with a political life when in the mid-sixties he ran for the Republican congressional nomination from a district on Long Island; however, he dropped out before the race even reached the primary election because it had become obvious early on that he had no chance of winning against William Casey.

In 1969 Gillies was hired by John Hay ("Jock") Whitney, another New York millionaire, to become president of the John Hay Whitney Foundation. A small entity in the larger Whitney organization, the foundation was responsible for giving out on a yearly basis several grants worth a few million dollars. Gillies kept the job until 1979, when he made two more forays into politics. In 1977 he ran as a Republican from Manhattan for a seat on the New York City Council—and lost. Next, in 1979 and 1980, he was involved in the presidential campaign of Barry Commoner, the candidate of the Citizen's Party, a quasiliberal environmentalist organization that never caught on with the American public. In the general election, Commoner pulled down a scant one percent of the popular vote.

In the wake of these two failures, Gillies was not sure where to go next in his career. He had left the Whitney foundation to focus on politics, and the two ventures he chose to pursue could not have been more disastrous. Faced with an uncertain professional future, Gillies decided that if the established world of politics was not going to welcome him, he would create his own political forum from which to speak. So, in 1982, he founded the World Policy Institute, a liberal think tank that espoused progressive politics and published those opinions in the *World Policy Journal*. Eventually, in 1984, he became so disillusioned with the Republican party—especially on the state level where the party was controlled by politicians like Al D'Amato—that he became a Democrat.

Gillies was still working as the president of the World Policy Institute when Hughes approached him about consulting for the Warhol foundation in the early fall of 1988.

In essence, though, what Gillies was, above all else, was a foundation man. Ensconced in an organization created by the wealth of someone else—someone like John Guggenheim or Henry Ford or Andy Warhol, geniuses who made a fortune and then left that money to the ultimate benefit of the public—foundation men tend to be conservative, small-thinking, careful to a fault, just the opposite of the kind of person who created the fortune that supports them. Where an entrepreneur thinks big, sees opportunities, takes risks, a foundation man does just the opposite: He conserves, plots, manages. Mostly he goes to meetings—lots of meetings, as many meetings as he can fit into a day. Andy Warhol hated foundation men. And Arch Gillies was an aspiring foundation man. Reserved and unimaginative, Arch had spent much of his life working within the strict confines of the foundation, where wearing a turtleneck instead of a button-down shirt is considered to be a radical, possibly even subversive, statement. Oddly enough, it was for this style of conformity that Fred had hired Arch. It would not be until later, when it was too late, that Fred learned firsthand that Arch could be petty and vindictive. Warhol would have never gotten that far with Gillies, however; he would have never gotten past his résumé.

To some, Gillies represented a particular class in America, especially prevalent on the East Coast, that saw as the central development in one's life the act of being listed in the Social Register. In many ways culturally conservative and socially regressive, this class of people seemed like a throwback to another era—to the fifties, or before. They were also a dying element in American society, being killed off in part by the radical social movements of the sixties, the sexual liberation of the seventies, and the openly aggressive entrepreneurship of the eighties. But Fred didn't care if Arch represented a dying class. In some ways Fred himself embraced that class. Anyway, maybe Fred just needed someone who knew how to take the minutes of a meeting, something so foreign to Fred it seemed almost otherworldly.

. . .

Not long after the Sotheby's sale, a cache of some three hundred pieces of jewelry was found in the bottom of a filing cabinet in Warhol's townhouse. Reports about the discovery appeared in the press—supposedly a Factory employee ran across the stash one day while he was looking around the house—and another, considerably smaller, auction was lined up. That auction took place in December, again at Sotheby's; it raised an additional $1.64 million. But some Warhol insiders believed that the second auction was merely an effort to respond to a serious allegation being made against the estate: that not *all* of Warhol's jewelry and furniture had been included in the Sotheby's auction. The first sale may have consisted of ten thousand items, yet countless pieces of jewelry and furniture that Warhol had bought through the years had not surfaced in the sale. "There was a lot of junk in that Sotheby's sale," says a buyer who sometimes bid against Warhol in auctions. "That second batch was junk too," contends another.

In the early seventies, Warhol went to auctions at Parke Bernet. One underbidder remembers three large, expensive pieces of furniture that Warhol purchased. "They were top items we were bidding on, top-quality merchandise," she says. "Andy bought these three big pieces of furniture. We're talking major pieces, even for back then—fifteen-to-twenty-thousand-dollar range. I think one was a Benet highboy. I'm ninety-nine percent sure they were not in the sale, because I was looking for them. In fact, there was nothing of their caliber. A lot of junk was in that sale."

Besides the John Lennon lithographs for which Warhol traded Frank Andrews, which didn't show up, there were more items that were never accounted for. Paige Powell remembers a piece of jewelry that she describes as "Andy's favorite diamond ring"—a solid stainless steel band with a small diamond set in it that Andy owned when he died. Sam Bolton recalls another ring, a modest five-hundred-dollar gold band that he gave to Andy. For years, Warhol collected the jewelry of Seaman Schepps. Store records indicate that over the years Warhol bought numerous pieces of Schepps jewelry. In 1975, he purchased, on separate occasions, a 618-carat emerald necklace for $6,500 and two emerald bracelets, one for $3,000 and one for $3,850. In February 1983 he bought a set of five fish made out of carved stone for $1,800. The following year he purchased a gold compact for $1,500 and a three-inch-high replica of a birdcage—which Schepps had created for his wife, who loved parakeets—for $6,000. These were only a few of Warhol's many Schepps pieces. Of all these items, though, only a handful were in the Sotheby's sale.

The buyer who was often Warhol's underbidder thinks it is possible that "twenty years from now, someone will open a letter and it will say, 'Now let me tell you where all the good stuff is hidden.' It'll be Andy's last laugh." But other Warhol associates have different ideas about where some of Warhol's collectibles may have gone. They point out that at a bank in Manhattan Fred Hughes, who proudly considers himself a collector, is rumored to have at least a half-dozen large safety deposit boxes full of jewelry, more jewelry than a person could ever imagine owning—unless the person was Andy Warhol.

The estate ended 1988 by making one last noteworthy sale—the townhouse on Lexington Avenue in which Fred had been living. As part of his payment for working for Warhol, Fred was allowed to rent the house at a drastically lower rate than what the property could have brought on the open market. According to a lease drawn up between Fred Hughes and Andy Warhol Enterprises, Inc., a lease that was neither dated nor notarized and that was signed not by Warhol himself but by Vincent Fremont, Fred was to pay $9,000 a year from 1982 to 1988, $15,000 a year from 1989 to 1992, and $21,000 a year from 1993 to 1996. The rent was to be paid "once annually in December." The lease, which ran from January 1, 1982, to December 31, 1996, was a standard one, the kind easily bought in any stationery store, except for two provisions that had been typed in at the end: "Tenant to have right of first refusal if building is offered for sale" and "This lease is in consideration of Tenants improvements." For all practical purposes, Hughes had the Lexington Avenue property tied up until 1996.

In early 1988 Hughes filed a petition, dated February 10, in surrogate's court explaining that he had a lease on the property through 1996; that his rent was so low the estate was losing money on the rental; that the property had been appraised for as little as $450,000 and as high as $800,000; and that he was willing to pay a purchase price of $513,419. It was not until November 17 that the surrogate, Renee R. Roth, issued a court order granting Hughes permission to buy the property. But Roth made two provisions in her order: Hughes had to pay $593,500 for the house—obviously she felt it was worth somewhat more than Hughes's bid—and he had to complete the sale by January 15, 1989. Hughes agreed to the stipulations, completing the deal.

Hughes had been able to buy a townhouse for just under $600,000 in a neighborhood where houses routinely sold for between $1 million and $2 million. What's more, he made the deal on the basis of an undated, unnotarized lease that the landlord himself had not signed.

5

WITH TEMPERATURES HOVERING IN THE SIXTIES, IT SEEMED MORE LIKE LATE spring than winter, but in fact it was early February 1989. The weather was a topic of conversation among the four thousand guests who had come to the Museum of Modern Art for a reception celebrating "Andy Warhol: A Retrospective," a major show that was scheduled to run through May 2, when it would begin touring the United States and Europe. Throughout his career, Warhol had longed for the respect as an artist that some of his contemporaries received. He especially coveted the admiration that the art press and the art establishment had given

Jasper Johns. Warhol believed that the quality and quantity of his artistic output warranted similar esteem, but he never got it, much to his disappointment.

The public persona Warhol cultivated made him internationally famous, yet it had also served to alienate him from certain sectors of the art world. "[Andy] had his own relationship with the public," Henry Geldzahler told a *New York Times* reporter that night at the reception, "something that makes museums nervous." More than likely, this speaks to why MoMA had never held a Warhol retrospective while he was alive—a professional accolade Warhol desperately wanted. So, on this evening nearly two years after his death, a crowd that included Dennis Hopper, Dominique de Menil, Keith Haring, Roy Lichtenstein, Baby Jane Holzer, Ultra Violet, Claes Oldenburg, Julian Schnabel, and art-world establishment figures like Agnes Gund and Blanchette Rockefeller strolled from room to room reviewing Warhol's career. "[This] is what Andy wanted all his life," Ultra Violet said that night, "and he had to die to get it."

What both this opening-night audience and the overflow crowds that came to the museum in the next few weeks saw was, as one of the museum announcements described it, "[an] exhibition [that] presents the full breadth of the artist's extraordinarily rich and prolific career." Starting with Warhol's fifties drawings, moving on into his pop work of the sixties, continuing with his celebrity portraits of the seventies, and ending with work from the eighties like *The Last Supper*, the retrospective did its best to represent the entire range of Warhol's art. The people who put the show together—Hughes and Hayes negotiated with the museum for the estate about which paintings would be used, and Kynaston McShine curated the exhibition—set out to prove that because of the "full breadth" of his "rich and prolific career," Warhol was a great artist. "Very few artists achieve the level of recognition that secures for them a place in the public imagination," McShine wrote in the introduction to the retrospective's catalogue. "Andy Warhol was an artist who did. However, this very celebrity of Warhol's, his sheer, inescapable fame, has often disguised the fact that he was one of the most serious, and one of the most important, artists of the twentieth century. He quite simply changed how we all see the world around us."

Reviewers agreed with McShine. "The exhibition underlines Warhol's enormous importance and gift," Michael Brenson wrote in *The New York Times*. "The Warhol effect derives from the casual inevitability of his images and the way raw, upstart ambition scratches soundlessly at the quiet, self-effacing surface." Even Robert Hughes, who for years had attacked Warhol's work in the popular press, found praise for Warhol in his *Time* review. "Warhol's power, uneven as it was, lay in an emotional narrative that contradicted its cold, fixed iconic surface," Hughes wrote. "He unskeined a story in which a horror of the world, verging sometimes on acute dread, mingled with an artificial calm and a desire for transcendence." Some critics were even more laudatory. "Warhol must be considered," Thomas Hoving wrote in *Fame*, "in the top rank of American painters of the twentieth century—indeed, one of the most refreshing, gifted, and significant painters on the world stage. In a brief burst of two or three years"—a reference to Warhol's period of intense creativity in the early sixties—"Andy Warhol changed art history forever."

It was accolades such as these that encouraged Fred Hughes and Charles Wright, the president of the Dia foundation, in a unique idea they shared: a museum devoted exclusively to the work of Andy Warhol. The Andy Warhol Museum would be located in the artist's hometown, Pittsburgh. If their plans came together the way they hoped, it would be the largest single-artist museum in the United States—a fact that would place Warhol alongside Picasso in terms of the importance of his contribution to art in this century.

Back in 1988, Wright and Hughes had approached officials at the Carnegie Institute in Pittsburgh to gauge their interest in the project. The Carnegie agreed not only to help buy and renovate an appropriate building to house the museum but also to manage the museum once it was opened. So, during 1988 and on into 1989, Hughes and Hayes drew up the legal framework from which the three parties—the Warhol foundation, the Dia Center for the Arts, and the Carnegie Institute—

could proceed to create the Andy Warhol Museum. Hughes and Hayes also assisted the Carnegie in choosing a suitable building in Pittsburgh that, through renovation, could be made into a museum. They picked an old eighty-eight-thousand-square-foot warehouse on the north side of the city, just a short walk from the central business district. The way they saw it, the museum would do on a permanent basis what the MoMA retrospective had accomplished for a few months in 1989: It would stand as a testament to the lasting value of Warhol's art.

At this time Hughes and Hayes solidified an overall plan for the financial future of the foundation. First, the foundation was to donate a large block of Warhol's art to the Warhol museum; by doing so, the foundation could satisfy the 5 percent rule—the law that says all tax-exempt public corporations must give away 5 percent of their assets each year to charity. This donation would cover them for years to come, perhaps as long as eight years or more. During that time, the foundation would judiciously sell off its art and nonart assets and build up a trust fund worth a hundred million dollars—or more. Then, when it had to start giving away money again, the foundation would be in a position where it would essentially only have to donate the money it would make off investing its principal, the financial base of which would never have to be touched. It was a solid, well-thought-out plan of action.

After the phenomenal successes of the Sotheby's auction and the MoMA retrospective, Hughes and Hayes decided that there would never be a better time to sell *Interview*. Since Hughes had fired Gael Love and replaced her with Shelley Wanger, the magazine had changed radically in its style and content. At one time the bible of hip, the magazine had become more literary, better written, more closely edited—and not nearly as much fun to read. Slowly the audience had dwindled from the record numbers the magazine had posted just before Warhol's death. So word was leaked to a small clique of wealthy New York publishers that *Interview* was up for sale. Malcolm Forbes and S. I. Newhouse expressed interest, but it was Peter Brant, the publisher of *Art in America*, who aggressively pursued the magazine. His bid of $12 million was much more than Forbes and Newhouse, who had not yet tendered firm offers, were even considering. Hughes and Hayes accepted Brant's bid and agreed to the fairly simple payout schedule Brant suggested. Brant would pay the Warhol estate $4 million in cash when he signed the contract; over the next several years, he would pay the estate an additional $8 million "less the amount of deferred subscription liability assumed by Buyer," to quote the contract. The estate would essentially finance the loan, on which Brant would pay interest. All parties accepted the deal, so the magazine was sold, seemingly for much more than it was worth.

Brant made his on-signing payment of $4 million. He also began to make his loan payments. But eventually he and the estate would fall into a serious dispute over how much he paid for the magazine and just how successful the magazine was when he bought it. (He would contend the circulation and advertising-page totals had been inflated.) It was a matter that would one day end up in court, not unlike several other business deals involving the estate and the foundation that would transpire in the coming months and years.

Since the multiple sclerosis had first manifested itself back in the late summer of 1988, Fred's health had progressively—and rather rapidly—deteriorated. First he had to walk with a cane; before long, he was often confined to a wheelchair, though on some days he was still strong enough to get around with a cane. Throughout his home and the Factory, Fred had workmen install handrails, hand-carved pieces of wood that looked like slender tree branches, so he could walk short distances on his own. At the same time, he had motorized seats installed alongside the staircases between all of the floors of his townhouse and between the Factory's first and second floors. If he had to go higher in the Factory, someone would have to carry him up the stairs. At any rate, an assistant would carry him from a building (his home, the Factory, or anywhere else he happened to be) to his car. The image of Fred being carried was poignant. For years he had been painstaking about his appearance—his clothes, his hair, his body. He was always impeccably dressed. Slender, dark-haired, handsome, he looked like a European aristocrat when he walked through a room. Now, all of that had changed. As the muscles in his body weakened, his physical appearance changed as well. His hair began to thin. His arms and legs became gaunt. His face withered and wrinkled.

As often happens with a patient suffering from multiple sclerosis, Fred became angry—with the disease, with his own body, with the people in his life. He was moody and temperamental; often he would fly into a rage if someone made the wrong comment. During meetings, he occasionally got so furious that he would scream at the top of his voice. On its most basic level, Fred's behavior was understandable, no matter how repugnant it may have been to those around him. After all, he had once been an energetic, fortunate man who could do whatever he pleased; now a disease was relentlessly eating away at his body's very ability to function.

Of all the episodes that came to represent the tragedy of Fred's physical condition, one incident stood out among those familiar with the situation. Ed and Fred had gone to Pittsburgh to attend a meeting with representatives of the Dia foundation and the Carnegie Institute to discuss the planning for the Andy Warhol Museum. It was a heady time for Fred. He was the key person on a small team of people who were building a museum that would be a shrine to an artist whose career he had guided for two decades. This day's meeting, held at the Duquesne Club, had been especially productive. Then, suddenly and unexpectedly, as Ed and Fred were leaving the club, Fred realized that he needed to go to the bathroom. Sporadic incontinence is one of the more embarrassing symptoms of multiple sclerosis. Fred, who was walking with a cane today, knew he had to get to the bathroom as quickly as possible, so he asked Ed if he would carry him there.

Ed understood the urgency. He took Fred in his arms—an amateur weightlifter, Ed often lifted barbells heavier than Fred, whose weight had dropped significantly as a result of the multiple sclerosis—and started for the bathroom. Halfway down the long hallway, Fred was no longer able to control his bladder. As Ed ran he could feel the urine soak through Fred's clothes and into his. In the bathroom Ed cleaned the two of them up as best he could. Still, it was a gut-wrenching moment. Fred's mood—understandably—had changed dramatically from the high he had felt only moments ago in the successful meeting to an almost unimaginable low.

When Fred got extremely sick, he became all but incapacitated—confined to his bed in a temporary state of paralysis that could last for several days. If his condition worsened, he would be hospitalized, since there was always the chance that his lungs would simply stop functioning. On days he was well enough to move about, he was often so irritable that he was difficult to deal with. His moody nature was only made worse by the medication he was forced to take in order to make himself strong enough to move around as much as he did—it had an effect similar to that of a huge dose of speed.

Throughout the summer of 1989, Fred was exceedingly abusive of Ed. He would become furious because Ed wouldn't go home with him at four o'clock in the afternoon (Fred now regularly went home early). He was jealous of the time Ed spent in the gym working out. He grew angry when Ed would not accompany him to social functions; in fact, Fred almost seemed to resent that Ed had a wife and a child at home. Maybe Fred was often angry and resentful because the disease made him feel more needy. Ed had another idea: He was sure that Fred had become more, not less, infatuated with him over time.

Though the tension that had developed between them was rather abstract, there was one specific sequence of events about which Hughes and Hayes ended up fighting bitterly. Since Warhol's death, the estate had maintained a policy—one that Hayes himself had championed—of authenticating any Warhol canvas that was submitted to it for verification. A person would show a canvas to the estate, and the estate—that is to say, Fred Hughes or Vincent Fremont—would examine the canvas to determine whether it was a Warhol or a fake. Standard authentication programs require the authenticator to stand by his decision; should it turn out that the canvas is not legitimate, the authenticator has to pay the person in full for the canvas as recompense. Hayes believed that an authentication program of this sort made the estate's artwork more valuable. After all, if dealers could feel confident in whatever Warhol art they were selling, they would be likely to deal in more Warhol art.

Sometime before the summer of 1989, Robert Miller, the owner of the Robert Miller Gallery, called on Hughes to authenticate a Superman collage supposedly created by Warhol; Miller was considering buying fifteen Superman collages that a man from Italy was offering for $175,000. In the process, Hughes somehow ended up with one of the collages for himself—for free. He then authenticated the entire batch. When Hayes found out about the deal, he was incensed. Regardless of what had actually transpired, according to Hayes the transaction created the appearance that Hughes had been given the painting in exchange for authenticating all fifteen. "I'm not going to take these kinds of chances with you," Hayes says he yelled at Hughes at one point. "I don't know *what* else you've done."

Some months after he had concluded his deal with the Italian, Miller learned beyond a doubt that the paintings were fakes. Because Hughes had authenticated them, Miller went to him to collect his $175,000. Hughes refused to pay—a decision that made Miller angry. How could Hughes not pay him? In purhasing the paintings, he had relied on the authentication. But just as suddenly as Miller had brought up the issue, he dropped it. When Hughes finally filled Hayes in on the situation with Miller, Hayes told him that the estate would have to pay; a deal is a deal, he argued. Hughes disagreed; he saw no reason why the estate should have to pay Miller off. Hughes claimed his authentication had only been informal. So Hayes went to Miller directly, and it was then that he learned why Miller had withdrawn his complaint so abruptly.

Hughes had conferred with Arch Gillies about the dispute, and afterward he had felt even more confident in his convictions. At some point it must have become clear to Miller that if he did not drop his grievance, the friction between himself and the estate and the foundation would prevent them from doing business together in the future. So Miller agreed not only to drop his complaint but also to sign a waiver agreement relinquishing all claims against the estate. Continuing to be concerned about the integrity of the authentication process, Hayes asked Hughes to change his mind. Hughes refused and asked Hayes himself to draw up the waiver. Hayes balked. This was not the way the estate and the foundation should be doing business, he argued—he was not going to have any part of it. Hughes took his problem to Gillies, who in turn approached Peter P. McN. Gates, his personal attorney and a senior partner in the firm of Carter Ledyard & Milburn, a high-priced Wall Street firm that specialized in corporate law.

In the end this disagreement between Hughes and Hayes would have a serious effect on their working relationship. At the same time, Hughes decided that perhaps he had an ally in Gillies. Hughes especially admired the hard-line position Gillies had encouraged him to take with Miller. Gillies had been a consultant to the foundation for over six months. He had been instrumental in setting up the foundation's grant program, the mechanism it was going to use to give away the 5 percent of its assets each year as required by law. The grant program had gotten under way in 1988 and was continuing to function well in 1989. Hughes started to think he should bring Gillies more fully into the operations of the foundation. Perhaps he should even offer Gillies a contract to work for the foundation on a permanent basis.

When Hughes mentioned this to Hayes, he was absolutely opposed to the idea. There was something about Arch Gillies that Ed Hayes didn't like. Gillies rubbed him the wrong way; to Hayes, Gillies seemed phony and superficial. Hayes didn't have much use for foundation men either. He had always had to fight hard to get what he wanted in life, and he had ended up with a lot—a house in Bellport, a townhouse in the East Eighties in Manhattan, a comfortable amount of money in the bank. But to Hayes, Gillies was complacent and lazy. "Arch Gillies has never broken a sweat in his life," Hayes would soon start saying. As for Gillies, he was beginning to develop a bad opinion of Hayes. To Gillies's way of thinking, Hayes was just an abrasive thug lawyer.

. . .

In November 1989 Hughes and Hayes had another disagreement, which dealt the final blow to their relationship. Because Fred's health was deteriorating, he was in constant contact with his doctors at New York Hospital. (It's curious to note that Fred continued his association with the hospital even though its standard of practice was questionable in light of the circumstances surrounding Warhol's death.) For over a year now, Fred had watched his body being destroyed by this disease. Often he seemed to be reaching out to Ed to help him cope with his illness. This had the effect of making Ed feel as helpless as Fred. Finally, at some point in November, as Hayes tells the story, Fred instructed Ed to talk to his doctor at New York Hospital. Maybe there was something that could be done.

One day, from Ed's office, Ed and Vincent—Ed was careful to have someone with him—telephoned Fred's doctor, who merely told them what they both already knew. Fred was extremely sick. To cope with his illness, Fred had to take medication. The illness—and more specifically the medication—would cause him to have wide mood swings. One minute he would be pleasant and congenial; the next, surly and vicious. Unfortunately, the doctor told them, at present the medical profession was just not able to treat multiple sclerosis any better. When Ed and Vincent hung up, they had not learned anything new. In fact, the conversation was rather depressing.

When Fred learned that Ed had talked to his doctor, he became furious—even though he had made the request. He called Ed into his office at the Factory. Ed sat down and looked across the desk at Fred, who suddenly lost control. "You think I'm crazy!" Ed remembers Fred shouting. Soon Fred was yelling so strenuously he could not keep from slurring his words. At the end of his tirade, he blurted out, "You think I should be put into an institution!"

Ed looked at Fred. He couldn't believe what Fred had just said. No one had ever considered putting Fred in an institution. "What are you talking about?"

"I talked to my doctor," Fred shot back. "He said you think I'm crazy."

"I don't know what the fuck you're talking about," Ed said. "I talked to your doctor because you told me to talk to your doctor. Fred, you're very sick. Your mood swings are enormous. You're always telling me to do more to help you. I can't do more. You said, talk to my doctor. I talked to your doctor and he said that you're sick and that you're taking medication and that you're going to have enormous mood swings. That was it. Vincent was in the room. Ask Vincent."

It did no good. Fred was now convinced that Ed was plotting against him. In Fred's mind, Ed was going to have him committed so that Ed could be in control of the estate and the foundation. "Fred was paranoid because he was taking these drugs at the time that make you paranoid," Hayes would later say to justify Fred's behavior. "Paranoia and hysteria are two symptoms of multiple sclerosis."

There was also the problem of the crush. Ed still believed Fred was attracted to him. According to Ed, on occasion Fred had been anything but subtle. Ed had repeatedly told Fred that he loved him as a friend, but *only* as a friend. Fred, however, would later say that he was *never* attracted to Ed; had Fred preferred men, Ed was just not Fred's type. Fred simply got tired of fighting with Ed about business matters, or so he would say. Ed would decide a business deal had to be conducted in a particular way and he would not consider Fred's opinion. Each negotiation turned into a painful ordeal. "I got tired of educating Rita," Fred later said. Whatever the source of tension between them, following the confrontation about the doctor it became clear that Fred was prepared to end their relationship.

And he did.

On that day in his office at the Factory, Fred told Ed that their association, as they had known it, was over. As far as Fred was concerned, Ed was no longer his friend. When Ed finally got up and walked out of Fred's office, he was not completely sure about what had happened. Whatever it was, he knew it wasn't good. So, to protect his own interests, he took steps to make sure that a large advance on his legal fee that had been approved by the surrogate—a payment of $1.6 million—would actually be issued to him. To date, Hayes had been advanced some $3.25 million on his fee, while Hughes had been given $2 million as an advance on his executor's commission; all of these payments had been cleared by the court. Hughes and Hayes had been paid this money because it looked as if Warhol's entire estate was going to be worth a great deal at closing—perhaps as much as $600 million. In fact, as their working relationship had gradually deteriorated between early 1987 and late 1989, the one issue on which Hughes and Hayes continued to agree was the value of the estate: Warhol was worth at least a half billion dollars when he died—or perhaps much, much more.

Within a few days of his falling out with Hayes, Hughes, angry and frustrated, went ahead with the one move he knew Hayes did not want him to make: He offered Gillies a permanent post. Starting in March 1990, Gillies would become the president of the foundation with a seven-year contract. His salary, $150,000 a year, would be twice as high as the one he earned at the World Policy Institute. Gillies accepted the job at once because, as a friend of his later told *The New York Observer*, "I think he got tired of being the poor relation in a rich family." To draw up his contract with the foundation, Gillies again turned to his friend and attorney Peter Gates, who had written the waiver agreement that Hughes had forced Robert Miller to sign. Gates was more than happy to comply; certainly it would be fortunate for him if, once Gillies had safely positioned himself at the foundation, Gillies released Hayes, who had been serving as the attorney for both the estate and the foundation, and retained Carter Ledyard. Following the stock market crash of 1987, business had become a lot more scarce for high-priced Wall Street law firms that specialized in corporate law. They were always on the lookout for clients with a good cash supply—clients like the Andy Warhol Foundation for the Visual Arts.

In an essential way, November 1989 marked a turning point in the development of the estate and the foundation. During the time they had worked together, Hughes and Hayes, despite whatever differences they might have had, made an excellent team, a fact proven by their accomplishments. The memorial service, the Sotheby's auction, the MoMA retrospective, and the sale of *Interview* were highly successful events that earned the estate money and prestige. The Andy Warhol Museum promised to be their most ambitious project yet.

As it turned out, laying the groundwork for the museum would be the last noteworthy act accomplished by the estate or the foundation. From early 1990 on, the tone and the activity of the Warhol organization changed drastically, as Gillies began to do what Hughes had never really expected him to do—exert control over the Warhol foundation. Beginning in early 1990 and throughout the next four years, the estate and the foundation would cease production of the kinds of events they had executed so brilliantly in the past. Instead, under the supervision of Gillies and a restructured board of directors, the foundation floundered as Fred found himself with less and less power to accomplish anything within the estate.

While the foundation and the estate went from one legal dispute to another during these years, the person who profited most substantially was Peter Gates of Carter Ledyard, who would find in the Andy Warhol Foundation for the Visual Arts the cash cow his law firm so desperately needed in a time of recession. In the course of these disputes, the foundation, and to a certain extent the estate, would willingly disparage both Andy Warhol's name and his reputation. It was a development that would be in direct opposition to what the museum was supposed to achieve when it opened in the late spring of 1994.

6

ONE MORNING IN EARLY MARCH IN 1990, ARCH GILLIES WAS SITTING AT HIS desk at the Factory. A modest-sized rectangular tiled room that opened onto a large work area—only a half-wood and half-glass partition gave Gillies some privacy—his office, located on the south side of the building, looked out onto East Thirty-second Street. From his desk, which was covered with several different neatly stacked piles of paper that were kept in place with rocks the size of eggs, Gillies could glance out of his large multipaned window and watch the crosstown traffic back up. Today, though, as he sat behind his desk, his back ramrod straight, he had to be relishing what this moment meant: He had become the president of the Andy Warhol Foundation for the Visual Arts. "This is great," a friend of his would later tell *The New York Observer.* "Arch finally got a real job."

In his career Gillies had worked for two men who had at their disposal vast fortunes. Gillies had merely indirect access to the money of Nelson Rockefeller and Jock Whitney; for all purposes, he was a middle-management administrator, not a chief executive officer. At the World Policy Institute, he had increased power, but because of the nature of the organization he did not have available to him the same sums of money he had through his jobs with Rockefeller and Whitney. The World Policy Institute barely financed its administration and its various political activities. Gillies did not have access to millions of dollars in business enterprises or endowment accounts. The institute hadn't been in existence long enough to build up the kind of reputation that would warrant that level of financial support.

Still, for years now, Gillies had been able to live a fairly untroubled life, although many of his friends would point to his wife, Linda, as a stabilizing force in their marriage. She certainly had done well for herself, ending up as the director of the Vincent Astor Foundation. Regardless of his actual social status, Gillies affected a genteel ultra-WASP air, one that was so well realized Fred Hughes had completely fallen for it. Tall, lean, and aloof, Gillies had kept his muttonchop sideburns long after they had gone out of style; he even refused to trim them, so they were always shaggy and unruly, lending him the look of an old yacht captain who had just come in to port from a long voyage at sea. Gillies cultivated this WASPy image in the press as well. Here's how a journalist would one day describe Gillies and his domestic life: "Archibald Gillies has danced with Brooke Astor in the Union Club. He plays golf in August in Maine; every other year he joins three friends from Choate Academy, where he prepped in the 1950's, to tee off at St. Andrew's in Scotland. His Central Park West apartment has a view of treetops, and is comfortably outfitted with a Steinway grand piano and antique French furniture, family legacies, which, he tells people offhand-edly in a way suggesting ease with money, he could not afford on his salary."

But this image of casual contentment that Gillies projected to his colleagues, friends, and journalists was not altogether accurate. In fact, he longed for a certain level of power and prestige that he had yet to achieve in his career. In the proper situation, Gillies could promote the political causes that were dear to him—he considered himself a cham-pion of free speech and artistic expression—while at the same time elevating his standing within his profession. With the Warhol founda-tion, Gillies had finally found the perfect arrangement. By using the foundation's grant program, Gillies could directly support organizations he felt needed help. By using the name of the Andy Warhol Foundation for the Visual Arts, Gillies could bring prestige not only to himself but to the causes he wanted to advance. Finally, because the foundation was set up the way it was, Gillies could have, if he placed himself strategically within it, direct access to the millions that would be flowing from the estate over the coming years. The one person in his way in the Warhol scenario—Fred Hughes—could ultimately, and fairly easily, be eliminated since, in the end, the foundation's money really wasn't his, either.

To solidify his place at the foundation, Gillies had to make several well-thought-out moves. The seven-year contract he had just signed gave him job—and financial—security. But he wanted more. To this end, he first had to get rid of Hayes. Gillies didn't trust Hayes, who, to Gillies, always seemed to have his own agenda. What's more, Hayes could not be manipulated; if Hughes had not been able to work on Hayes—and he hadn't—then Gillies himself didn't have much of a chance. Gillies could not tell Hughes how to run the estate, but he did have the authority to make changes within the foundation. Since 1987, Hayes had been the attorney for both the estate and the foundation. Now, before Gillies did anything else, he wanted to remove him as the foundation's lawyer. So, on this morning in March 1990, Gillies got up from his office chair and lumbered toward Hayes's office near the front lobby of the building.

When Gillies entered Hayes's office, Hayes was sitting at his desk doing paperwork. For some time, he had expected Fred to fire him as the lawyer for the estate. Earlier in the year, Hayes had gotten his payment of $1.6 million, funds issued by Hughes and approved by the court. Still, it had been over four months since Ed and Fred had had their falling out, and in that time their working relationship had not improved at all. As he had done with other people with whom he had had professional disagreements—Gael Love and Paige Powell, to name only two—Fred now went out of his way to have nothing to do with Hayes. He refused to be in the same room with him alone; he would barely even speak to him if they were forced to attend the same meeting. As a result Hayes also did his best to avoid Fred.

With Gillies taking over the foundation, Hayes had no idea what was going to happen next. During the last few weeks, while Gillies prepared for his job as president, Hayes felt a little apprehensive whenever Gillies wandered into his office, as he did this morning.

"Hello, Ed," Gillies said, after he had come in. "Can we talk a minute?"

"Sure," Hayes said. "Have a seat."

Gillies sat down in the chair in front of the desk and, as Hayes recalls, got to the matter at hand. "Look, Ed," Gillies said, "we want new counsel for the foundation. We'd like to go out and line up independent counsel." Gillies spoke in a singsongy yet businesslike tone of voice, as if he were always in the middle of some urgent negotiations.

Hayes looked across the desk at Gillies, who was clearly nervous about how Hayes was going to respond.

"I think that's a great idea," Hayes said, leaning back in his chair. "Fred and I haven't been getting along for some time. Anyway, I think the foundation really needs independent counsel."

Hayes was being cooperative, which was surprising. Gillies had prepared himself for a bitter confrontation—and it hadn't happened. In fact, Hayes almost seemed relieved to be giving up his position at the foundation. Gillies's sour expression relaxed a bit. "Well, we'll keep you on as a consultant for a year," he said.

"Okay, but the only thing I really want is to stay on the museum committee."

"I'll check into that. As you know, that's Fred's territory."

Gillies stood to leave. He cut an imposing if lanky figure, standing there in Ed's office. He seemed pleased with the way their meeting had gone. Ed wouldn't have been surprised if Arch had turned, lined himself up, and, using an imaginary club, gone through the motions of a golf swing, à la Johnny Carson at the end of his opening monologue, for Arch often did this when he was happy.

"By the way," Hayes said, catching Gillies before he could go, "do you have any objections with me staying on with the estate? Do you have any problems with my contract? I'm just curious."

"Absolutely not," Gillies said. "As long as the surrogate has no problems with it, I don't either."

"Good," Hayes said. "I'm glad to hear that."

With this, Gillies left Hayes's office.

In the next day or so, Gillies asked Hughes if Hayes could continue to serve on the museum committee. Hughes said no.

Now that Gillies was free to hire whomever he wanted to represent the foundation, he chose as independent counsel Carter Ledyard, the firm that had as one of its senior partners his longtime friend Peter Gates. Apparently, to Gillies, while it was a conflict of interest for Hayes to represent both the estate and the foundation, it was not a conflict of interest for Gates to represent both the foundation and Gillies. Gates himself had drawn up Gillies's contract with the foundation—the very organization he was now, as its attorney, supposed to protect from Gillies.

It was at this time that Gillies began to persuade Hughes that he should expand the board of directors. Since 1987, the board had been made up of the three trustees Warhol himself had named in his will: Hughes, Fremont, and John Warhola. But Gillies believed that the board was too select. Gillies would one day tell Bob Colacello the advice he gave to Hughes at this point. "I said to Fred, 'The foundation is soon going to receive major assets from the estate, and you will need three things: first and foremost, an independent board; secondly, a strong staff with experienced executive leadership; and thirdly, the best possible advice you can get on everything, whether it's lawyers, accounting, art dealing, commentary on the art itself—just make sure it's topflight." As far as Gillies was concerned, Hughes now had "experienced executive leadership"—Gillies—and the "best possible advice" on legal matters—Carter Ledyard. What Hughes needed next was an independent board.

So, during the spring and early summer of 1990, Gillies began casting about for potential board members. When he did, he came up with two possibilities. One was Agnes Gund, an art collector, a wealthy arts patron, and a member of the board of trustees of the Museum of Modern Art, among other boards. (Eventually she would become MoMA's president, which, some argued, in itself presented a conflict of interest.) A woman who at times seemed scatterbrained and unfocused, she might not have appeared to be a logical choice to serve on some of the most powerful art boards in the country. The other candidate was Brendan Gill, an elderly journalist who had spent most of his career reporting for *The New Yorker*, often on architecture. Now in his late seventies, Gill liked to tell stories about going out drinking with his good friend J. D. Salinger ("Jerry," as Gill referred to him), in the old days back when Salinger's work was first being published in *The New Yorker*. Hughes did not immediately agree to the addition of these two candidates, but he was certainly interested. As charmed by social status and intellectual panache as ever, Hughes was impressed with Gund, because she was rich and well placed socially, and Gill, because his name was nearly synonymous with the prestigious magazine.

One of the main activities that the board was to oversee was the process by which the foundation would give away 5 percent of its worth each year. The foundation planned to meet this legal requirement primarily through a grants program. In fact, the reason Hughes had originally hired Gillies back in 1988 was to have him research the various methods by which the foundation could conduct a grant program that would meet all of its legal obligations. Gillies presented several programs to Hughes, who selected the most appropriate one. Gillies put together a series of advisory panels that gave him input on possible grant programs; the list of art world figures who participated in these panels included the artists Jasper Johns and Ashton Hawkins, Peter Palumbo, and Kynaston McShine, who had curated the MoMA Warhol retrospective. Ultimately Gillies and Hughes decided on a grant program that would award grants in three different areas: curatorial, educational, and historic preservation and parks. The first category would allow the foundation to give money to "curatorial programs at museums, academies, universities, and other organizations to assist in the innovative presentation of the visual arts"; the second, to "organizations seeking to improve the teaching of the visual arts"; the third, to "organizations seeking to preserve and enhance parks and historic buildings." The awards would be given out twice a year, in the spring and the fall. Applicants were supposed to submit a two-page letter describing their project. If interested, the foundation would get in touch with them.

The foundation awarded its first grants in the spring of 1989—sixty-one grants totaling $2.3 million. In the fall it gave out its second set—fifty-seven grants totaling $1.7 million. With these grants the foundation exceeded its annual requirement to give away 5 percent of its worth. The money that was being used to fund the foundation—and in particular the grant program—was drawn from the estate as it liquidated Warhol's real property. But even by early 1990 it had become apparent that the most valuable asset in the estate was going to be Warhol's art. As curators and art handlers—and Hughes and Fremont—had gone through Warhol's work, they had discovered nothing short of an astonishing collection of art—some 4,100 paintings, 4,500 drawings, 19,000 prints, 60,000 photographs, plus countless videos and films. In terms of sheer size, it was an art collection second only to Picasso's. In fact, the collection was so large that a troubling question had presented itself: Exactly how much was all this art worth?

In 1988 Hughes and Fremont had put a tentative value of $250 million on Warhol's collection of art. Using this figure, they fixed the value of the entire estate, including cash and real property, at some $297 million. Now that sum seemed modest. Anyway, for legal purposes, the Hughes-Fremont appraisal was not applicable. The estate would have to commission a reputable independent appraiser, preferably Sotheby's or Christie's. Hughes spoke to both auction houses. Then, six weeks after Gillies had taken over as president of the foundation, Hughes decided on the company he wanted to perform the appraisal.

On April 17, 1990, Hughes wrote a letter to Martha Baer, the administrator at Christie's who would be responsible for an appraisal of Warhol art, in which he documented the conditions Christie's should consider in conducting a fair-market-value appraisal of the Warhol art owned by the estate as of February 22, 1987, the day Warhol died. "In determining fair market value," Hughes wrote, "Christie's should be guided by what a willing buyer would pay a willing seller, neither being under any compulsion to buy or sell and both having reasonable knowledge of relevant facts. Christie's should apply such discounts, if any, whether for blockage or otherwise, as it deems appropriate in determining such fair market value. Christie's should prepare its appraisals with a view to updating said appraisal from time to time, in whole or in part, as the Estate may require." To execute the agreement, Hughes requested that Christie's "submit at your earliest convenience [an] agreement setting forth the fees which Christie's will wish to charge for the initial date-of-death appraisal, but subject to a ceiling for such fees which would be acceptable to Christie's." As evidence that Christie's and the estate accepted these terms, Hughes and Baer each signed an "agreed to" addendum the following day.

Then, on April 25, Baer submitted a formal contract detailing the fees Christie's planned to charge. The company had agreed to drop its rate for a specialist from the standard $1,800 a day to $1,500, but to that rate Christie's added "a fee per administrator of $1,000 per day, based on time." In addition, Christie's would charge "a fee per typist of $30 per hour." The company did place a limit on the total fee that could be charged: It would "not . . . exceed $150,000." Again, Hughes and Baer signed the fee contract, finalizing the deal.

As it turned out, Hughes, Hayes, and Gillies all had a vested interest in the value Christie's placed on the Warhol art. Hughes and Hayes wanted the Warhol estate to be appraised at as high a figure as possible. Under New York State law, as the executor Hughes was entitled to 2 percent of the value of the estate at closing; according to the terms of his contract with Hughes—a contract that had been updated on three separate occasions—Hayes was also entitled to 2 percent. So, if a particularly large value was placed on the whole estate—$600 million, say—Hughes and Hayes could be entitled to $12 million each. On the other hand, Gillies had a strong motivation for a lower appraisal. The foundation was going to be required by law to give away 5 percent of the value of the estate on a yearly basis. Should the value reach $600 million, the foundation would have to give away $30 million each year, an amount that would be all but impossible to meet. Gillies also had to be aware of the 2 percent fees that would be due Hughes and Hayes at the estate's closing. For either or both of these reasons, Gillies had more than a passing interest in making sure that Christie's considered the foundation's wishes paramount. It just so happened that an old friend of his, Stephen Lash, was now a high-ranking administrator at Christie's. Gillies decided that it was time to call Lash.

Apparently, someone with the foundation had spoken to Lash—if not Gillies, then another person of influence—for on April 10, 1990, seven days *before* Hughes wrote the letter to Martha Baer confirming that Christie's would be doing the appraisal, Lash sent a confidential internal memorandum to Linda Izzo, another Christie's administrator. Recently, Lash said in his memo, he had received a telephone call from Frank Harvey—he continued to do legal work for the estate—who wanted to talk to him about the methodology that Christie's intended to use in evaluating the Warhol art. "He (oddly) seemed comfortable in calling me to ask about the basis for our values," Lash wrote. "It is clear to me that he was concerned about issues such as blockage discount, etc. I said nothing except that I wanted to discuss the matter with my colleagues. My own view is that we should raise this with Carter Ledyard, who, in fact, represent our client, the Foundation. I do not see how we can be having discussions with the Estate lawyers on this subject at this time, and that is what I propose to tell them. Please let me know if you disagree in any way." A sequence of events obviously had transpired that led Lash to believe his company's client was the foundation, not the estate. What's more, he had formed this opinion one full week before Hughes had formally commissioned Christie's to do the work on behalf of the estate.

Throughout the summer of 1990, Gillies and Hughes had more on their minds than the Christie's appraisal. In fact, Hughes was beginning to wonder whether he had made a mistake by hiring Gillies. As it happened, Gillies really didn't know anything about art or the business of art. Though he had not thought so at the time he and Gillies had had their first lunch, Hughes now felt it would seem logical that, to run a foundation created by an artist and devoted to the support of the visual arts, Gillies should have at least *some* professional expertise in this area, but he didn't. Hughes would try to have a discussion with him about a topic involving art, and Gillies would be completely unable to hold up his end of the conversation. Hughes soon learned that Gillies didn't know anything about Andy Warhol, either. He didn't even seem to *like* Warhol—his art, his films, the person he was, what he stood for. Finally Hughes realized that Gillies apparently planned to do what he had never imagined Gillies would: He fully intended to run the foundation as if it were his own. He was not going to do what Hughes had expected he would do: take orders from Hughes and merely carry out his wishes. Hughes was not entirely sure how this had happened. Despite the fact that Hughes had worked with Gillies for over a year (Gillies consulted one day a week for an annual salary of $30,000), Hughes felt he should have checked more thoroughly into Gillies's background before hiring him to run the foundation full-time. Still, Hughes hoped it was not too late to rectify the situation.

It was Gillies's understanding at this point that he would also become a director when the board was expanded. Even though the foundation's bylaws authorized up to fifteen directors, the estate had told the surrogate that its initial expansion would stop at five; those two seats would be filled by Gund and Gill. Gillies must have sensed that Hughes would not be inclined to seek an additional seat for him on the board. Because of this, he acted quickly to replace an existing director, a move that would solidify his position at the foundation. Hughes and John Warhola were not going to step down; Gillies knew that. Fremont, however, did not seem as keen on being a director.

In the summer of 1990, Ed Hayes was beginning to get a bad feeling about the process Christie's was using to appraise the art. Two years before, Hughes and Fremont had put the value of $297 million on the entire estate; with the art market still hitting highs, Hayes had decided that the art—and therefore the estate—was worth a lot more. As the early drafts of the appraisal began to come in, Hayes could see that Martha Baer was placing prices on Warhol's work that Hayes considered to be drastically below market value. Hayes also had the strong sense that

Baer was going to apply to the overall appraisal a substantial blockage discount, a concept in the art business by which an appraiser can enforce a discount on the value of an artist's work if a large block of that work is going to be sold at one time. Baer was now working on the date-of-death appraisal, which would eventually be filed in October 1990, but that appraisal would be used as the basis for the date-of-transfer appraisal, the appraisal that would determine the value of the estate on the days the art was transferred from the estate to the foundation. It would be the second appraisal—the date-of-transfer—that would be used to determine the fees paid to Hughes and Hayes.

Just as Hayes was becoming most concerned about the appraisal, he read a small item in the *New York Law Journal.* "Robert Mapplethorpe estate executor and Manhattan solo practitioner Michael Stout has been awarded $1 million in commissions on the late photographer's estate," the item read, "which court papers value at approximately $240 million. The commissions, awarded July 6 by Manhattan Surrogate Renee R. Roth, are an advance on what Mr. Stout will receive under the Surrogate's Court Procedure Act once the estate is disposed of. He could earn as much as $4.8 million, according to the statutory formula. That figure would rise if the estate increases in value." From this item Hayes knew that Stout had submitted to the court at least a preliminary appraisal from Christie's—a document that might prove useful in trying to understand how Christie's was going to appraise the Warhol art collection. That Christie's was appraising the estates of both Robert Mapplethorpe and Andy Warhol at the same time was telling about the state of contemporary art—and ironic, too, for Warhol had never particularly admired Mapplethorpe's photographs.

Through his contacts, Hayes got a copy of a Christie's letter to Stout that revealed not only the total sum Christie's had placed on the Mapplethorpe estate but also the methodology it had used to arrive at it. Written to Michael Stout by Andrea Krahmer, an assistant vice-president at Christie's, the letter, dated June 4, 1990, began by noting that "the total value of the appraisal is $228,806,800." But the pertinent information appeared at the end of the letter. "In preparing this appraisal," Krahmer wrote, "we have also considered whether a blockage discount should be applied to this appraisal. In view of the business plan for the Estate, it is our belief that a discount is not appropriate in this instance. The Estate and residuary beneficiary intend to sell these photographs over an extended period of time, rather than to have the entire body of work appear on the market simultaneously. Therefore, the valuation should reflect individual sales over time, which is the basis for our figure of $228,806,800."

While this may have been the public position Christie's took—that the "business plan for the Estate" didn't call for a blockage discount—an April 20, 1990, internal memorandum from Krahmer to Patty Hambrecht, a Christie's administrator involved with appraisals, indicated that Christie's did not apply a blockage discount because Michael Stout didn't want them to. The memo read:

> I spoke with Michael Stout and Burt Lipskay (the tax attorney . . .) regarding blockage discount on the Mapplethorpe appraisal. They said that a blockage discount was not of interest in this situation and that the IRS, as soon as they saw that the beneficiary was a Foundation, would not be concerned with the values on the tax return. I explained that in order for us to submit what we felt was a responsible appraisal, the blockage discount issue would need to be addressed. Stout and Lipskay are set against this, and as an alternative they have suggested that we provide a covering statement explaining that all of our values given reflect fair market for the items individually, if they were sold one at a time, rather than as a collection. I think that this should cover us in this instance. Do you agree? Do you have any suggestions for specific language that we should use in our covering statement?

The June 4, 1990, letter provided enough of a basis for Hayes to decide that it was time to sit down with Christie's. In early August 1990, he set up a meeting at the Factory with Hughes, Gillies, Fremont, Gates, Michael Frankel (a colleague of Gates's at Carter Ledyard), and Martha Baer. After all, there were millions—his millions—at stake.

When he walked into the second-floor conference room just down the hall from Fred's office at the Factory, Hayes had in his pocket Xerox copies of Krahmer's letter to Stout about the Mapplethorpe estate. He was ready to hear what Baer had to say and, if he had to, to ask her about the methodology Christie's was using with the Warhol estate. It would have been hard to determine what exactly Baer expected when she walked into the room. Charmingly ditzy, Baer sometimes seemed to have a memory about as short as her attention span. Maybe that's why she could give the appearance of being nervous and jumpy; she was often responding to a situation as if it were completely new to her, to a person as if she had never met him before, whether she had or not. This was for sure: Today she hoped the meeting would go smoothly. But then again, Baer frequently seemed to look on life's bright side, out of either optimism or naïveté.

As soon as everyone was in the room, Baer started the meeting by explaining that Christie's was well into the process of formulating the unit-to-unit prices for the Warhol artwork—numbers, she said, about which she was absolutely certain. Then she explained how she was going to arrive at her final figure after all the items in the collection had been appraised. Since the collection was so large, she said, she felt that it was necessary to apply a blockage discount.

"We always use a mass sale concept," she said, a mass sale being one where an enormous quantity of material is sold at once, as Sotheby's had conducted the sale of Warhol's collectibles. "And we never compute appreciation into the figures. This is the way to do it. This is the way we always do it."

Baer was going to take the unit prices (soon Hayes would contend that those prices were one third of the prices Hughes and Fremont gave the work in their day-of-death appraisal), add those numbers up, and then apply a blockage discount to the total. There was only one problem with this theory: The Warhol estate and foundation did not intend to have a mass sale—not under *any* conditions. One third of Warhol's work would be donated to the Warhol museum; the rest would be sold judiciously, for good prices, over time. The sale of that art could take twenty to thirty years, if not longer.

Sitting around the conference table, the men in their suits said nothing. So Baer continued. When she reiterated that Christie's always used blockage discount, Hayes finally stopped her. "Look," he said, "are you sure this is the way you always do it? It doesn't sound logical to me."

Baer, whose routine arm and facial gestures were often erratic, seemed especially startled. She had not anticipated the challenge. Her mouth twitched slightly. "That's the way we always do it," she said. "There is no other proper way to do it."

Hayes pushed his point. "It seems to me if we do it this way we'll be criticized. You've ignored the creation of the museum. You can't include those paintings in a fictitious mass sale. They're not going to be sold."

"It doesn't matter," Baer said. "We have to do it this way."

There was a pause.

Hayes looked around the room. The men at the table still said nothing. "It doesn't matter?" he asked.

"No. It doesn't matter."

"Are you sure?"

"I'm positive."

"You are?"

"Yes, I am," Baer said. "I've been doing this a long time."

Hayes paused. "Okay." It was as if she were on the stand, under cross-examination. "The other thing I'm concerned about are your unit prices. They're a third of what Fred and Vincent came up with. Your numbers are completely out of line with what Warhol got when he was alive."

But Baer was just as sure of the unit values she was placing on the art. On this subject she was unflappable. So Hayes returned to the issue of blockage discount. "Did you check and see," he asked, "if Christie's has ever done an appraisal in which you take into consideration the idea that the art is going to be sold over time to maximize its value?"

Now clearly unsettled, Baer was beginning to get impatient with Hayes. "No," she told him. "We *always* do it this way."

Hayes looked at her across the table. "Are you sure?" he said.

"Yes," she said, now fed up. "I checked."

Hayes straightened in his chair. "That's funny," he said, reaching into his pocket as though he were about to pull out a gun and shoot her. "I have in my pocket here a copy of the Mapplethorpe appraisal. In it, you took the position that because they were going to sell the photographs over time, you didn't have to take a blockage discount. Can you explain this to me?"

Hayes slapped a copy of the Krahmer letter down on the table with a thud. Then he slid it over to Baer. Normally fidgety, Baer sat completely motionless, all of the energy suddenly drained from her body. She stared at the paper lying there before her, unwilling to make even the slightest effort to pick it up. Perhaps if she didn't touch it, it would go away.

Meanwhile, Hayes passed out Xerox copies of the letter to the others at the table.

"I'm not going to read this," Gillies said.

"Neither am I," Frankel said.

So Hayes focused his attention on Baer, who still said nothing. She barely moved; she made no effort to pick up the letter. In fact, as Hayes stared at her, he was sure she was turning pale; she looked as if she might even faint. When he realized that she was not going to answer his question, he became furious. "I don't think you're acting appropriately!" Hayes nearly shouted at Baer. "You're not answering my questions!"

Alarmed, Gillies interrupted. "Ed," he said, "I think you're being harsh with Martha."

Hayes turned and glared at Gillies. "If this woman thinks she can come in here and play me for a fool, she better think again."

Baer had heard all she was going to take. Without warning, she got up from the table and rushed out of the room. In turn, Gillies, Fremont, and Hughes (who on this day was walking with a cane) followed her out to check on her. Hayes was left in the conference room with Gates and Frankel.

"This isn't right," Hayes said to Gates. "It seems to me she's acting on somebody's instructions. This can't be a logical way to do things."

"You're just picking on her, Ed," Gates said. "She's a very talented woman."

The three men sat in the room in silence until Baer returned, again followed by Gillies, Hughes, and Fremont. It was a somber if curious procession. They all took their places at the table.

"I'm going to leave now," Baer announced slowly.

"I think you're going to have to answer these questions sooner or later," Hayes said to her. "It would be better if you answered them now."

It did no good. Baer gathered her belongings and left.

When she was gone, Hayes looked at the other men in the room. "If we do not appraise the value of this estate correctly," he said, "we're going to get in a lot of trouble. It was phony appraisals that got the Rothko people into trouble." Hayes paused. "Gentlemen, if you think you're going to take advantage of me, you're out of your fucking minds."

The meeting was over.

If Christie's appraised Warhol's work as low as it seemed they would, it would cause serious damage to the Warhol art market at a time when it could not afford to be hurt at all. During 1987, 1988, and 1989, the market had been solid. In those years, some $61 million worth of Warhol artwork had been sold at auction around the world. In addition, Hughes and the estate had sold another $30 million. But, beginning in 1990, prices had started to slip—not dramatically, but just enough to cause Warhol insiders concern. A heavily discounted appraisal could plunge the Warhol market into a dangerous depression.

The morning after the Baer meeting, Hayes brought this up when he,

Gillies, Hughes, and Gates reconvened in the conference room for another round of discussions. First, though, he had to face criticism for his behavior the day before.

"Martha was very upset," Hayes recalls Fred saying. "You didn't act in a gentlemanly fashion."

"She was physically ill after she left," Gillies joined in.

There was an image: Martha was so upset with Ed she had become queasy. In all honesty, Ed was amazed it took so little to turn her stomach. "Look," Hayes said to the men, "I want to tell you right now. This art is incredibly valuable. Sooner or later, someone will demand a proper accounting. I promise you, if it appears we are trying to avoid that, we'll all be in trouble. There's no way in the world I'm going to go along with this."

What may have been foremost in Hayes's thoughts was his plan to run for public office someday. If the appraisal hinted at anything illegal or unethical, it could taint his candidacy. Perhaps this provided motivation for his zeal, but it came with an undeniable benefit: By pressing for an undiscounted appraisal Hayes put himself in a position to make an enormous amount of money.

On October 4, several people with Christie's—Martha Baer, Linda Izzo, Patty Hambrecht, Judith Bresler, Frank De Biasi, Liz Fanlo, and Victoria Bjorklund—met with Michael Frankel and Toni Thomas of Carter Ledyard. There were no representatives from the estate present at the meeting, even though the meeting's purpose was to discuss the appraisal, which, technically speaking, had been commissioned by the executor of the estate. Still, according to a confidential memorandum written by Linda Izzo four days later, they discussed several topics vital to the development of the appraisal. "Carter Ledyard was pleased with the blockage approach of discounting different categories at a different rate," Izzo wrote about the meeting. "We are to prepare an additional summary page for the appraisal which lists the summary of discounts. The Drawings and Prints will also be discounted by category." At the meeting, it was even decided just how Christie's could justify applying blockage discounts. "It is the view of Carter Ledyard that the Foundation business plan should not impact on Christie's valuation," Izzo continued. "It is not relevant what the Foundation does with the property. They are seeking a true Fair Market Value appraisal. Subsequent valuations of the assets of the Foundation will be influenced by the business plan. The Foundation will require yearly appraisals." As of the writing of this memo, Izzo was anticipating a meeting scheduled for the next morning between Martha Baer's Christie's group and Ed Hayes and Frank Harvey; David Oxman and Jim Lloyd of Davis Polk & Wardwell (Hughes's counsel); and Michael Frankel and Toni Thomas of Carter Ledyard. The purpose of this meeting was "to give Ed Hayes the opportunity to tell us the factors he would like us to consider in our valuation," Izzo wrote. "We are to listen to his comments. Hayes would like the business plan considered. Martha should make a laundry list of everything that was considered while doing the valuation."

The meeting took place as planned on October 9. The Christie's people listened to what Hayes had to say. But they did not tell Hayes—or anyone else at the meeting, for that matter—that the Christie's and the Carter Ledyard representatives had already met to confirm the form of the final appraisal. Nor did they reveal that this meeting with Hayes and others from the estate was little more than window dressing since all of the vital decisions had already been made.

During the late summer of 1990, as the drama with Martha Baer was developing, Peter Gates—at Gillies's request—approached Hughes and Vincent Fremont with a potential problem neither had anticipated. For years while Warhol was alive, Hughes and Fremont had sold more of Warhol's art than any other dealer; they continued to sell the art after Warhol died and to collect hefty commissions. Each had made an excellent living for some time from this arrangement. Now Gates told Hughes and Fremont that they could not continue to serve on the board and sell art—since the situation created a potential conflict of interest—unless they both agreed to sell the art in compliance with a set of complicated monitoring procedures. IRS regulations prevented them from being able to maintain the arrangement they had had up until now. So Gates presented Hughes and Fremont with an ultimatum: Comply with the new monitoring scheme or resign from the board. For Hughes and Fremont, this was not a small consideration, since Hughes and the estate had sold $30 million worth of Warhol art between 1987 and 1989. After some thought, Hughes decided that he didn't want to comply with any guidelines; still, he could not bring himself to resign from the board. After all, if he stepped down, he would have no say at all in how the foundation would be run in the future. But Fremont was in a different situation. With a wife and a family to support, he badly needed the income he received from selling Warhol art.

At the October 1990 board meeting, two new trustees were elected—Agnes Gund and Brendan Gill. At the meeting's conclusion, Fremont let it be known that he wished to continue as a dealer of Warhol art. If he had to resign from the board, then that's what he would do. To help him make up his mind, Gillies and the board offered him what appeared to be a deal too good to turn down: Should Fremont resign, Gillies would make him the *exclusive* agent for Warhol art around the world. This would mean that on every piece of Warhol art sold by the foundation anywhere in the world Fremont would collect a commission. Fremont jumped at the offer. Gillies interviewed two other potential agents, though some would say Gillies did not ever seriously consider giving the job to anyone besides Fremont.

According to the terms of the contract, Fremont's tenure as agent would last from December 11, 1990, until December 31, 1995; Fremont was "engaged as the Foundation's exclusive agent for the sale of Andy Warhol's works of art throughout the world, meaning that [he] would receive the commission not only on sales [he] effects but on all other sales as well"; he would receive "10% of the sale price on all sales during the exclusivity period"; and he was "to be paid $131,850 for the period from December 11, 1990 through December 31, 1991 and thereafter an annual fee as the parties agree for each year"—at least "$125,000 for the year 1992 and $75,000 for each year thereafter." It was, for Fremont, an excellent deal.

By now, Hughes had become highly distrustful of Gillies. His maneuvering had tipped his hand: Hughes believed that Gillies's objective was to entrench himself in the foundation to the point where he would have more power within the organization than Hughes. His election to the board might be all he needed. Because of this, Hughes determined to oppose Gillies's efforts to become a trustee. But Hughes had one serious problem. The two new board members were not likely to vote against Gillies; neither was John Warhola. Since Gillies had cut a deal with Fremont, Fremont would not be in a position to oppose him. If only Fremont would stay on the board, Gillies would not have a seat to take. Fremont, however, had made his decision. He would resign at the next meeting—the meeting at which Gillies would make his move to get on the board.

The meeting took place in early December. After Fremont resigned, the other directors at the meeting—Gund, Gill, Warhola—voted in favor of Gillies joining the board. Only Hughes opposed Gillies. As of this moment Gillies became a trustee. Hughes might launch a campaign to get rid of him, but he would have an extremely difficult time. Hughes was so livid he could hardly control himself. "Vincent *could* have sold the art," Hughes said later, all but confirming that he had been duped by Gillies and Gates. "I now have better legal advice. [The conflict of interest] was easily overcome. That's when I first had doubts about the value of Mr. Gillies' advice." Not exactly. Hughes had been suspicious of Gillies for some time. What Hughes knew by December 1990 was the following: He had hired the wrong man to run the Warhol foundation, and now it was going to be all but impossible for him to fire him. For his part, Gillies would always plead ignorance—"I have no idea," he'd say—when it came to explaining why he and Hughes had had their falling out.

7

IT WAS THE DEAD OF WINTER—JANUARY 15, 1991—AND THE BEGINNING OF a new year. Arch Gillies sat at a table in a Manhattan restaurant having lunch with Stephen Lash, his old friend. Gillies had been foundation president for almost a year now and a board member for about five weeks. Over the next several months, Warhol's artwork—his paintings, sculptures, collaborations, prints, drawings, photographs, videos, and films—were supposed to be transferred from the estate to the foundation, where all assets would ultimately reside. A tentative plan had been put together for their transfer: The paintings and sculptures would be passed from the estate to the foundation on February 1; the prints and related material on April 1; and the drawings, photographs, videos, films, and archival material on May 1. As these various transfers were made, Christie's would be submitting drafts of the appraisals that Baer and other Christie's employees had been working on since April 1990. These date-of-transfer appraisal figures would determine the commissions Hughes and Hayes would receive as well as the amount of money the foundation would be required to give away to the public each year. Naturally Gillies was keenly interested in what figures Christie's was going to place on Warhol's art. Two weeks before the start of the transferral, Gillies decided he needed to set up a lunch with Lash, who, of course, was not only a friend but also an influential decision-maker at Christie's.

At this point in his life, one of the integral elements of Gillies's personality was his tendency to play the role of the wheeler-dealer. It was not unusual for him to pepper his conversations with lines like "Well, maybe we can do business together." (Of course, Gillies himself had never been *in* business.) Today's performance at lunch would be no different.

At the start of their conversation, Gillies and Lash caught up on their personal lives. Then they got down to the subject at hand: the appraisal. First Gillies sketched in the tentative plan by which the estate was going to transfer the art; next he pointed out that the foundation would need these appraisals done on a yearly basis. "You know," Gillies said over the noise in the restaurant, "the fee income Christie's will generate from this will be like an annuity."

Gillies moved on to other topics. He mentioned the foundation's art advisory committee (Kynaston McShine, Robert Rosenblum, Trevor Fairbrother, and Kasper Koenig), which served to advise Gillies on what pieces should be donated to the Warhol museum. One third of the existing Warhol collection would go to the museum, but one third of the remaining two thirds, Gillies told Lash, would be sold. Gillies did not have to state the obvious: Christie's would be a logical house to sell that art. His wheeling and dealing was in full swing.

With this, Gillies raised perhaps the most pressing topic of the lunch: blockage discount. One of the more nebulous concepts in the art business, it is essentially a mechanism by which an appraiser can put almost any price he wants on a piece of work since blockage discounts can range from 5 to 90 percent (or more) and since the application of a discount and the percentage of that discount are usually decided solely by the appraiser. An appraiser, for example, may value a work at a million dollars, but if the piece of art is to be sold in a block of work by the same artist the appraiser can reduce the appraised value of the million-dollar painting to as little as one hundred thousand dollars—or less.

Gillies was careful with his words. "I don't have to remind you," he said, "that Christie's didn't take a blockage discount with the Mapplethorpe appraisal"—a decision that could pose a serious problem for the Warhol foundation. If Christie's did not apply a blockage discount to Mapplethorpe, how could Baer justify applying a discount to Warhol?

"Ed Hayes is aware of the fact that Christie's knows the details of the foundation's business plan," Gillies continued, reminding Lash that the business plan did not call for a one-time mass sale—the one factor that would demand the application of a blockage discount. "Perhaps someone from Christie's should speak with Michael Frankel at Carter Ledyard. He's an expert on this. I just want to make sure your lawyers are up to speed on blockage discount."

Lash noted Gillies's suggestion.

"Will you follow up on the Mapplethorpe appraisal?" Gillies asked.

"Yes," Lash assured him.

"I have to emphasize, Stephen," Gillies said, "that I have no particular brief for high or low values. I simply want to ensure that the appraisal reflects the correct market values. Ed Hayes is, of course, arguing for high values, and the only grounds for this are the calculation of his legal fees, which are two percent. I'm hopeful that the attorney general will dismiss these fees as excessive."

Before the two men finished their lunch they agreed to meet again in a month or so. But the lunch had had an effect on Lash. Two days later, he wrote a detailed four-page confidential memo to key staff members at Christie's in which he recapitulated the meeting with Gillies, whom he described as "the President and Chief Executive Officer" of the Warhol foundation. In the memo he observed that because blockage discount "is a major issue in this appraisal . . . we must reopen this point." On that same day, Lash wrote a short letter to Gillies. "Many thanks for an enjoyable and useful lunch," Lash said. "I think we accomplished a great deal, and I hope and trust that this will permit us to provide the Foundation with an even better product. I look forward to working with you. . . . Let me also take this opportunity to wish you a happy, healthy and prosperous New Year."

By summer, Gillies saw his lunch with Lash pay off when drafts of the appraisal started to come in with numbers indicating that the final figure Christie's would place on the 4,118 pieces of art was going to be drastically lower than what Ed Hayes had expected. "Pursuant to your instructions, Christie's has valued these works as of February 1, 1991, the date of their transfer to the Foundation," Baer wrote to Hughes in a cover letter that would eventually be dated, for official purposes, October 14, 1991. "In making this fair market value appraisal, Christie's has been guided by what a willing buyer would pay a willing seller, neither being under any compulsion to buy or sell and both having reasonable knowledge of all relevant facts." Christie's, Baer said, took into consideration a number of other factors, among them "any appropriate discount . . . if all the paintings, sculptures and collaborations transferred to the Foundation were sold on or within a reasonable period of time after the Valuation Date." In the last two and a half years, 615 Warhol paintings and sculptures had been put up for sale at public auction at either Christie's or Sotheby's, Baer stated. Out of that number, 523 sold. "These numbers are significant to the determination of how readily the market could absorb the 4,118 works transferred. In making this determination, Christie's gave greatest weight to absorption rates closest in time to the Valuation Date."

To arrive at the individual unit prices, Christie's relied heavily on sales records from the New York and London offices of Christie's and Sotheby's for the twenty-one years between January 1, 1970, and June 15, 1991. Baer and her colleagues also used sales invoices provided by the estate for the years 1985 to 1991. Once Baer had determined individual unit prices, she then made her decision about blockage discount. "In light of the factors outlined above," she wrote, "Christie's does not believe that the art market as of February 1, 1991 would have had the capacity to absorb the 4,118 paintings, sculptures and collaborations on or within a reasonable period of time after the Valuation Date without a significant decrease in the price a willing buyer would have paid. . . . Stated differently, these 4,118 works could not have been offered on or within a reasonable period of time after the Valuation Date without severely depressing the market for Warhol's works. After taking into account the factors listed above . . . and cross-checking its analyses, Christie's determined that a discount of 60% is appropriate." With this information in hand, Baer set the worth of the majority of Warhol's work. "Based upon the foregoing, it is Christie's opinion that the total fair market value of the paintings, sculptures and collaborations by Andy Warhol distributed by the Estate to the Foundation on February I, 1991 was $77,927,440, which reflects the application of a 60% discount to the undiscounted value of $194,818,600."

The draft appraisal for another large group of Warhol's art—2,628 drawings, 9,612 prints, and 62,960 photographs—also came in around this time. "In light of the factors outlined above"—the same as with the paintings, sculptures, and collaborations—"Christie's does not believe that the art market as of May I, 1991 would have had the capacity to absorb the 75,205 drawings, prints, and photographs on or within a reasonable period of time after the Valuation Date without a significant decrease in the price a willing buyer would have paid," Baer wrote in her cover letter, this one to be officially dated December 16, 1991. "Based on the foregoing, it is Christie's opinion that the total fair market value of the drawings, prints, and photographs by Andy Warhol distributed by the Estate to the Foundation on May I, 1991 was $14,092,444, after applying the discounts by category set out in Exhibit B, which yield a blended discount of approximately 70% overall, to the undiscounted value of $47,242,758."

These numbers angered Hayes, who believed that the value of Warhol's art was considerably higher than the $92 million Christie's said it was worth. Straightaway Hayes decided to hire his own expert to do an alternate appraisal. The person who came most highly recommended was Jeffrey Hoffeld, an art advisor who had owned his own gallery in Manhattan. At the time, Hayes didn't know Hoffeld; he was only told that Hoffeld was a close friend of Agnes Gund. Hayes hired Hoffeld to begin an appraisal at once.

By the fall of 1991, Hughes was so fed up with Gillies—his personality, his style, his manner of running the foundation—that he treated him with open disrespect. It was not at all unusual for Gillies to come into his office at the Factory in the morning only to discover that pieces of his furniture had been removed the night before—under orders from

Hughes. It was also commonplace for Hughes to lose his temper with Gillies in meetings, sometimes yelling and hurling insults at him. Hughes regularly denigrated Gillies to anyone who would listen. Often referring to him as a "not-for-profit profiteer," Hughes had one line about Gillies he used so frequently it got picked up in the press: "To know Arch Gillies is to loathe him."

As of October 1991, Gillies had had enough of Hughes's badmouthing. That month, Gillies put in several telephone calls to Hughes to try and set up a meeting with him, Peter Gates, and Tom Melfe, Hughes's attorney. Hughes didn't bother to return Gillies's telephone calls. Finally Gillies typed out a letter to Hughes. "The reason I have been trying since Friday morning to arrange a meeting with you, Tom Melfe and Peter Gates," Gillies wrote, "is to discuss the attached 'protocol' before the [board] meetings tomorrow. My hope was that, in this private meeting, you would commit to me your determination to comply in the future with the three numbered paragraphs going forward. If you did that and supported me at the meetings as stated in the last paragraph, I would report to the Board that we had settled our differences. If you do not do that before the meeting, I will be compelled to bring the subject before the Board."

To the letter, Gillies attached his protocol. It is one of the more stunning documents that the head of a public corporation—especially a foundation president and a self-professed champion of free speech—would try to force a colleague to sign, no matter how rude and distasteful that colleague was. The protocol began by saying that because Hughes had displayed a "pattern of increasingly hostile and damaging behavior" certain "commitments are required of Fred Hughes . . . to forestall" any more damage to the foundation's reputation. "[First,] Fred Hughes will not communicate to persons outside the Foundation complaints about or criticism of (a) Arch Gillies as President of the Foundation or (b) the management or operations of the Foundation, unless legally compelled to do so. *In no event* will Fred Hughes convey such information, complaints or criticism to members of the press or media." Second, Hughes would make criticisms only to Gillies or the board and "will not address to the staff criticisms of the staff, or give directions to the staff." Third, Hughes would adhere to "guidelines established by Arch Gillies from time to time respecting the care and handling of Foundation property." Hughes would show that he was willing to live by these rules "by voting in favor of Arch Gillies as a Member and Director of the Foundation and in favor of Arch Gillies continuing as President."

Hughes read the protocol and promptly disregarded it. There was no way Gillies was going to coerce him into remaining silent about the foundation he, more than anyone besides Warhol, had helped to create. As it happened, not too long after this, I telephoned Hughes to request an interview for an article I was planning to write on the Warhol estate for *New York* magazine. For years Hughes had refused to give interviews to journalists, deferring instead to Warhol. After Warhol's death Hughes had continued to turn down interviews. To my surprise, he agreed to talk to me and arranged a meeting. At the time, of course, I didn't know about the protocol. In retrospect, I can't help believing that Gillies's attempt to silence Hughes was what made him suddenly decide to sit for an interview with me.

On a cool, pleasant November morning, I arrived at Hughes's Lexington Avenue townhouse. I was met at the door by a handsome young man who gave me a tour of the impressive four-story building. He ended the tour by escorting me to the third-floor sitting room, where I met Hughes. For years, Hughes's suave style and dark good looks regularly stopped conversation when he walked into a room. Now, with his "wobbly legs," as he would call them, he could not even get out of his wheelchair without the help of an assistant. At his direction, I sat down at a table he used as a desk while he positioned his wheelchair beside me. Wearing a tailored black-and-white jacket, black slacks, white shirt, and tie, he still affected the look of a continental businessman as he sat slouched in his wheelchair, the victim of his own failing muscles.

"So what have you written that I would know about?" he asked.

"Well, I just published a biography of Sylvia Plath."

Excited, Hughes began to question me about Plath, whose work he knew. While he talked, I noticed that his hair, slicked back, was now thinning; that the motions he made with his hands were jerky and unsure; that his voice often quivered and cracked. To overcome this, he spoke in an exaggerated way, as if he were a contract actress in a forties B picture. His assistant brought in coffee. When Hughes placed his cup in the saucer, the china clattered.

The conversation soon turned to Warhol. I asked him how many of Warhol's paintings would be sold and how many would go to the museum.

"Numbers!" he exclaimed. "Some of Andy's paintings will go to the museum, and some will be sold for the continued benefit of the foundation. There's not a large amount. Andy was much more of a hand-to-brush and brush-to-canvas painter than he wanted people to know. He wasn't a factory turning out paintings. He liked to give that impression, which is quite an artistic thing. But there aren't that many paintings."

I asked him about the process of liquidating the estate.

"It's pretty simple," he said. "You get the stuff, you sell it, and it goes to the foundation."

Then why was the process taking so long?

"There was no rush," he said. "The dirtiest word in my vocabulary is 'rush.' I have transferred the art assets to the foundation. Eventually, all of the money will be put into the foundation—bank accounts, the sale of the real estate." But when I tried to get him to be more specific, he turned surly. "A number." He sneered. "What does that *mean?*"

"Are you happy with the board of directors?" I asked.

"I have enormous respect for Brendan Gill and Agnes Gund. Mr. Fremont was convinced to resign against my wishes. Archibald Gillies was added to the board when Vincent Fremont resigned. I did not vote for him like the rest of the trustees. I just felt we needed someone with experience in the visual arts." He sounded so diplomatic, something for which Hughes wasn't exactly known. I tried to get him to comment further. "No. I don't think it's appropriate at this time to speak on [the board], and I've been asked by the foundation's attorney not to." Hughes paused for a while before adding slyly, "I certainly don't want to *offend* anyone."

"And what about the falling out with Hayes?"

"The less I say about Mr. Hayes, the better. He doesn't make the decisions; the executor does. The power of an executor of a large estate in New York is not inconsequential." A pause. Then a homily: "Tell the truth. You will confound your friends but confuse your enemies."

"Would Warhol be pleased with how his money is being spent?" I asked.

"Andy—" Fred Hughes began, then stopped. "You had to work hard to get what he really thought. He really thought very clearly and incredibly honestly. I think he would have been terribly proud—not necessarily with the way things are now but with the way things are going to be."

Later, at the end of our conversation, I again mentioned Hughes's longtime colleague Fremont.

"I have a name for him," Hughes roared. "Benedict Arnold! And you can quote me on that."

In the fall of 1991, the estate was hit with a multimillion-dollar judgment in the most disastrous financial deal it had made since Warhol's death. Back in late 1987, the estate had signed a licensing agreement with Schlaifer Nance, an Atlanta-based company, run by Roger Schlaifer, that was best known for marketing Cabbage Patch Kids. Roger Schlaifer had immediately begun to design and market Warhol-related products, mostly notebooks and calendars. At first Hughes and Schlaifer were able to agree easily on the kinds of items Schlaifer would market. Then, six months into their relationship—about the same length of time it would take for Hughes to become disillusioned with Gillies—Hughes and Schlaifer started to have disagreements over just how they should continue to market Warhol's name and image. Schlaifer wanted to move their operations into the area of fashion, but when he produced his first ideas Hughes was horrified. Ripped T-shirts, rhinestone-studded sweaters, sequined blouses, all with Warhol images—Hughes felt they were some of the ugliest articles of clothing he had ever seen, and he told Schlaifer just that.

Throughout 1988 Schlaifer submitted a series of products to Hughes for his approval, but Hughes routinely rejected them. By 1989 Hughes had stopped speaking to him, putting himself in effect in breach of the licensing agreement that legally required him to confer with Schlaifer. Hughes didn't care. He had grown so tired of dealing with Schlaifer, whom he now viewed as a totally inappropriate choice to market Warhol products, that he simply refused to speak to him anymore. By early 1990 Schlaifer had filed breach-of-contract lawsuits against the Warhol estate in New York City and Atlanta. After several months of discussions between lawyers, the case was scheduled to be heard before an arbitration board beginning in early 1991. Initially Schlaifer said he would settle the case for $7 million; however, when Hughes was deposed, he came across so poorly—as so arrogant and hostile and clearly all but impossible to work with—that Schlaifer changed his mind. He now wanted $12 million to settle.

As soon as it convened, the arbitration board ruled that Schlaifer could not sue for lost profits, one of the main points in his suit, so the likelihood of his getting a large award was not good. Still, in the spring, Gillies recommended to Hughes and Hayes that the estate pay Schlaifer $6 million. Hayes questioned this. He was sure the arbitration board would come in with a much smaller figure, an amount that would more or less cover the money Schlaifer had invested in the project. So Hayes never made Schlaifer the offer. In August 1991, the arbitration board issued its decision. Saying that the estate acted "in bad faith and in willful disregard of [Schlaifer Nance's] rights" and that "numerous sublicensees and potential sublicensees were put to substantial futile efforts because of the Estate's willful determination to cause the contract to fail," the board ruled in Schlaifer Nance's favor. Schlaifer would receive $2.4 million in out-of-pocket expenses, $1.6 million in punitive damages, and about a quarter of a million in interest. At the same time, he would also have to pay back to the estate $700,000 in profits for merchandise that had been shipped but had not yet been collected on. The net award, then, was about $3.5 million.

Schlaifer reacted immediately by filing civil RICO—racketeering—suits against Hughes, Hayes, and Fremont (who had been involved on a minor level with the licensing program). Schlaifer claimed that the three men had used the estate to defraud him, a charge that was going to be extremely difficult to prove. Even so, over the next two and a half years, the case dragged on, requiring numerous conferences with the judge who was handling the suit, Louis Stanton. Schlaifer incurred substantial legal fees, possibly as much as the foundation, which spent at least $2 million. Finally, in February 1994, Stanton dismissed the case. In his opinion he could find no evidence that Hughes, Hayes, or Fremont had used the Estate of Andy Warhol to defraud Schlaifer. The $2 million Schlaifer had put into the civil RICO case had more than depleted the punitive damages and interest he had won from the arbitration board, meaning that Schlaifer had worked on the Warhol project since 1987 and probably ended up losing money.

Only the lawyers profited.

In late 1991, another piece of litigation was concluded, this one involving the wrongful-death lawsuit that in 1987 the Warhol estate had brought against New York Hospital and several members of the medical staff connected with Warhol's care, among them Denton Cox. Originally, Cox had been left out of the suit, but the estate lawyers added him at the last minute. Since 1987, there had been numerous meetings and depositions and pretrial conferences that generated thousands of pages of court records, until the dispute finally culminated in a trial in New York City before Judge Ira Gammerman. Of all the witnesses to take the stand, the most compelling—and poignant—was Dr. Cox.

On his first day of testimony, Cox sat on the stand, focused and intent. He was also in deep conflict: His devotion to Warhol had sometimes put him at odds with his hospital, which had to defend itself vigorously against claims made by Warhol's estate. Today Bruce Clark, an estate attorney, was questioning him. "These are the notes by Min Cho," Clark was saying. " 'Two A.M. He's back asleep,' right?"

" 'Two A.M.,' " Cox repeated, reading from Warhol's hospital chart. " 'Blood pressure 120 over 80. Pulse 80. Respiration is 20. No complaint. He's back to sleep. IV runs okay. He refuses'—something—'medications.' "

"Pain medications," Judge Gammerman corrected Cox.

" 'He continued sleeping,' " Cox said.

"Then," Clark asked, "no observation until four-thirty A.M., right? That is recorded?"

"Yes, correct," Cox said.

"The patient appears 'pale more.' "

"Yes."

"Now, even in somebody as pale as Andy Warhol, more pale is an ominous sign, is it not?"

"Yes," Cox said.

"It is something that could alert you, right, and at that time, she felt his pulse?"

"Yes."

"And no recording of what amount the pulse was, right?"

"Correct."

"No recording of blood pressure?"

"None."

"No recording of respirations?"

"She just said 'okay,' " Cox pointed out, still looking at Min Cho's notes on Warhol's chart.

"Then at four forty-five, he's even more pale, and this time there is no pulse recorded, right?"

"From what I can read, he appears 'more pale. Listen pulse.' "

"Says 'okay'?" Gammerman tried to decipher the chart.

"Now, Doctor," Clark said, "at each one of these instances, at four-thirty and four forty-five, Andy Warhol was still savable, wasn't he?"

"I would have hoped so, and believe so," Cox said without hesitation. This was the crux of Cox's argument: Andy Warhol had died of an unexpected—and unexplained—heart attack while asleep in his bed at New York Hospital, yet Min Cho, had she been more observant and realized that Warhol was having a heart attack, could have saved his life by immediately calling for the hospital's emergency cardiac team.

The estate had a different theory about how Warhol died. Doctors for the estate believed that while Warhol had indeed died of a heart attack as Min Cho was attending to him, the cardiac arrest was brought on by specific circumstances. According to these doctors, the hospital's medical staff had not properly monitored the fluids that were pumped into Warhol's body before, during, and especially after his surgery. As a result Warhol had been overhydrated; he had effectively drowned in his own body fluids. That would explain why, doctors for the estate argued, Warhol's lungs were suspiciously heavy. Cox—and cardiovascular experts lined up by New York Hospital—thought this theory was untenable and pointed to the same autopsy as evidence to support the claim that the origin of the attack was sudden and unknown, in the same way as it was with one hundred thousand deaths each year in the United States. All of the experts who had actually studied the body or the autopsy at the time of Warhol's death, Cox noted, were sure that, while the cause of the heart attack had been unknown, it was clearly not the result of overhydration, or fluid overload. Cox asserted that the estate had concocted this story of overhydration so that the estate and Steve Hayes, Ed's brother, who had been hired to handle this litigation, would have a better case.

Later, as he was being questioned by Glenn Dopf, his own attorney, Cox was asked to describe the visit he made to Warhol just after Warhol had been returned to his room from surgery. "I wait until my patients are really able to understand and retain [what I say] and I give them reassurance," Cox said on the stand. "That's why I timed my visit to occur after Andy came out of the recovery room and was in his room. And he had been in it just a few minutes when I saw him."

"Would you turn to that part of the chart that reflects your visit?" Dopf asked.

"Did you write the note?" Gammerman asked Cox.

"Yes, I did."

Then, looking at the note, his description of the last time he saw Andy alive, Cox could no longer maintain his composure. Slowly his eyes clouded over, and he began to cry.

"I am sorry. I apologize," he said, losing control. "I didn't want to do this. . . . But I cared."

"You want a break?" Gammerman asked him.

"No, I think we can go on." Cox hesitated. "I just cared so much and tried so hard."

Now sobbing, Cox couldn't speak.

"Let's take ten minutes," Gammerman said.

When the trial resumed, Cox was able to finish his testimony. In the end, though, his efforts on the stand were irrelevant. Several days later, following the decision of the hospital and Thorbjarnarson to settle and under pressure from the hospital's attorneys, Cox reluctantly agreed with the hospital's resolution to offer the estate a settlement. Cox had wanted to continue to fight, but Min Cho had kept such poor records that the hospital could not prove conclusively that Warhol had *not* been overhydrated. So, to avoid an even larger potential award, the hospital agreed to pay the Warhol estate $3 million. Naturally, that sum was actually paid by the insurance companies that represented the doctors and the hospital.

As it happened, all of the money, except for legal fees, went to Warhol's two brothers. Unhappy with Warhol's will, Paul and John Warhola had threatened to contest it until Hughes and Hayes had reached a compromise with them. In exchange for not contesting, the brothers would receive all of Warhol's retirement money—about $330,000 went to Paul, $430,000 to John—and split whatever damages the estate recovered from the hospital in the wrongful death suit. Also, because John had been named as a trustee to the foundation's board, he was entitled to receive a salary of $75,000 a year. The brothers would have liked more money, of course; but considering the fact that Warhol had explicitly made only small provisions for them in his will, they had to be content with what they could get.

The Warhol foundation ended 1991 by electing two new directors to its board: Kinshasha Holman Conwill, the head of the Studio Museum in Harlem, and Kathy Halbreich, the head of the Walker Arts Center in Minneapolis. That brought the total number of board members to seven.

As Christmas approached, the conflict between Hughes and Hayes was about to enter its third year. From February 1987 to November 1989, they had been with each other constantly—working at the Factory, going on business trips, socializing outside the office. After their falling out, however, Hughes and Hayes had never even been alone in the same room—until this day in late December. In the second-floor conference room at the Factory—the same one in which Hayes had had his confrontation with Martha Baer—Hughes and Hayes were meeting with Tom Melfe, Hughes's attorney. More than anything else, Melfe seemed to want Hughes and Hayes to work out their differences. It would certainly be better than having their dispute resolved in court. As if to put more pressure on them to reconcile their disagreements, at one point Melfe got up and left the room.

Initially, neither seemed sure what to do. Then, as Ed remembers, he took out a picture of Avery, his daughter, Fred's goddaughter, and handed it to Fred. Fred took the photograph from Ed and looked at it. Avery, now four, was a beautiful child—blond, personable, happy.

"I'd like to see Avery," Fred said, glancing up at Ed.

"I'd love for you to see Avery," Ed said. "You know, if you can't have a relationship with me, you can have one with my wife and my daughter. She *is* your goddaughter."

"Why don't you have Susie call and arrange to bring Avery by," Fred said.

Then there was a pause.

"Fred, I feel bad about this whole thing," Ed said, picking up the conversation. "I've never had a rupture with a friend before. If I've hurt you in any way, I'm sorry."

"I don't know if we can be friends again," Fred said halfheartedly. It was as if he wanted to repair their friendship but didn't know how he could; too much damage had been done.

"Let's just forget about it," Ed said. "Go on with your life. It's no big deal." He waited. "I'll have Susie call to bring Avery around to see you."

In a few days Susie Hayes called Fred and asked if she could bring Avery by in the next day or so. He told her it was not a good time. Susie never called Fred again.

8

EARLY IN 1992 GILLIES TURNED HIS ATTENTION TOWARD HAVING HUGHES removed as chairman of the board of directors. Gillies had more than ample evidence to support the removal. By then, Hughes had become impossible to work with; he was so insulting, so critical in his comments, that both his colleagues and Factory employees went out of their way to avoid being around him. The final blow came with the appearance in late January of the *New York* magazine cover story I wrote. In it, Hughes was highly critical of the foundation. "Your piece came out," Gillies says, "and there was a revolt, if you will. Everyone was up in arms about it. I sent out a letter saying we had to consider removing Fred from the board." At the same time, Gillies let it be known that he felt the foundation would be better off if Hughes would at least step down as the board's chairman. Meanwhile, the board approached Brendan Gill to offer him the job of chairman—and a $35,000-a-year stipend. Finally the board met and Hughes was presented with an option: Either he could voluntarily resign as chairman of the board—to become honorary chairman—or his fellow trustees would vote him out. Hughes resigned, effective February 11, 1992. (Afterward, he would contend he was happy to give up the job.) At that meeting he was replaced by Gill.

By June 1992 Ed Hayes had to know that he was never going to reach an understanding with either Hughes or Gillies. Technically, he was still the attorney for the estate—he had never been fired—but because of his strained relationship with the men, a situation made worse by the fact that Hughes and Gillies were also not speaking, the prospect of his reaching any kind of reconciliation with the estate and the foundation looked slim. In 1987, 1988, and 1989, Hayes had been paid a hefty fee for the legal work he and various attorneys who worked for him had done—$4.85 million. The large payment of $1.6 million, made to him just before Gillies took over as president of the foundation in early 1990, was the last payment Hayes had received. Still, according to the terms of the retainer agreement he had signed with Hughes, Hayes was entitled to more: 2 percent of the value of the estate at closing. The feedback he'd been getting from Jeffrey Hoffeld indicated that the estate could well be worth as much as $500 million to $600 million, or even more. If the estate were worth $600 million, Hayes would be owed some $12 million. That would mean the estate or the foundation, the estate's sole beneficiary, would have to pay him an additional $7.15 million.

The legal options available to Hayes to collect more money were not numerous, but there was one that could bring him relief: He could file something called an SCPA 2110 petition in surrogate's court. A motion that asks a judge to fix an attorney's legal fee, a 2110 petition is in effect a request for the payment of fees. On June 11, 1992, with the estate and the foundation locked in bitter conflict and the chances of the estate being closed in the near future all but nonexistent, Hayes filed the petition.

"My representation of the Estate entailed substantial personal sacrifice," Hayes wrote at the beginning of a thirty-page affidavit that explained both what he had done as the estate's attorney and why he deserved more money than the nearly $5 million he had already received. "The hours were demanding and unpredictable; the personalities were difficult; the problems were complex and wide-ranging. Warhol died suddenly on February 22, 1987, leaving behind a huge business enter-

prise, in disarray because of his death, and a single man in charge—
Frederick Hughes, his key advisor for twenty years. I accepted the
responsibilities that Hughes offered in return for a written fee arrangement that was modified over time but always reflected a basic premise:
my compensation would be measured as a percentage of the Estate's
value. This standard gave me the incentive and motivation to marshall,
maintain, and, in fact, increase the value of the Estate"—a motivation
not unlike the one Dottie Payne had given Hayes years ago in her
restaurant in Smithtown, Long Island, when she paid him not by the
hours he worked but by what he actually accomplished. How his life
had changed, though! "The fee that I seek is substantial," Hayes
wrote, "a $12,000,000 fee on a $600,000,000 (or greater) estate."
Part of that money would go to Frank Harvey, Hayes's associate, who
had done much of the daily legal work for the estate through the
years. Still, how in good faith could Hayes ask for so much money—
surely one of the largest legal fees in history? "Its reasonableness must
be judged by the unprecedented nature of the services rendered, the
difficulty and variety of the problems addressed and solved and the
measurable value that has been added to the Estate's assets as a result
of my legal guidance." Hayes also made one final point: Since Hughes
had demanded all of his time, he had in essence given up his legal
practice to represent the Warhol estate. Between 1987 and 1992,
Hayes had had essentially no other clients.

On July 14, 1992, through Thomas Melfe, his attorney at Donovan
Leisure Newton & Irvine, Hughes answered Hayes's 2110 petition.
Hughes said that "[the] Petitioner has long ceased acting as legal counsel
for the Estate of Andy Warhol under the terms of all agreements relating
to Petitioner's retention, thereby nullifying such agreements"; that "[the]
Petitioner breached his fiduciary duty to the Executor by entering into
agreements and charging a fee for legal services which a lawyer of
ordinary prudence would deem in excess of a reasonable fee"; that "[the]
Petitioner's request for legal fees is unreasonable and inconsistent with
the standards set forth in *Matter of Freeman*," one of the precedent-setting
cases in the field of estate law; that "the retainer agreement of Petitioner

and Frederick W. Hughes, as Executor of the Estate of Andy Warhol, constitutes an unconscionable agreement and should be deemed null and void as a matter of public policy"; and that "The Petitioner is barred in whole or in part by operation of the doctrine of unclean hands," a legal term that says a party is guilty of improper business practices. Because of these—and other—reasons, Hughes requested that the court not only dismiss ("with prejudice") Hayes's petition but also direct Hayes "to refund to the Estate of Andy Warhol such amount as the Court may determine was paid to him in excess of the fair value of services, together with interest" and to grant "other and further relief as the Court may deem just, proper, necessary, or appropriate under the circumstances."

The decision about Hayes's legal fees—and other matters that would come up as a result of the 2110 petition—would be made by a woman whose regal manner and authoritative presence caused her to be the focus of attention when she walked into her courtroom in surrogate's court. Adjectives like "aristocratic" and "commanding" had been used to describe her in the past, but the one detail about her life that usually created the most comment—a detail she did not play down since she was deeply proud of her family heritage—was the identity of her uncle: Otto Preminger, the legendary Hollywood director whose films included *Exodus, Laura, Porgy and Bess, Hurry Sundown,* and *The Man with the Golden Arm.*

Eve Preminger was born in 1935 in Austria, the daughter of Ingo and Kate Preminger. During her childhood and youth she was known to her family as Eva—a beautiful, charming, and intelligent child. Like those of all Austrian Jews, her life was changed permanently on March 12, 1938, the day Hitler invaded Austria. Somehow her father was able to sneak his family through Czechoslovakia to Switzerland, where they met up with Ingo's parents, who had escaped by a different route. From there they traveled to New York City to join Ingo's brother, Otto. An immigrant to America years before, Otto was making a name for himself as a movie and theatrical director. At the moment, he was in New York preparing a play.

When the Premingers arrived in the United States, however, they discovered they could only secure visitor's visas, since the quota for permanent visas had already been met. One day Otto got a call from Tallulah Bankhead, whose father was the Speaker of the House of Representatives and whose uncle was a senator from Alabama, her home state. Bankhead suggested that Preminger go see her father and uncle in Washington. "I met with the two Southern gentlemen," Otto Preminger later wrote, "and they told me that they were ready to introduce a special bill which would permit my parents and my brother and his family to become Americans regardless of the quota. A few weeks later they went to Canada for a day, applied for their visas, and returned as immigrants. When I went to see Tallulah and expressed my thanks she drawled, 'Oh it's nothing, daaahling!' "

Eve Preminger grew up in New York and eventually studied law at Columbia, where she served on the *Columbia Law Review*. After graduation she entered private practice, specializing in entertainment law, which seemed a natural choice given her uncle's success and the fact that her father had become a respected talent agent. In 1976 she was appointed to the criminal court of the city of New York. Two years later she was named acting supreme court justice, only to be elected to the supreme court three years after that. While on the bench, she heard a number of cases that became well known, among them the CBS murders and the shooting of New York City police officer Steven McDonald. Finally, in 1990, though her candidacy was opposed by *The New York Times*, which supported a more conservative candidate, she was elected as a surrogate of New York County. During all of these years, as the *Times* noted, she had not lost the liberal—that is to say, humanitarian—politics that she had been taught as a young girl in Austria. On the subject of her politics, she is described this way in her official court biography: "Judge Preminger was a member of the Founding Board of Advisors of the Gay Men's Health Crisis in 1981, the Board of Directors of Project Green Hope, and numerous other community organizations. She has served on the Supreme Court Committee on Gender Bias, the Governor's Advisory Council on Alcoholism, Women in Criminal Justice, and various committees of the Association of the Bar, the New York City Lawyers Association, and the American Bar Association. She is a member of . . . the National Association of Women Judges."

In many ways Preminger was the perfect judge to try to resolve the dispute over Warhol's estate. Sophisticated, liberal, the product of an artistic family, she better than most judges would be able to appreciate the value of an artist's body of work.

Not long after Melfe submitted Hughes's reply to Hayes's 2110 petition, Robert Abrams, the attorney general of the state of New York, issued his opinion on the matter of the Hayes petition. In a legal brief whose language was often harsh and accusatory, Abrams said that "the undated Retainer Agreement of Edward W. Hayes with Frederick Hughes, as Executor of the Estate of Andy Warhol, is not binding on the charitable beneficiary of the Estate, the Attorney General, or the Court, and is of no force and effect"; that "the Retainer Agreement constitutes an unconscionable, unreasonable, and unfair agreement and a contract of adhesion, and is unenforceable, illegal, and void"; that "the Retainer Agreement should be deemed null and void as contrary to public policy"; that "the petitioner [Hayes] has effectively been discharged as counsel for the Estate, thereby nullifying the Retainer Agreement"; that "[the] petitioner breached his fiduciary duty and his duties of loyalty and reasonable care to the Executor and the charitable beneficiaries of the Estate by seeking to enforce an unconscionable and unfair retainer agreement and continuing to demand an outrageous legal fee unrelated to the necessary legal work performed"; and that "the petitioner engaged in fraud and overreaching in inducing the Executor to enter into the Retainer Agreement."

Some of the positions the attorney general took were simply wrong. The retainer agreement, for example, *was* dated, as were two of the three updates. Other positions seemed extremely hard to defend; it would be difficult to prove that Hughes had been the victim of fraud when he willingly signed four different versions of the retainer agreement over a long period of time. Abrams appeared to know this too, despite the fury with which he attacked Hayes, so that at the end of his brief he added, almost as an afterthought, his opinion on who should have to pay Hayes in the event the retainer agreement was judged enforceable. Because "the Executor of the Estate has breached his fiduciary duty of reasonable care and loyalty to the charitable beneficiaries of the Estate by imprudently entering into the Retainer Agreement, thereby subjecting the charitable beneficiaries to additional expenses in opposing the instant Petition as well as the risk of substantial, unwarranted payments to the Petitioner as requested in the Petition," Abrams believed that "any fees awarded to the Petitioner pursuant to the instant Petition should be the personal responsibility of the Executor, and should not be assessed to the Estate." It was not a unique position for an attorney general to take—in many cases an executor has been held personally liable if he has mishandled an estate—but it certainly exposed Hughes to a major risk. If Preminger determined that Hayes was due anywhere near $7.15 million and Hughes was held accountable for even a good portion of the award, Hughes could be destroyed financially.

At a conference in Preminger's chambers in the early fall, the subject of the attorney general's brief was raised. Preminger had called all of the parties into her chambers to talk about the possibility of a settlement— something, she made clear, she wanted more than anything else. In the meeting were Hayes, Frank Harvey, and their attorney, Charlotte Fischman of Kramer Levin; Tom Melfe and David Jewell from Donovan Leisure; Beth Jacob, Toni Thomas, and Mike Frankel from Carter Ledyard; and David Samuels, Pamela Mann, and Laura Werner from the attorney general's office. Usually the charities bureau of the attorney general's office monitors the operations of public corporations like the Warhol foundation, but, because of Hayes's 2110 petition, the attorney general had become directly involved in the legal dispute. Samuels, the assistant attorney general assigned to the case, took a single position to the exclusion of all other issues involved in the disagreement: Hayes should be paid no more money—no matter what.

The discussion was going so poorly that Preminger was beginning to think there was little hope of a settlement. And then Samuels brought up the fraud allegations that the attorney general had mentioned in his brief. "We think Mr. Hayes obtained his contract fraudulently," Samuels said, explaining why the attorney general would not even be willing to discuss a settlement with Hayes. "We also wonder if Mr. Hughes obtained any of the paintings he says he owns fraudulently."

Preminger stopped the discussion. "These are extremely serious allegations, Mr. Samuels," Preminger said. "What evidence, for instance, does the attorney general have to make such an allegation against Mr. Hayes in his brief?"

Samuels seemed surprised to have been asked the question. A hypertense man who was known for blurting out inappropriate comments at inopportune times, Samuels could also act almost childishly, especially if his integrity was called into question. He appeared to be a virtual caricature of the bumbling government bureaucrat—the kind of professional who can make it in the government but nowhere else. In this instance, he merely tried to avoid answering Preminger. "Well, we're investigating how Mr. Hayes got his contract," he asserted.

"What do you mean?" Preminger said, anger slipping into her voice. "What evidence do you have to charge him with fraud? Where is the evidence?"

"Well, we're looking into it."

"I said, what evidence do you have?" she demanded.

"Well . . ." Samuels said, his voice trailing off.

"Mr. Samuels," Preminger said, "I can only assume that you have no evidence whatsoever to support any of your allegations."

What Samuels should have known, but obviously didn't, was that Preminger's husband, Theodore Friedman, a personal injury attorney, had himself been prosecuted by New York County District Attorney Robert Morgenthau on charges that, a jury had decided, were in effect trumped up. Friedman was representing a tenant who was injured in a housing project. Morgenthau claimed that during the trial Friedman had tampered with a witness, so he filed charges against Friedman on extremely thin evidence. When the case came to trial, the jury not only acquitted Friedman but also read a letter aloud in court that criticized Morgenthau. (Eventually, in a strange twist, this case would be used in a successful attempt to have Friedman disbarred.)

Preminger knew what it felt like to be the victim of unsubstantiated allegations. Then again, her family had a history of defending people who had been unfairly accused of crimes. In fact, it was her father and her uncle who helped to break the blacklist in the late fifties. Otto was scheduled to direct *Exodus*, a picture based on the Leon Uris novel. Uris had written a screenplay that Preminger had rejected. When Otto began to scout around for another screenwriter, Ingo recommended Dalton Trumbo, one of his clients. A member of the Hollywood Ten, Trumbo had been blacklisted for years, even though in 1957 he won an Academy Award for *The Brave One*, a screenplay he had written under a pseudonym. Otto hired Trumbo, and when the picture was released he insisted on listing Trumbo in the credits. "The reason I fought censorship," Otto Preminger later wrote, "was not because I thought that a few cuts or changes in a film would destroy an artistic masterpiece, but because I believe that permitting those cuts would be a step, no matter how small, toward the loss of our liberty." That's also why he championed the cause of someone like Dalton Trumbo, and why his niece Eve, a refugee from Nazi oppression, might have had a deeper than usual sensitivity to random accusation.

At Carter Ledyard, the responsibility for the work that resulted from what became known as "the Ed Hayes problem" fell to Beth Jacob. Gates would oversee Jacob, but she was in charge of the day-to-day business of the case. A former Manhattan assistant district attorney, Jacob had been at Carter Ledyard long enough for Gates to build up trust in her, even though she gave an impression of fragility and was pathologically soft-spoken. In the fall of 1992, just as *Hayes* v. *The Andy Warhol Foundation* was coming into being, Jacob was involved in another Carter Ledyard case that was making the papers, although in the end she surely could not have wanted it to. Several years before, the Hospital for Special Surgery had fired a doctor. Upset with the hospital's treatment, he had filed a wide-ranging lawsuit charging everything from libel to defamation of character. As the trial date approached that fall, the hospital, Jacob's client, became worried about the case and authorized Jacob to offer the doctor a significant out-of-court cash settlement. Though settlements were discussed, Jacob convinced the hospital administrators that they should allow the case to go to trial because it was highly unlikely that the hospital would lose. (It should be noted that within the legal profession some lawyers prefer not to make settlements since it means they can't continue to bill their clients for their services.)

The case went to trial. At one point, Dr. Nigel Sharrock, a doctor with the hospital and therefore Jacob's client, was seen talking in the hallway to one of the jurors and reading that juror's EKG. Jacob witnessed the conversation but did not report it to Louis Freeh, the judge in the case. Freeh learned of the conversation when another attorney reported the exchange. Freeh put Jacob on the stand, where she told the judge that she had not reported the incident because she thought it was a joke. From the bench, Freeh told Jacob that she had behaved "inappropriately" and "unprofessionally." To make matters worse, when the jury came in from deliberations at the end of the trial, they leveled a $9.2 million judgment against the hospital—well more than what the hospital could have settled the case for before it went to trial. Immediately after the verdict, Beth Jacob and Carter Ledyard were fired.

During 1992 and on into 1993, Jacob regularly appeared along with her boss Peter Gates at the board meetings of the Warhol foundation, where she told the members, as confidently as she had told the administrators at the Hospital for Special Surgery, that there was no way they were going to lose their case. Hayes was incompetent. He was responsible for the Schlaifer Nance mess. He had bungled the *Interview* sale—the reason Peter Brant had stopped paying his mortgage on the magazine about a year after the deal had been completed. Finally, nobody was going to doubt the reliability of the Christie's appraisal, the cornerstone of their case. The board believed Jacob—even Anthony Solomon, a former advisor to two U.S. presidents who had been elected to the board at the November 1992 meeting. In fact, in some ways Solomon had actually been brought on the board to take care of "the Ed Hayes problem." An old, sickly man who was often in and out of the hospital, Solomon was sometimes seen attending foundation events wearing a neck wrap (for medical purposes). Like so many other people now involved with the foundation, he was a part of the establishment elite who were used to having access to power and money and at the same time completely unaccustomed to having someone challenge them in the way Hayes now was. Stubborn Arch Gillies with his wheeling and dealing ("You bet I'm stubborn," he would proudly proclaim), nervous Martha Baer with her fleeting memory, old Anthony Solomon with his neck wrap, jittery David Samuels with his darting eyes, reticent Beth Jacob with her inaudible mumbling—it was an odd lot of characters worthy of a Warhol movie, only, in all likelihood, at some point Warhol would have become horrified by the plot of the story and turned the camera off.

As Hayes's case progressed toward an actual trial, Charlotte Fischman's firm developed a potential conflict of interest with Hayes through another—separate—case, so Hayes hired Robert Jossen to replace Fischman. A partner at the firm of Shereff, Friedman, Hoffman & Goodman, Jossen had gone to law school at Columbia with Hayes. Unlike Hayes, he had been one of the top students in his class and served on the *Columbia Law Review.* After law school, he had clerked for a federal judge, then ran the appeals bureau of the United States attorney general's office. If the case did go to trial, Jossen would make a formidable adversary. At least he spoke loudly enough to be heard in a courtroom—unlike Jacob. "She'd be in a courtroom," says a detective who used to work with her when she was an assistant district attorney, "and if the court reporter said it to her once he said it a thousand times, 'Speak up!'"

9

RECENTLY MARTHA BAER HAD LEARNED THAT FRED HUGHES HAD PUT UP TEN of his Warhols to be sold at auction. Rumors had been circulating about these paintings for some time. Larry Gagosian had made Hughes an offer for the paintings—an offer Hughes refused. "I tried to get those paintings," Gagosian later said. "I made him a very nice offer, but he wanted to gamble with the auction house." The house with which he had gambled was not Christie's, either; it was Sotheby's. That's why Baer was annoyed. Christie's had four Warhols listed in its spring catalogue, but it made her angry that after all the work she had put into the Warhol appraisal Hughes had not even bothered to discuss his paintings with Christie's before giving them to Sotheby's. She picked up the telephone in her office and called Vincent Fremont.

"I was calling to find out about Fred's consignment of the Warhols to Sotheby's," Baer said when Fremont got on the telephone.

"He's his own man," Fremont said.

"Well, what are the chances of a possible consignment to Christie's in the future?" Baer said.

"Don't hold your breath."

It was not what Baer wanted to hear.

That same day, Baer wrote a pointed interoffice memo to a colleague, which she copied to Stephen Lash, in which she spelled out her feelings on the matter. "I will call Fred Hughes tomorrow to ask why we were never consulted," Baer wrote. "Right now both Stephen and I think we should discuss whether to continue with the appraisal. No doubt it will end up in litigation and Ed Hayes would make and is a powerful enemy...."

Can we get out of this gracefully? Stephen and I would like to discuss this with you soon. Please let me know when you have time."

The next day, Friday, April 16, Lash had lunch with Gillies. In the event Christie's reneged on the appraisal, it could have disastrous consequences for the foundation, now that it seemed the conflict was going to end up in court. If Gillies had not known of Christie's trepidation before yesterday, Baer's call to Fremont had to have tipped him off. So, at lunch with Lash, Gillies made the situation perfectly clear: Should Christie's be displeased because Hughes had given his Warhols to Sotheby's, perhaps the foundation could make up for Hughes's decision in the future.

"We may not be selling anything right now, except to museums," Gillies told Lash, "but the foundation will become commercial sellers in June of 1994. At that time, there will be sixty million dollars' worth of art to be sold."

"How can we assure that the foundation will sell through Christie's?" Lash asked.

"Martha Baer and Patty Hambrecht should meet with me and the foundation lawyers," Gillies said. "Also, Christie's should make a presentation to the board."

That seemed to be all Lash needed to hear. With a potential $60 million future sale only a year off, he was certainly not going to allow Christie's to back out of the appraisal at this point. That following Monday he wrote Gillies a letter thanking him for the lunch and the check for $30,665 Gillies had sent him as a partial payment for the appraisal services. "I can only assume that this is a direct outgrowth of our lunch of Friday for which I am most grateful," Lash wrote. "The amount of $33,102.25 remains outstanding from the Estate, and I have enclosed a copy of the invoice dated March 25, 1992. . . . I also wanted to let you know that you will be receiving a letter under separate cover, and a bill in the amount of $50,748.98 from Martha Baer for services rendered to the Foundation for the second half of 1992."

Whatever had transpired between Gillies and Lash at their lunch calmed the reservations Lash and other Christie's officials were beginning to feel about the Warhol appraisal. Christie's would go forward, and Lash would make sure that he and Baer did their best to land the $60 million worth of art.

On the night that Hughes's ten Warhols—along with another two that had been included at the last minute from unidentified private collections, *Tunafish Disaster* and *Self-Portrait (Green Camouflage)*—went on sale at Sotheby's, the auction room was crowded with bidders and spectators. Some in attendance had also been present in the spring of 1988 when the sale of Warhol's massive collectibles collection made headlines and set auction records. Since Warhol's death the prices for his paintings had gone up steadily. In 1988, his paintings were regularly fetching over a million dollars each. Then, in 1989, Christie's set a record when it auctioned *Shot Red Marilyn* for $4.1 million, the highest price ever paid for a Warhol. Though the market leveled off somewhat after that, Thomas Ammann paid $2.1 million for *210 Coca-Cola Bottles* in May 1992, and later that same year, in November, Sotheby's sold *Marilyn X 100* for $3.7 million.

The excitement in the room, however, was tinged somewhat with apprehension. After all, some of Hughes's Warhols seemed to be uncompleted works in progress, and they were all minor compared with the major paintings Warhol was producing at the same time all of these were done in the early sixties. What's more, of the ten canvases, only two were signed. Within the confines of the art world, gossip makes its way quickly. This is possible in part because the core group of people who actually run the art world is so small—perhaps as few as three thousand people, as Tom Wolfe once estimated. The animosity that existed between Warhol's estate and the foundation was no secret. Most potential buyers knew that there was a strong possibility that litigation would develop over the value—and perhaps even the content—of the estate before it was closed out. Why would someone knowingly buy a Warhol from Hughes—and an unsigned one at that—when the painting might actually end up being a part of a lawsuit?

That question was answered when the first Warhol was put on the block. A strange stillness fell over the large room as a significant period of time passed during which nothing happened. No one was bidding on the painting. "Do I have any bidders?" the auctioneer asked repeatedly from the podium. More time passed; more silence. The auctioneer moved on. The first of Hughes's ten Warhols had not sold.

A buzz ran through the room when the situation became clear: These Warhols were not going to sell. Of the ten, only the two signed works found buyers. The two Warhols from private collections remained unsold as well. Perhaps this was the beginning of the end of the Warhol art market. Perhaps Warhol was not as important—and bankable—as many dealers and historians had been saying since his death. Perhaps Warhol *was* just a fad, as so many of his critics had claimed through the years.

The next night, at Christie's, fears about the collapse of a Warhol market were not quelled. Not one of the four Warhols put on the block sold. "Andy Warhol got yet another 15 minutes of fame," *The New York Times* reported afterward, "but it wasn't the kind the artist would have liked. When 16 of his works went on the auction block in New York in a 24-hour period with disastrous results—only two sold, and they went for very low prices—it was the talk of the art world."

What no one could agree on was just why it had happened.

Not long after the debacle at the spring sales, in May 1993, I went to Fred Hughes's brownstone to have lunch. A year and a half had passed since I'd last seen him; during that time, his multiple sclerosis had progressed considerably. MS is aggravated by stress, and recent events had obviously taken their toll. His speech was slower than I remembered it, his diction more slurred, his muscles weaker. As we talked, I found myself lighting one cigarette after another for him. "Light me up a fag, butch," he'd say. Despite his physical deterioration, he had not lost his mental faculties. In many ways he was still as cunning, clear-thinking, and savvy as ever. Many art world insiders blamed Hughes for the disaster at the spring sales. Gillies believed that Hughes made a mistake by flooding the market with Warhols. The Warhols didn't sell, Gillies claimed, because there were too many of them to buy. "It's a collector's market," Gillies said. "When ten or twelve paintings are put up at once, it's not hospitable to the serious collector. They get nervous."

I asked Hughes about the spring sales.

"Of course, it was a big flop," he said slowly, his tone thick with irony. "I was selling my favorite paintings so that I could make ends meet. I needed money. But they didn't sell. It was worth it, though. I let people know I'm still out there." He took a sip of coffee, his hand shaking as he picked up the cup. "So, do you want to buy a Warhol wholesale? You've come to the right place."

"How much of a discount?" I asked.

"Well, quite a lot," he said. "It depends on what you want. Seriously, they're available. As soon as the auction was over I got lots of offers. I certainly don't want to give the impression that I'm stuck with a Macy's basement fire-sale thing. No way, José. If necessary, I'll get out and sell my body on the street. Do we hear any comers for that? You're gonna have to pay for it." Finally he got serious. "It was my gamble," he said. "The fact is, I was surprised they didn't sell. Then again, so were Sotheby's and Christie's."

"Why didn't they sell?" I said.

"Because," Hughes said, drawing out the word and raising his voice in mock anger, "people didn't *bid* on them!" Then he changed his tone. "There's an enormous amount of speculation as to why. People are looking for a discreditation. A lot of your average millionaires—and some below average—who didn't buy Warhol are happy to see that they were right after all."

"Since you need the money, couldn't you use the executor's fee that you'll receive when the estate is closed out?" I said.

"Well, every little bit helps," he said. "I've got to somehow pay my creditors. Laundry is not what it used to be here on the fashionable Upper East Side. So, yes, if you want to do me any favors, you'll say that Frederick W. Hughes certainly wants this estate to be closed."

"At this point, what do you think of Gillies?"

"Surely the man must have some idea of something else to do for a living." He paused, then continued. "Well, he married well. She's the president of the Vincent Astor Foundation. You know, just about the time I was going to dismiss him he engineered a strategy—he convinced Fremont to retire from the board—to become a trustee over my very calm objections to the other trustees. I don't know what hold he had over the trustees at the time. I know what he was trying with most people. I was the only person with an objection."

"Do you ever feel like you've built a foundation that other people are now living off of?"

"*Y* for Yosemite, *E* for Ecuador, and *S* for—in this case, it starts with *S* and ends in *T.* Okay?"

"Do you ever think about Warhol?" I asked near the end of our lunch.

"Yes, and I'll tell you this," Hughes said, his voice becoming softer. "I really miss the old bugger. Dominique de Menil told me once that there are certain people in life, they never leave. They're there. I feel that way about Andy. He's still here in a million ways. I'll be at the office and I'll say, 'Wait till that son of a bitch comes in here—am I going to give him hell!' Then I'll realize he's not going to come in. . . . Our lives are financially, spiritually, and mentally intertwined. What can I say?"

On April 14, 1993, Thomas Melfe submitted a 2110 petition—the same sort of petition Hayes had filed in the court about a year before—on behalf of his firm, Donovan Leisure. Hughes had hired Davis Polk & Wardwell after his falling out with Hayes in November 1989 to handle the legal affairs for the estate, even though Hayes was technically still the estate's attorney; but, when he had a disagreement with them over their fees about a year later, he hired Donovan Leisure. Now, in his 2110 petition, Melfe was asking Judge Preminger for "payment of the sum of $148,646.31 for legal services rendered to, and costs incurred by such firm on behalf of, the Estate," approval of "payments already made to Donovan Leisure in the amount of $403,382.93," and an additional payment of $5,537.18 for legal services rendered by Donovan Leisure in the Schlaifer Nance matter. "To date, 34 of Donovan Leisure's partners, associate attorneys, legal assistants, and law clerks have accumulated approximately 2100 hours of time charges working on the various Estate issues," Melfe wrote. Melfe himself put in "475.75 hours on the case, at a cost of $150,481.25." Jonathan Koslow, a former partner, devoted 231.5 hours, worth $62,768.75; Nina Myers, Laura Benzoni, and Anne Barnett 600 hours, worth $127,008.75; David Jewell 275.5 hours, worth $89,537.50; and Peter Smith 106.25 hours, worth $29,218.75. Besides these lawyers, a group of a dozen other attorneys put in 151.75 hours, worth $42,425, and even more attorneys "in the various practice areas as well as law clerks" worked 174.75 hours, worth $25,912.50. "For the foregoing reasons," Melfe wrote—in the 2110 petition he listed reason after reason—"I . . . respectfully submit that the reasonable amount to be paid to Donovan Leisure for legal services rendered to the Estate of Andy Warhol is $148,646.31 and an additional $5,537.18 for services rendered in connection with the [Schlaifer Nance] RICO action, and that it is reasonable to approve the prior payments to Donovan Leisure of $403,382.93 for legal services rendered to the Estate." In so doing, Melfe sought to absolve Hughes from any personal liability he might be held for as executor, since Hayes was still recognized as the attorney for the estate; in addition, he wanted to have Hughes's estate-issued payments approved.

Almost a month later, Beth Jacob answered Donovan Leisure's 2110 petition on behalf of the foundation. "We write to request that this petition be treated as a claim against the Estate and determined in the context of the executor's account, rather than handled as an independent proceeding," Jacob wrote, reminding Preminger that in a conference in her chambers on March 4 Preminger had decided to treat Hayes's 2110 petition as a claim against the estate. "Millions of dollars have been paid to other lawyers for other legal work done for the Estate," Jacob added. "The extent to which this work was required and to which neither Mr. Hayes's nor Donovan Leisure's work was redundant is another question which must be answered in all three proceedings."

That same day, in his own court papers, Hayes responded through his attorney to Donovan Leisure's 2110 petition not by attacking Donovan

Leisure or the estate but by accusing the foundation of, in essence, gross mismanagement. "The Andy Warhol Foundation for the Visual Arts has adamantly refused to engage in good faith to resolve Mr. Hayes' SCPA 2110 application or to conclude an informal accounting of the Estate," Hayes's attorney contended. "Indeed, the Foundation has rebuffed the efforts of this Court to assist in settling the outstanding disputes with Messrs. Hayes and Hughes and has rejected mediation as a potential means of reaching a settlement. By its intransigence, the Foundation has fostered and encouraged unnecessary and wasteful litigation, forcing the Executor to incur legal bills. . . . The Foundation itself has incurred legal fees in excess of one million dollars in opposing Mr. Hayes' SCPA 2110 application and quarrelling with Mr. Hughes. Thus, the Foundation's President, Archibald Gillies, was quoted in *Art & Auction*'s February 1993 issue as follows: 'The only money trouble we're having is Ed Hayes's lawsuit, which is costing us around $1 million.' " Moreover, Hayes's brief continued, to keep from paying high fees to Hughes and Hayes, the foundation has "denigrated [Warhol's] work . . . instead of promoting [him] as one of the great masters of the Twentieth Century."

By now, to much of the art world and to a portion of the New York legal community, the Warhol case had become a joke. So, on May 14, 1993, the day of the Donovan Leisure 2110 hearing, when the bailiff called out the name of the next case to be heard in Preminger's court—"Andy Warhol"—the spectators, mostly lawyers waiting for their cases to come up, moaned audibly. One even laughed. The attorneys representing the various parties got up and took their places at the long lawyers' table. Vast and spacious, Preminger's courtroom in surrogate's court is one of the most elegant in all of the courthouses in downtown Manhattan, with its wainscoted walls, ornate chandeliers, and two fireplaces. Preminger often sits on the bench surrounded by two or three legal assistants since the two New York County surrogates have support staffs larger than most other federal or municipal judges.

Today, the hearing looked to be brief: Preminger would listen to

Donovan Leisure's arguments as to why the firm should be paid the "reasonable amount of $148,646.31 and an additional $5,537.18 for legal services in the RICO case and to approve prior payments of $403,382.93." Those sums came to a total of $557,566.42 for services that the firm rendered only between May 2, 1991, and April 1, 1993. Tom Melfe, the lawyer for Donovan Leisure, stood at the lawyers' table and presented his case to Preminger. As attentive as ever, she listened to him argue that Donovan Leisure had been representing Hughes for some time, that the firm had done extensive work for the estate, and that he and his colleagues deserved to be paid by the estate. On the bench Preminger seemed completely unmoved by his argument. When he was finished, she offered her opinion immediately. "Your petition is denied," she said. Donovan Leisure's bills would be taken up with all of the other claims against the estate—such as Hayes's 2110 petition—at a later date.

The Donovan Leisure attorneys were horrified.

"But Your Honor, should we continue to work for Mr. Hughes?" Melfe asked.

"Do whatever you think is appropriate," Preminger said, and then moved on to her next case.

Within days, Hughes fired Donovan Leisure, or perhaps the firm was no longer willing to work for him without a guarantee that they would be paid. After this, Hughes hired the third law firm he had used since his falling out with Hayes: Winthrop, Stimson, Putnam & Roberts. There, his main lawyer would be Mark Rennie, a young, intelligent estate law expert who, like so many other attorneys in this case, took his degree from Columbia's law school.

A week earlier, on May 7, 1993, Attorney General Robert Abrams had amended the brief he filed with Judge Preminger the previous year. The clause that accused Hayes of fraud and overreaching was amplified to address the concerns that Preminger had so vehemently raised in her chambers. "The petitioner engaged in fraud and overreaching," Abrams wrote, "in inducing the Executor to enter into the Retainer Agreement by falsely representing to the Executor that an executor's commission is the customary fee in the State of New York for legal services rendered in the administration of a substantial estate." Actually, Hayes claimed he did not represent to Hughes that a percentage contract was customary—he simply suggested that this was one way to do it—but, even if he had, surrogates in New York have ruled that percentage contracts are appropriate. "As this Court has observed on any number of occasions in the past it is the law of the State of New York that a 'time clock' approach not be applied to fee matters," wrote the surrogate of Monroe County in a case involving Ruth Barry, a local resident who had died. David Samuels felt differently. "In general, other surrogate court judges have ruled against percentage contracts," he says. "The size of the estate is the only factor that you take into consideration. We don't agree on the size of the estate. We're just not convinced that the estate is this large. We represent the interests of charitable beneficiaries. We try to represent the public interests here. We regulate charity operations in the state of New York."

In fact, after Christie's had submitted all of its individual appraisals—for Warhol's photographs, paintings and collaborations, drawings, and prints—it appeared the appraisal for Warhol's entire body of art was going to be some $95 million, drastically lower than Hayes's minimum figure of $600 million. The one fact both sides agreed upon was this: Warhol's nonart assets—his real estate, collectibles, stocks, bonds, cash, films, and videos—were worth $119 million. The total value of the Warhol estate, then, according to Christie's and the foundation, was some $220 million; the attorney general also endorsed this figure. Hayes now put the total estate—the art plus the nonart assets—at some $700 million or more.

Since this dispute had begun back in 1991, Hughes had sided with Hayes on the issue of the estate's value even though the two men weren't speaking. After all, the larger the estate, the larger Hughes's executor's commission. Hughes had even gone along with Hayes and filed a draft accounting as recently as January 1993 that put the estate's worth at $650 million. But Hughes was worn down by the lengthy dispute. He was also getting sicker. It was fairly routine for him to have to be rushed to a hospital for immediate intensive medical care. Many of his friends felt it was only a matter of time before Fred would bow to the pressure and work out a settlement with Gillies and the foundation. He would not, however, do this for less than the right price. His position was clear: He deserved to be paid for all those years he had helped Andy build his empire.

As the airplane descended toward Venice, Italy, Mark Rennie, Hughes's personal attorney at Winthrop, Stimson, looked out on the magnificent city stretched out below. It had been a long trip over from New York, and he was anxious to get on with his business in Italy. He had an extremely tight schedule. In fact, he would have little time to do anything other than meet with his client, who was summering in Venice, discuss their immediate business, and then get on a return flight to New York. Hughes was to sign a settlement agreement Rennie had negotiated with the foundation. The time had finally come when Fred felt it was appropriate to settle. For a while now, Gillies must have been concerned that Hughes and Hayes would join forces to take on the foundation in what appeared to be an inevitable legal action. No doubt the fear of having to fight both men in court had persuaded Gillies to seek a settlement with Hughes. In doing so, Gillies would not only disarm Hughes but completely isolate Hayes as well. For several weeks, lawyers at Winthrop, Stimson and Carter Ledyard had met to work out an agreement acceptable to both parties. At last they had that document in hand. So, only a few days before Rennie headed for Venice, Fred did what he could have done since late 1989, the time he and Ed had had their falling out, but didn't: He had a letter sent to Ed relieving him of his duties as attorney for the estate.

When Rennie arrived in Venice, he went directly to the mansion of Giovanni Volpi, where Hughes was staying. Unexpectedly, Hughes had become so ill from his multiple sclerosis that he had to curtail drastically his vacation plans. Rennie found him weak and bedridden. In the dull heat of the Italian summer, Hughes lay motionless in his bed. This had been an especially bad flare-up, and as a result he was partially paralyzed. Pulling up a chair, Rennie sat down next to the bed and explained to Hughes that he had reached a settlement with the foundation. Rennie had sent over drafts of the agreement, but he now had the final document. In the agreement Hughes would be given a total of $5.2 million as his executor's commission; because he had already received $2 million in advances since 1987, he would be entitled to another $3.2 million. What's more, the foundation would agree that a group of Warhol paintings—Hughes was to provide the list to the foundation at a later date—would be found to belong to Hughes, not the foundation. In addition, the foundation agreed to pay the legal bills from Donovan Leisure. In return, Hughes was to stipulate that the Warhol estate was not worth $600 to $700 million, as Hayes was claiming, but the $220 million that Christie's was contending. Even though for years Hughes was in agreement with Hayes that the Warhol estate was worth closer to $700 million than $220 million, even though he had just filed a draft accounting saying the estate was worth $650 million, and even though by agreeing to the low figure Hughes would probably end up doing further damage to the Warhol art market, one that was already dangerously soft, Hughes didn't see that he had a choice. He was sick. He needed money. He was weary of the long fight. In the guest room in the mansion in Italy, Hughes took the document and, with his hand shaking, he signed it. More than some of Warhol's inner circle would say that this was the moment when Fred Hughes sold Andy Warhol out.

On the day after Hughes signed the agreement, a group of lawyers gathered in Preminger's chambers for a meeting she had scheduled to determine whether the estate should have a contested public accounting. At this conference, besides Steve Weiner and Susan Kohlmann from Winthrop, Stimson, were David Samuels; Beth Jacob and two other Carter Ledyard attorneys; and Hayes and Harvey, along with their lawyer, Robert Jossen. Before the meeting began, Weiner asked if he could provide the judge with information that would affect the very issue they were about to discuss.

"The estate and the foundation have reached a separate agreement," said Weiner, a balding middle-aged man who looked the part of an estate lawyer. "We have both agreed that the value of the estate is $220 million."

At the table, Samuels smiled proudly. From his point of view, he believed the attorney general's office had won a great victory in siding with the party that forced Hughes to accept a lower appraisal of Warhol's work. It was a major development to help prevent Ed Hayes from getting any more money—the one thing Samuels wanted more than anything else.

Preminger was unfazed. "Well, this is rather odd," she said. Then, after a long silence, she asked, "Can I meet with the parties separately?"

All parties agreed. It would be the last time Preminger spoke with the parties separately.

When the foundation and the estate met with her, they told her that Hughes had accepted a $5.2 million executor's fee with no art to be used to supplement his fee. "We're giving him no art," they explicitly told the judge. Later, as Hayes, Harvey, and Jossen met with Preminger, Hayes told the judge that he was certain that Hughes would be getting art as part of his payment in addition to the $5.2 million.

Preminger reconvened all of the parties.

"I can tell that we are not going to be able to settle this," she told the roomful of lawyers. "But we'll try one more time next week. If we can't, then there will be a trial. In the meantime, the foundation and the estate should supply both Mr. Hayes and me with copies of the settlement agreement."

The following day, as she read the agreement, Preminger discovered that along with the $5.2 million the foundation intended to pay Hughes—minus the $2 million in advances he had already received— the foundation "accepted Hughes's assertion that the property listed on a schedule which Hughes is delivering to the Foundation simultaneously with the execution of this Agreement, which is in the possession of the Foundation, is owned by Hughes individually and never properly constituted property of the Estate or the Foundation." There was to be a second list as well. "Within 30 days after the date of execution of this Agreement, Hughes shall provide the Foundation with an affidavit listing all works created by Andy Warhol (other than as set forth on the [previous] schedule) which Hughes owned individually as of the date of Warhol's death or owns as of the present time."

This is how Hughes would describe the agreement in a press release he issued at the time: "As executor of the Warhol estate I am claiming the full commission to which I am entitled by law based on the Christie's appraisal I alone commissioned over two years ago. The calculations of the value of the estate and of my commission are thus entirely my own. In addition, the foundation offered me an additional payment of $800,000 in recognition of my sales efforts and other significant contributions I made to the estate beyond my services as executor. I accepted their offer. The foundation is also returning to me at my insistence property of mine that had been improperly transferred to the foundation."

When Preminger studied the two lists accompanying Hughes's agreement, she realized that the foundation was recognizing Hughes's ownership of hundreds of Warhol paintings. Hayes, in a separate lawsuit against Hughes, filed a motion to prevent the foundation from making the payments due Hughes as part of the settlement agreement. Preminger scheduled a hearing on the matter of the Hughes agreement for November 3, 1993, just two weeks before the start of the trial that would determine the merits of Hayes's 2110 petition. She had ordered that the trial would be in two parts: First, she would decide the authentic value of the Warhol estate; if the value was indeed more than $220 million, she would resolve the issue of the worth of Hayes's legal advice in the trial's second part. At the November 3 hearing, Preminger heard Hughes's lawyers argue that Hughes needed the money he was to receive from the foundation for medical expenses. Jossen argued that since the trial was imminent Preminger should wait until its conclusion to authorize payment to Hughes. Preminger agreed. In her written opinion she stated: "The Executor is restrained from paying himself commissions pursuant to the settlement agreement until the determination of the issue of the valuation hearing." In effect, Preminger had frozen the assets—the cash and the art—Hughes was supposed to receive as a result of his signing the agreement at least until the first part of the trial was over.

During 1993, the ongoing dispute between the foundation and Peter Brant over *Interview* came closer to being resolved because of a decision made by a federal judge. When Hughes and Hayes sold the magazine to Brant in 1989 for $12 million, Brant had paid $5 million in cash and taken a loan from the estate for the rest. He had paid the loan for a year; then in the summer of 1990 he stopped. Brant charged that Hughes had defrauded him by not turning over audio tapes of interviews Warhol had conducted for the magazine as he had promised and later denying that they were part of the deal, and by lying about the number of paid subscribers to *Interview*. Brant called Hayes, listed his complaints, and suggested that the estate reduce his note from $7 million (approximately what he still owed) to $4 million; in return, Brant would put up some land as security. Hayes was inclined to take the deal—he had heard rumors that Brant was in financial trouble—but because the foundation now shared assets with the estate, it was involved in the decision-making process; in short, Hayes did not have the authority to accept Brant's offer without clearing it first with Gillies. When Hayes approached Peter Gates, at Gillies's insistence, Gates resisted. It seemed that the security Brant wanted to put up was not unencumbered.

Enter more lawyers. For roughly the next eighteen months, the foundation's lawyers—Gates and his colleagues—met with Brant's lawyers, accomplishing nothing. Finally, in early 1992, the foundation decided to sue Brant. With Gates overseeing, Carter Ledyard lined up another firm, Coblence & Warner, to handle the litigation. Not long after Coblence & Warner filed the suit, a series of mistakes dating back three years came to light. When Hayes had executed the original contract for the sale on July 26, 1989, he listed as a party to the contract Andy Warhol Enterprises—the company that actually owned *Interview*. One day earlier, however, on July 25, papers had been filed dissolving Andy Warhol Enterprises. As soon as the mistake surfaced in the course of the

Brant litigation, Hayes dismissed it as a mere "scrivener's error"—blaming it on a secretary's typographical goof—but its consequences snowballed. In fact, Hayes was lucky. While the dissolution papers were filed on July 25, 1989, the certificate of dissolution was not registered with the New York Department of State until August 6, 1990—the day, according to New York State law, that the company would have been considered officially dissolved.

In their complaint, the Coblence & Warner lawyers failed to include as a plaintiff Andy Warhol Enterprises, even though it was a party to the contract. Brant's lawyers moved to have the case thrown out because the proper party wasn't named. Furthermore, they argued, the sale of *Interview* by a defunct corporation was not a legitimate transaction, and therefore Brant owed the estate and the foundation no more money. The judge hearing the case, Kenneth Conboy, dismissed it in mid-1992, instructing the foundation's lawyers to file their suit properly next time.

At this point Winthrop, Stimson, which had started doing some work for Hughes, took over the case. On April 6, 1993, the amended complaint was filed in Conboy's court, this time with Andy Warhol Enterprises listed as a petitioner and documentation attached showing that the company had legally been in business until August 1990. Brant's lawyers moved again to dismiss the amended complaint.

About a month later, when Gates and Gillies were interviewed for a BBC documentary about the Warhol foundation, they attacked Hayes for the legal work he had provided the estate and the foundation. Specifically with regard to the *Interview* sale, Gillies said that Hayes had given them "abysmal legal work" and held him accountable for the original "scrivener's error." In fact, the foundation had already filed a separate legal malpractice suit against Hayes over this very issue.

Finally, in December 1993, Judge Conboy dismissed Brant's motions to block the foundation's lawsuit, clearing the way for the foundation to attempt to collect the $7 million. In the time since the lawsuit had commenced, the foundation had received no money from Brant, whose financial situation had gotten considerably worse. Furthermore, it had spent hundreds of thousands of dollars—maybe close to a million—in legal bills to three different law firms. Gillies had authorized the payment of fees to Coblence & Warner, then to Winthrop, Stimson; throughout the time these two firms were working on the case he was also authorizing payments to Carter Ledyard.

Back in 1989, when Peter Gates drew up the contract for his friend Arch Gillies and the Warhol foundation, he never could have imagined the millions his law firm would make off Gillies and the foundation over the next four years. But the biggest payoff was yet to come. The prospect of a trial in surrogate's court was not unpleasant for Gates, whose firm during the preparation for the trial and the trial itself would bill the Warhol foundation a rumored $300,000 a month.

During his lifetime, Andy Warhol hated lawyers.

This is why.

The year 1993 ended on an odd note. In November, it was widely reported in the press that forty-five Warhol drawings, all done in the 1950s, that were to have been included in the retrospective at the Museum of Modern Art in 1989 had never been returned to the estate or the foundation. In late 1988 they had been shipped, along with all the other artwork for the show, to the museum, where they were put into storage. Ultimately the museum decided not to include them in the show. But in May 1989, when MoMA workers were shipping art back to the estate, the forty-five drawings were discovered missing. "It's sort of a mystery," a MoMA insider told a journalist in November 1993. "They were there and then they weren't. It's an embarrassment to the Modern. They'd rather not have it ballyhooed." No one at the museum, the estate, or the foundation ever reported to the police that the drawings were missing. Certainly Agnes Gund was pleased the missing drawings were never reported, a move that spared MoMA humiliation in the wake of the success of the retrospective. Then again, through the years Gund had realized indirect benefits from her position on the Warhol board. One of her pet projects, Studios in the School, as well as MoMA, received grants totaling several hundred thousand dollars. Daniel

Shapiro, the lawyer married to Gund, counts Christie's among his clients. Finally, Gund bought from the foundation something called *The Lips Book*, a sizeable collection of Warhol drawings of lips. Gund paid $60,000 for the book, though people familiar with the drawings would contend the book was worth perhaps as much as five times that amount.

Instead of reporting the lost drawings to the police, the foundation merely filed a claim to collect insurance on them, one that took some time for the insurance company to act on. "Enclosed please find the executed 'Receipt and Release' form regarding 45 Andy Warhol drawings lost while on loan to the Museum of Modern Art," Jane Rubin, administrator of collections at the foundation, wrote on July 29, 1993, to Graham Miller International, the adjuster that handled claims for the company that insured MoMA. "Thank you for processing these papers so that we can receive payment in final resolution of this long-standing claim."

The "Receipt and Release" form, which Gillies had signed, said that in exchange for a sum of $1,091,000 "the Foundation hereby releases MoMA and Underwriters from any and all liability to the Foundation respecting the 45 drawings . . . which are owned by the Foundation and were lost while the same were on loan to the MoMA, and the Foundation hereby releases and transfers to Underwriters all its right, title and interest in the Drawings, except for the following three Drawings"—the foundation listed the drawings—"which continue to be the property of the Foundation and which, if found by MoMA or otherwise coming into its possession or control, will promptly be returned to the Foundation without charge to the Foundation."

For years now, the foundation, the estate, and Hayes had been arguing about the value of Warhol's art. This insurance claim, then, should have indicated the value that the foundation believed these drawings were worth. According to the foundation's total claim of $1,091,000 for forty-three drawings, each drawing was worth $25,372. In the Christie's appraisal, Baer had valued the same drawings at eight hundred dollars apiece.

10

AFTER YEARS OF FIGHTING AMONG THE ESTATE, THE FOUNDATION, AND Hayes, after countless delays engineered mostly by the foundation through Carter Ledyard, Preminger finally fixed a start date—November 17, 1993—for the two-part trial. It had been well over six and a half years since Warhol had died, and, despite all of the legal and financial maneuvers that had taken place during that time, maneuvers that had run up millions of dollars in fees of various sorts, the Estate of Andy Warhol was still not settled. Now, for all practical purposes, only one key outstanding issue remained—Hayes's 2110 petition—to interfere with a settlement.

About a week before the trial was set to begin, Beth Jacob filed a motion with the court asking that the public be barred from reading any of the affidavits or hearing any of the testimony pertaining to the appraisals or prices of Warhol artwork. "The Foundation has moved this Court for sealing and protective orders to maintain the confidentiality of evidence and information regarding the identity, number and unit values of the Artworks," Jacob wrote, referring to a previous order she had submitted in May. "The issue of confidentiality concerns not only the sealing of the records but the protection of confidential information during the hearing." Jacob would contend that the number and value of the foundation's Warhol artwork was equivalent to a corporation's "trade secret." If this information was not kept private, she said, the business of the foundation could be severely damaged. Whether or not this was true, the following can't be debated: Arch Gillies, the former president of the World Policy Institute and the president of a public corporation, a man who had openly endorsed the fundamental right of free speech in the past, had instructed his attorney to file court papers to deny the public access to large portions of the upcoming trial.

Almost immediately, Hayes made his official plea that the trial be kept open to the public. Pointing out that all legal proceedings for the estates of both Mark Rothko and Robert Mapplethorpe had been open, Hayes stated that he had his own theories about why the foundation would not want a public trial. "The only true answer," Hayes wrote, "is that it would hurt the Foundation management . . . to be exposed as having accepted low-end appraisal valuations (which *reduce* the amount that the Foundation is obligated to distribute to the public). In short, this desperate attempt to bar the public . . . is designed to save Foundation management from public accountability (and personal embarrassment)." To underscore his belief that a public trial would not affect the value of the art, Hayes closed his papers by saying that "nothing would make me happier than an award that included art."

When I learned about the foundation's request to close the trial, I contacted Leon Friedman, general counsel to PEN American Center and a member of PEN's Freedom-to-Write committee, on which I also serve, and explained to him what the foundation was trying to do. Friedman said he would take immediate action—and he did. First he conveyed the particulars of the situation to George Freeman, a senior attorney at *The New York Times,* who agreed to write a brief in support of a public trial and to appear at a November 16 pretrial hearing Preminger had scheduled to consider the issue. Next Friedman contacted lawyers at Random House, my publisher, who also agreed to appear in court.

November 16 was unseasonably warm in New York City—warm enough, in fact, that a topcoat was not necessary. Tom Wolfe walked into surrogate's court at eleven-thirty that morning wearing a black-and-white checked cotton suit accented with a high-collared button-down white shirt, a thin-cut lime green tie, black loafers, and a black fedora. He milled about with the small crowd until the court clerk opened the door leading to the judge's chambers and announced, "All rise. The Surrogate of the County of Manhattan, the Honorable Eve Preminger." The attorneys, clients, and spectators stood and faced the bench as the judge—strong and commanding—walked from her chambers down a short railed-off passageway and up the three steps to her bench. "You may be seated," the clerk said, and those in the room took their seats.

Wolfe sat in the back row, scribbling notes. For several years, an essential ingredient in the myth of Ed Hayes had been his friendship with Tom Wolfe. In his own way Wolfe had relished the role he had played in the myth. Now, on this pivotal day in Hayes's career, Wolfe was there for his friend. Actually, even their outfits were complementary. Wearing a chalk-striped gray suit, a red tie, and a brown fedora, Hayes looked not so much the "gangster lawyer" as the gangster.

After some brief opening remarks, Judge Preminger directed David Samuels, the assistant attorney general, to state his position on closing portions of the trial. Shifting from one foot to the other, Samuels stood at the lawyers' table and launched into a criticism of Ed Hayes; the only point he sought to make was that Hayes had been paid too much money. When Preminger interrupted him to ask if he had an opinion on whether the trial should be open to the public, Samuels said he would leave it to the discretion of the court. Preminger seemed amazed. Was Samuels telling her that the attorney general didn't have a position on this vital issue? Samuels had to admit that, even though the attorney general always had sided with the foundation, he could not bring himself to support them on this issue, which was clearly a violation of the public's right to know. As a result he was simply not going to take a position. Preminger was incredulous. As Samuels started in on yet another attack on Hayes, Preminger told him to sit down.

Then Preminger turned to Jacob, who argued that a "limited" portion of the testimony—the part that contained any reference to the value or number of Warhol artwork—should be off limits in order to protect the foundation's "trade secrets." Preminger interrupted her. Exactly how would Jacob propose to accomplish this? The courtroom should be cleared each and every time numbers were going to be discussed, was Jacob's suggestion. That's all Preminger needed to hear. She moved on to Hayes's side.

Robert Jossen stood. There were no good reasons to close this trial, said Jossen, a stout, articulate man. Little would be revealed that art world insiders didn't already know, since through the years numerous lawyers and appraisers had combed through the Warhol estate. Anyone in the art world who wanted to know which works were held by the estate already did.

Next Preminger recognized Leon Friedman, who spoke on my behalf. Standing at the lawyers' table, Friedman argued that there was no "compelling" reason to close the case, a requirement for a trial to be closed. "It's relevant information," Friedman said, gesturing with both hands, "and we the public have a right to see what's going on." Friedman turned the floor over to George Freeman from the *Times*. "It's remarkable that the foundation would seek to keep from the public, not from competition, the number of different types of Warhol artwork," said Freeman, a bookish man in his late thirties who argued with sureness and authority. "It's a question of supply and demand, and buyers should not be deprived of these facts." In conclusion, Freeman added that in the fifteen years he had been representing *The New York Times* he had never seen a request like the one being put forth by the Warhol foundation.

Preminger was about to call a recess when she stopped to ask Jacob if she intended to appeal her decision. "Yes," Jacob said. When Preminger asked Jossen if he planned to appeal, Hayes answered for him. "No, Your Honor, we don't." Preminger called a ten-minute recess.

When she returned to the bench, the judge read her decision. "Balancing the competing considerations herein, most particularly the substantial public interest in these proceedings and the almost insuperable problem of conducting a fair and orderly trial with relevant portions of the testimony constantly interrupted for immediate *in camera* hearing or subsequent *in camera* disposition, the Court denies the Foundation's motion to close the trial. The Court grants the Foundation's request, at least temporarily, to seal the inventory exhibits attached to the affidavits unless and until the matters in said exhibits are demonstrated by trial testimony to be relevant."

The trial would be open. Only the Christie's appraisal would be sealed, though witnesses could be questioned about its contents. Preminger stood and left the bench. In the red leather chair in which he sat near the far end of the lawyers' table, Hayes leaned back and smiled.

That afternoon, the foundation's lawyers appealed Preminger's decision to the appellate division of the state supreme court. In the chambers of Judge Israel Rubin, Robert Malaby of Carter Ledyard and Robert Jossen argued whether the trial should be postponed to allow the foundation time to make a full appeal. Since the foundation wanted only "partial closure of the court during certain narrowly specified testimony," Malaby believed that Preminger had "erred" in ruling to open the trial to the public. Jossen argued that legal proceedings involving both the Rothko and Mapplethorpe estates were open to the public. The elderly judge stopped the discussion. "Well," he said in a quiet, even voice, "we usually keep these things open." The request for a postponement was denied. The beginning of the trial would take place the next day as scheduled.

On the morning of the seventeenth, not long before the trial was set to start at ten o'clock, Beth Jacob called in sick. Through her clerk, Preminger let Carter Ledyard know that the trial would begin at two-thirty on the afternoon of the eighteenth, with or without Jacob.

By the start of the trial, both sides had made their positions clear, partially because the trial's direct testimony had been submitted to Preminger in the form of affidavits. Ed Hayes now believed that Warhol's art was worth as much as $708 million, based on the evaluations provided by his experts. Furthermore, because he felt Warhol's art would increase in value over time and because the business plan of the foundation did not call for anything approaching a mass sale of Warhol's art, Hayes argued that no discount should be applied to the appraised value.

In the trial, Hayes would be opposed by the foundation, the estate, and the attorney general. All three parties supported the appraisal conducted by Christie's, which set the value of Warhol's art at $95 million, a figure Christie's arrived at by applying substantial blockage discounts. Christie's felt it was justified in applying these large discounts because a mass sale of Warhol art would seriously depress the market. The foundation would argue that holding the art for the years it took to sell it would put the foundation's collection at a similar risk. Why were Gillies, Hughes, and the foundation's board prepared to argue that Warhol's work—the chief asset of their endowment—was a risky investment? Why was it not in their interest to see the highest value possible assigned to the estate?

One reason was obvious: They did not believe Ed Hayes should be paid any more money under any conditions. They contended that Hayes had not properly served the estate as its attorney. "Mr. Hayes was uninterested in the artistic aspect of Warhol's estate, resented and sometimes even fell asleep at meetings and dinners involving art, had no appreciation of Warhol's art and no knowledge of other contemporary artists," attorneys from Carter Ledyard would later write. "In fact, people who worked with Mr. Hughes have said that Mr. Hughes's falling out with Mr. Hayes was at least in part over Mr. Hayes's ignorance of, lack of sensitivity to, and total lack of interest in Warhol's art other than as a source of money." The foundation contended that Hayes had little involvement with the Sotheby's sale, the MoMA retrospective, and the Warhol museum. In addition, the foundation found cause to cite Hayes for legal malpractice in his handling of the Schlaifer Nance licensing agreement and the sale of *Interview* to Peter Brant. "The Estate has been forced to expend substantial legal fees in trying to enforce the promissory note [with Brant] in federal court. . . . The Schlaifer Nance mistake is clearly a legal mistake—Mr. Hayes, as lawyer for the Executor and the Estate, permitted Mr. Hughes to enter into a contract which was heavily skewed in favor of the other party, had few protections for the Estate, and contained misrepresentations on behalf of the Estate."

But perhaps there was another motivation to suppress the value of the estate, one stronger than the desire to keep Ed Hayes from getting any more money. By 1993, the foundation was losing money. Beyond the obligation to award 5 percent of its assets, the foundation was spending a lot more than it was earning—between the years of 1990 and 1993, their overhead had tripled, they had incurred legal bills in the millions, and since the sale of *Interview* very little cash had been generated. The foundation, through mismanagement and gross expenditures (many incurred in the course of preparing for this trial), was running down its assets. Shortly after he became president, Gillies rejected the business plan Hughes and Hayes had devised that would have built up a cash reserve whose interest alone would have met the annual 5 percent requirement. Instead, he began to spend the modest cash reserve they'd begun to build up. Starting out with $26 million in 1990, by mid-1993 Gillies had allowed the foundation's cash position to drop below $10 million. As a result, in 1993, after giving away nearly $4 million in 1990, $6 million in 1991, and $4 million in 1992, they were only issuing a little over $1 million in grants. If a value of $700 million were to be placed on the estate, the board would have to give away $35 million each year, a herculean task and one that could bankrupt the foundation. Perhaps the only chance to keep it alive was to plead poverty.

To accommodate the claims of the various parties, Preminger had decided to divide the trial into two parts. In the first part, she would hear testimony about the value of the estate; at the end of that part, she would issue her opinion on the estate's value, fixing an exact amount. In the trial's second half, she would determine the worth of Hayes's legal services. In a sense, the integrity of the Warhol foundation would also be on trial—not just Ed Hayes's worth as an attorney. Most important, though, Preminger would settle the squabble over the value of Warhol's estate and in the process go so far as to help determine the ultimate value of Warhol as an artist.

Every seat in the courtroom was taken as Ed Hayes delivered his own opening statement. "This is not a trial," he said, standing at the lawyers' table, "this is an appraisal"—an appraisal of the importance of Warhol's work. Hayes assumed the role of critic, making a case for the enduring quality of Warhol's art. Since Campbell's soup was the sort of food poor immigrant mothers fed their children when they came home from school, he said, "maybe the Campbell's soup can represented his mother's love." Likewise, as for those shoes Warhol drew in the fifties, "maybe they represented the shoes of his mother." From examples such as these, Hayes drew the conclusion that "the thought behind Warhol's art is timeless." The Queens accent was controlled; his tone was forceful, precise, and uncharacteristically genteel. Hayes asserted that he had formed one overriding opinion during the past six and a half years: that Andy Warhol was a masterful artist whose work was of the highest caliber of the twentieth century. "History will show," Hayes said in conclusion, "that there are not *enough* Warhols."

Samuels spoke next. In what was becoming a familiar routine, Samuels attacked Hayes in language that bordered on character assassination. Finally Preminger stopped him. "Mr. Samuels," she said, "what is the attorney general going to prove in this case?" In a brief but rambling response, Samuels stated that even though "the attorney general does not purport to be an expert on art" he believed that in this case the use of blockage discount was appropriate, "given the amount of [Warhol] artwork." Again, Preminger interrupted. "Is it your position that the attorney general wants to accept the Christie's appraisal?" Yes, was his reply.

In a voice that was nearly inaudible, Beth Jacob began her opening remarks. She made four points: one, this case was "not about the value of Warhol art"; two, because Christie's was famous the auction house's appraisal should be accepted without question; three, blockage discount was "required by the principle of economics"; and four, there was just one person who would "win or lose" in this case—Ed Hayes.

The first witness Hayes called to the stand was Jeffrey Hoffeld. An art expert, a former gallery owner, and now an art appraiser for the Internal Revenue Service, among other clients, Hoffeld had spent months studying the Warhol estate, item by item. For his work since 1991, Hayes had paid him over $100,000 in fees, only a portion of the nearly $700,000 Hayes would end up spending on the litigation resulting from his 2110 petition—a stultifying sum for which he went through all of his available cash and most of his savings and retirement accounts.

For the 4,118 paintings, pieces of sculpture, and collaborations, Hoffeld came up with two totals, which he called "high" and "low." His high was $391,200,000; his low, $295,900,000. These numbers compared drastically with Christie's undiscounted total of $194,818,600 and discounted total of $77,927,440. The total Hoffeld placed on Warhol's 5,103 drawings was just as dramatically different. Hoffeld believed the drawings, ranging from the fifties (the drawings that were lost by the Museum of Modern Art, for example) through the eighties, were worth $91,285,000, compared with Christie's undiscounted value of $15,333,845 and discounted value of $4,943,288. The drawings were a significant area of disagreement between the two appraisals.

Hoffeld cited examples of paintings and silkscreens that he believed were grossly undervalued by Christie's. On February 7, 1991, only a week after the Christie's valuation date, the foundation sold a painting called *Tiger* to a dealer for $200,000; Christie's had appraised the same painting at half the price. The foundation had sold *Double Hamburger* for $400,000; Christie's had appraised it at $150,000. Similarly, there were *Frog*, which sold for $150,000 compared with an appraised Christie's price of $100,000; *Rhino*, which sold for $175,000 compared with an appraised price of $100,000; and *Beatle Boots*, which sold for $150,000 compared with its appraisal at $60,000.

If the variances between the appraisal prices and the recent market prices were so glaring, why wasn't the attorney general's office investigating the discrepancies? Apparently this did not concern David Samuels. When he cross-examined Hoffeld, Samuels asked him one question after another about the difference between conducting an appraisal for a taxpaying client and a nontaxpaying client. Some of Samuels's questions were so vague that even Preminger didn't understand them. Finally he sat down.

Jacob took her place at the podium, her voice now weaker than it had been during her opening argument. She posed question after question, but Hoffeld held his own on the stand. More than once Preminger told Jacob to abandon a line of questioning. "Go on to something else or we'll never get done," she said at one point. At last, Hoffeld grew angry, for the design behind Jacob's questioning became clear: She was determined to prove—and attempted to have Hoffeld corroborate on the witness stand—that Warhol's art was a fad, that it was declining in value *at this very moment*, and that as a result it was a bad investment. There was an unseemly quality to what Jacob was doing. Here was an attorney representing the organization that bore Warhol's name, not to mention paying her bills, and yet it seemed her objective was to destroy Warhol's reputation as an artist. After a long stretch of cross-examination by Jacob, Preminger recessed the court for the day. The spectators filed out of the courtroom, not exactly sure what they had seen.

The following day, a Friday, Dale Stulz, a photography expert hired by Ed Hayes, was allowed to take the stand before Jacob had finished with Hoffeld because Stulz needed to return home to Los Angeles for the weekend. Under cross-examination by Samuels, Stulz testified as to what he felt the foundation could get if at one time it sold off its entire collection of Warhol photographs, all 66,000 of them: $80 million. Then Robert Malaby of Carter Ledyard took over. More polished and poised than Jacob, Malaby tried to discredit Stulz's evaluation of Warhol's photographs, noting that the Christie's appraisal of the photographs came in at a mere $107,000. At the height of Malaby's attack, he asked Stulz at how much he had valued the 19,879 black-and-white photographs taken by Warhol.

Eleven million dollars, Stulz replied.

So would Stulz advise Hayes to accept the photographs as a settlement? Malaby asked.

"I would tell him to consider it," Stulz said.

"You mean to tell me—" Malaby started.

Jossen stood up. "Objection, Your Honor."

"Sustained."

"—that you would have Mr. Hayes take these photographs *instead of getting paid*," Malaby asked sarcastically.

"Sustained!" Preminger said sternly. "Perhaps you didn't hear me."

Malaby was done, though. His question about taking the photographs as payment may have been cynical, but it also introduced into the trial itself the solution that had been used in the Rothko case: Perhaps the dispute could be settled by paying Hayes off in art.

On redirect examination, Jossen asked Stulz, who had founded the photography department at Christie's in 1978, about the Christie's appraisal. Because Christie's considered Warhol to be a painter, Stulz testified, the company did not regard him as a photographer. The fact that he had published countless photographs in *Interview* and two photography books of his own somehow seemed beside the point to the auction house. Because of this, Christie's originally valued many of the photographs at one dollar each and many of the Polaroids at a nickel each. Interestingly, fifty-five of the one-dollar photographs had been consigned by the foundation to the Pace/MacGill Gallery, where a sales price of $7,500 had been put on each print. Finally, in its actual appraisal, Christie's decided to reconsider the photographs; Baer fixed values on them ranging from $200 to $2,000 each. "I believe I have taken a conservative approach," Stulz said of his own $80 million estimate.

Jeffrey Hoffeld was back on the stand to conclude his cross-examination by Jacob, who once again led him through a mind-numbing litany of questions that seemed to have little to do with placing a value on the Warhol estate. Finally Preminger got fed up. "I'm going to preclude the questioning," she said, effectively telling Jacob to sit down. "I have no further questions, Your Honor," said Jacob, a rail-thin, high-strung woman, as she gathered up her papers, although judging from the stack of typed-out questions she had on the podium in front of her she had plenty to go.

Then Jossen asked Hoffeld to select the one estate with which

Warhol's could be compared. There was only one: Picasso's. "Warhol may well outdo Picasso in his number of subjects," Hoffeld said.

At the end of the Friday session, Preminger called all of the attorneys to her bench for a private sidebar. She suggested that perhaps the foundation and the attorney general should start thinking about ways they could save face in the proceedings; she then dismissed the court until the following Tuesday afternoon when Gillies was scheduled to testify. On Monday morning, however, Preminger's office contacted the four sides—the estate, the foundation, the attorney general, and Hayes—and asked to see them at once. Hayes requested that Agnes Gund attend the meeting, but Jacob said the foundation would bring whomever they pleased.

When the Carter Ledyard team of lawyers arrived at the judge's chambers that afternoon at three-thirty, they had with them, instead of Gund, Arch Gillies and Brendan Gill. Right off, Preminger asked if she could meet alone with Hayes and his attorneys. Jacob objected to the judge meeting with any one party alone. As a result Preminger called the whole lot into her office. Preminger raised the possibility of paying Hayes off in art, citing the proposal Malaby had presented to Stulz. Would the foundation be willing to give Hayes the black-and-white photographs in order to end the litigation? The foundation was categorically opposed to giving *any* art to Hayes as a settlement. Gill, who during the trial often spent time making architectural sketches of the courtroom in a large notebook as he sat in the gallery (when he wasn't dozing off), spoke vehemently about how it would not be appropriate to pay Hayes off in art. The foundation needed the art for revenue, so it could continue to support charitable causes. But wasn't the foundation having to sell its art to cover the enormous legal bills incurred in fighting Hayes's 2110 petition? The foundation attorneys didn't have an answer for that one.

The meeting ended. The trial would go on. The billing hours would resume.

. . .

Calm, confident, controlled, Arch Gillies looked the part of a foundation president, with his handsome blue suit, accented tie, and starched white shirt. As he sat on the witness stand and began to answer questions posed to him by Jossen, it seemed as though he had been well rehearsed for his appearance. Jossen, compact and expensively dressed, volleyed questions at Gillies, who answered each with as short an answer as possible. The questions were not ones Gillies could have felt comfortable answering, but he never tried to offer an amplification of his answers.

"Your current salary, sir, is $189,000 a year?" Jossen asked.

"Yes."

"And in addition to that, you receive a twenty percent pension participation, correct?"

"Yes."

"[At the World Policy Institute] you earned approximately $75,000 a year?"

"Yes."

"So you doubled your salary when you moved from the World Policy Institute to become president of the Andy Warhol Foundation?"

"Yes."

Did he have any particular training in art or art history? No. Was he an expert in art in any way? No. When he suggested to Hughes that the foundation needed a president, was he the only candidate he had in mind? Yes. In December 1990, was he elected to the board of directors to fill a vacancy created by Fremont's resignation? Yes. Had Fremont resigned to become the exclusive agent for Warhol art because Gillies said Fremont could not remain on the board and continue to sell Warhol art? No, Gillies answered emphatically, but the implication of Jossen's question was clear.

"Now, just before your election to the board," Jossen said, "you had a falling out with Mr. Hughes. Isn't that correct?"

"Yes."

"That was around November of 1990 that you had a falling out with Mr. Hughes."

"He had a falling out with me," Gillies answered.

How long did their relationship remain strained? Through 1991, 1992, 1993, Gillies said. As part of the settlement agreement between the estate and the foundation, reached in the summer of 1993, did the foundation relinquish all claims against Hughes? "I don't know," Gillies replied. Back in 1991, did Gillies attempt to force Hughes to sign a protocol that would have limited Hughes's ability to criticize Gillies? Yes, he had, Gillies said, because Hughes was degrading Gillies "not only to the press but to anyone within his earshot." Did Hughes sign the protocol? "No," Gillies said, "he did not."

"Isn't it true, Mr. Gillies," Jossen asked, "that before you became president of the Andy Warhol Foundation, you had never had any experience in running a foundation where there were assets that had to be managed?"

"Yes," Gillies replied—an answer that resonated through many of the events that had happened over the past three or four years.

Jossen moved on to the sale of Warhol art. Did the foundation consider selling off all of its collection in 1991, the reason Christie's could justify applying a blockage discount to its appraisal? "No," Gillies admitted. Had the foundation ever sought one single buyer? No. Had the foundation ever entertained a proposal from one single buyer? No.

Pointing specifically to the foundation's 1991 tax forms, Jossen noted that Christie's had applied to the appraised total of the entire Warhol collection—$160,712,260—a blockage discount of $97,586,961, meaning that the foundation was obliged to give away 5 percent of $63 million, instead of 5 percent of $160 million—a difference in charitable donations of roughly $5 million a year. Jossen asked Gillies to turn to a page of the 1991 tax return, a document that he had signed as the president of the foundation.

"All right. There is an amount under line IE of $97,586,961; right?"
"Yes."
"That's a blockage amount; right?"
"I can't answer that. Sorry."
"Doesn't that amount—the $97 million—get deducted for blockage?"

"You are leading me through a calculation that I have not done before and I am not an expert about, and I can't help you. I'm sorry."

When Jossen quoted the totals for the artwork and for blockage, Gillies apologized for not being able to help him "with specific figures."

Finally Preminger interrupted and asked Gillies if he could explain the general concept of applying a blockage discount. Gillies complied. Does the application of blockage discount allow the foundation to donate a smaller sum of money every year? Preminger asked. "Yes," Gillies answered.

On October 4, 1990, Jossen reminded him, a meeting took place between representatives from Carter Ledyard and Christie's. A separate meeting was held between Christie's and Hayes, who was still the lawyer for the estate, a few days later. "Had Mr. Hayes been invited to attend that meeting?" Jossen asked.

"I don't know," Gillies said.

"Had Mr. Hughes been invited to attend that meeting?"

"I don't know," Gillies said.

"Had anyone on behalf of the estate been invited to attend that meeting?"

"I don't know."

"Did you ever ask?" Jossen queried.

"No," Gillies said.

The implication was not subtle: Christie's was having separate—secret—meetings with the foundation because they intended to satisfy the foundation, not the estate. Gillies's answers did little to contradict the unstated contention. The trial was in danger of doing untold damage to the auction house, not just the foundation.

Next Jossen mentioned the January 1991 luncheon between Gillies and Stephen Lash. "You invited Mr. Lash to lunch?" Jossen asked.

"I did."

"You suggested the lunch?"

"Yes, I did."

"And was there anyone at this luncheon from the estate?"

"No."

Jossen then asked Gillies if during the lunch he and Lash discussed the idea that the fee income Christie's would get from appraising the foundation's art would be like an "annuity."

"It doesn't sound like me, but we undoubtedly talked about the fact that there would need to be annual appraisals of the work," Gillies said.

Jossen handed Gillies an internal Christie's memo that summarized Lash's lunch with Gillies. "It appears Mr. Lash put the word 'annuity' in quotes to attribute to you," Jossen said.

"Yes."

Jossen then asked Gillies if he and Lash also discussed the Mapplethorpe estate.

"I see from Mr. Lash's memorandum that I did talk about it," Gillies replied. "Yeah, I'm sure I did."

Did Gillies tell Lash at their lunch that he wanted a blockage discount applied to the Warhol appraisal?

"I don't recall," Gillies said.

Soon after this, Jossen indicated that he had reached a cutoff point for the day. He wanted to resume questioning following Thanksgiving recess; the judge granted the request and recessed the trial. On his first day on the stand, Gillies had created a curious impression. Even though as president he was responsible for running the foundation, Gillies seemed to be an unengaged, ineffective, almost disinterested administrator. In creating his wealth, Warhol had been intimately involved in the business dealings in all areas of his empire. In running the foundation endowed by Warhol's lifetime earnings, Gillies seemed content to give the impression that he was as removed from its day-to-day operations as Warhol had been involved.

The trial resumed on the Wednesday after Thanksgiving. When Gillies was back on the stand, Jossen took his position at the podium, asking him if he had ever told Lash that he wanted to sit with Christie's and talk about the specific unit values of the Warhol artworks they were appraising.

"No," Gillies said.

"Did you ever tell Mr. Lash that you wanted to sit with representatives of Christie's to discuss blockage discount?"

"No," Gillies said.

"Are you sure?" Jossen asked, but Gillies couldn't answer before Jossen posed the next question. "In May of 1991, did you have a conversation with Mr. Lash in which you told him that you wanted to sit with Christie's to discuss specific unit values for the pieces of art?"

Suddenly Gillies changed his approach. "I don't recall." His reply sounded nervous.

"In May of 1991, did you have a conversation with Mr. Lash in which you told him you wanted to sit with Christie's and discuss blockage discount?"

Gillies realized there was no way out. "In the spring of 1991," he said, "I requested that Christie's, the estate, the foundation, all sit together for the purpose of having any interested party that had standing to say whatever they wanted to say about the draft appraisal."

Did Gillies tell Lash that the attorney general wanted to discuss unit values? "Yes, in the context of my previous answer."

And to discuss blockage discount? "Yes, in the context of my previous answer."

Jossen moved on to a letter written by Martha Baer to the attorney general. In the letter Baer made the claim that from the time the appraisal was completed in 1991 until January 1993, the month she was writing the letter, the value of the art she was appraising had actually declined by 20 percent. Did Gillies agree with Christie's reassessment of its appraisal?

"I don't either agree or disagree," Gillies said. "I accept the appraisal."

"You have no opinion?" Jossen asked.

"That is correct."

"Did you know the basis of Christie's new opinion?"

"No," Gillies said.

"Did you discuss it with the board?"

"No."

"With anyone on your staff?"

"No."

"Did you ever discuss it with Mr. Hughes?"

"No."

"With Mr. Hayes?"

"No."

"Was this something you were concerned about?"

"No."

"Was this something you gave *any thought to at all?*"

Both Samuels and Jacob leapt to their feet to object.

Coolly Preminger looked at Gillies. "Was it a matter of concern to you, Mr. Gillies?" she said, a hint of contempt in her voice.

"No," Gillies replied, unperturbed.

With this established, Jossen got Gillies to acknowledge that he routinely compared Christie's appraisal prices with foundation sales records. Was Gillies aware of the discrepancies that existed between Christie's appraised value of series like *Endangered Species* and *Shadows* and the actual sale prices of paintings in those series?

"Yes."

"Did those differences ever cause you to wonder about whether or not the appraisals that you had gotten from Christie's were accurate?"

"No."

"Had you ever questioned anybody in Christie's about that discrepancy?"

"Certainly not."

"Had you ever mentioned it to Mr. Hughes?"

"No."

Jossen's next focus was the settlement agreement between the foundation and Hughes. Had the foundation agreed that a body of Warhol art belonged to Hughes? "I don't know if you're stating that exactly right," Gillies answered.

Then Jossen produced an affidavit, written by Hughes to comply with the settlement agreement, in which he listed page after page of art that he claimed was his.

"How many pieces of art were on that list?"

"I don't recall."

"Did you ever make a determination of the dollar amount?"

"No."

As a part of the settlement, did the foundation also agree to give Hughes additional artwork? Yes.

How much was *that* worth? One hundred thirty-four thousand dollars—based on the Christie's appraisal.

Jossen finally had Gillies detail a part of the settlement agreement in which Hughes had agreed to *return* three pieces of art to the foundation. Did the attorney general ever investigate why Hughes had this art? No. Did Gillies ever ask the attorney general to investigate Hughes? No. Did Gillies ever even *talk* to Hughes about the art? No.

To establish that Gillies knew little about important foundation matters, Jossen brought up the 19,879 black-and-white photographs that Christie's had valued at $107,000 and Stulz at $11.6 million.

"Now, you believe, as you sit here, that that's an accurate appraisal number"—the $107,000?

"As of May 1, 1991, it is."

"And as of today, is it higher or less?"

"It may be higher, it may be less."

"Mr. Gillies, is it your testimony, then, that you have no idea as to whether or not this is an accurate appraisal?"

"As of May 1, 1991," Gillies said, but he also testified that the foundation still had not decided if the photographs were art or simply archival material. Should the photographs be dismissed as archival material, he said, they would be considered worthless. What's more, he really didn't know *when* the foundation would decide if the photographs were worthless, if they were still worth $107,000, or if they were actually worth much more than that.

Preminger stopped Gillies. After listening to him for hours, Preminger seemed angered by his apparent refusal to form an opinion on vital issues pertaining to foundation business. She was especially troubled that he was unable to put a price on the black-and-white photographs. "As I guess you know," Preminger said, "I'm sitting here trying to decide how much these photographs are worth. Are you telling me there is no way to know, at any time since the death of Mr. Warhol, whether they had any fair market value?" Later, Preminger added, "I am at a loss for how this Court is supposed to make any rational decision about the value of these photographs."

Gillies launched into a long, clumsy explanation about why he had not yet been able to establish a concrete price for the black-and-white photographs. He ended his monologue by asking Preminger, "Does that help?"

"Not at all," Preminger said, indignant.

At this point, Jossen saw a way of forcing Gillies to admit that he *had* formed an opinion on the value of the photographs—and that in fact he had expressed such an opinion within the past two weeks. In order to accomplish this, however, Jossen would need to question Gillies about the off-the-record meeting that had taken place in the judge's chambers before Thanksgiving. This was the meeting in which Gill had lectured Preminger about why the foundation would not consider paying Hayes in art and at which Gillies *did* appear to endorse a value for the photographs. But Jacob, who saw the direction in which Jossen was headed, promptly objected.

Preminger considered the objection. Then she overruled it.

"A week ago Monday," Jossen said, "didn't you sit in Her Honor's office, and weren't you asked the question by Her Honor, 'Do you agree that the 19,000 black-and-white photographs are worth $107,000?' " Jacob objected again, pointing out that if Preminger permitted this line of questioning to continue, the judge would become a witness in her own trial and would therefore have to recuse herself from the case. Because there had been no court reporter at the meeting, everyone in attendance was a witness to the conversation, including the judge. Preminger sustained Jacob's objection and called a brief recess.

During the recess, the Carter Ledyard attorneys huddled in a private meeting room on the fifth floor, along with the Winthrop, Stimson lawyers representing the estate. Meanwhile, Samuels put in a call to the attorney general's office. Hayes paced restlessly in the hallway outside the courtroom. Finally the recess ended, the judge took the bench, and Gillies resumed his seat on the stand. But before Jossen could ask a question, Jacob made an oral motion. Standing at the lawyers' table, she said that she "hated" to do this, especially now that the case was nearing a conclusion, but because she believed that "the Court is too personally involved" she had no choice but to ask for a mistrial.

A strange silence fell over the courtroom. The friction between the judge and the foundation, the estate, and even the attorney general had now for the first time been openly acknowledged. Because Preminger had taken too pointed an interest in the case, Jacob was saying, she should dismiss herself from any further proceedings.

Preminger stared at Jacob. "Motion denied."

Samuels stood to "join in the motion."

"Your application is denied," Preminger said, her voice free of emotion.

Finally Steve Weiner stood. "The estate joins in the motion for a mistrial," he said.

"Similarly denied," Preminger said again.

There was a surreal quality to the exchange, as if the dialogue had taken place not in an actual trial but in a movie or a play. One spectator observed in a loud whisper, "They just slit their throats." It was a pivotal point in the trial. Preminger could not have been clearer: She had seized control of this case and intended to take what *she* considered to be appropriate actions.

But Jacob had also shown her hand. It seemed that she was already acknowledging an imminent defeat. Now she was laying the groundwork for her appeal.

The most damaging line of questioning was yet to come for Gillies. Jossen asked him to explain a sequence of events that transpired in April 1993. On April 15, according to an internal Christie's memorandum, Martha Baer confirmed that she had spoken with Vincent Fremont to ask why Fred Hughes had used Sotheby's rather than Christie's for the sale of his Warhol paintings. When Baer asked Fremont if there was a chance of getting a consignment in the future, Fremont had told her, "Don't hold your breath." If they were not going to get any art to sell, Baer believed, then Christie's should withdraw from the appraisal.

Just at this time, Gillies had had lunch with Lash and let him know that after June 1994 the foundation would have $60 million worth of Warhol art to sell. By April 20, 1993, Christie's had decided to stay with the appraisal, according to another internal Christie's memo. "It was stressed that the next step [for Christie's to take] is for Martha and Patty [Hambrecht] to meet with Arch and the Foundation's lawyers," the memo stated. "A presentation should also be made to the board." Gillies's move had worked. With a potential $60 million art sale dangling before them, Christie's silenced their fears about the appraisal. Perhaps the oddest element to this story was how that one sale could be worth $60 million when, according to the Christie's appraisal, the entire Warhol art collection was worth, with a blockage discount, only $95 million.

How did Gillies respond to Jossen's questioning about the Christie's internal memo that resulted from his lunch with Lash?

"This is not an accurate description of my lunch with Stephen Lash."

Jossen was finished. Next Jacob questioned Gillies, but the presentation did little to counteract the damage Jossen had done. The trial broke for lunch.

In the afternoon session, Peter Falk, a prints expert hired by Hayes, testified. He told Samuels that in his opinion the 19,000 Warhol prints were worth $100 million, compared with Christie's undiscounted estimate of $29.8 million and discounted estimate of $7.2 million. On redirect examination, Hayes himself questioned a witness for the first time in the trial. Focused and forceful, he fired off questions so fast that Beth Jacob hardly had time to rise to her feet to object. The tone of the trial was elevated to a new level of spiritedness. Unfortunately, it was short-lived. When Falk was finished, the foundation called its first witness, Victor Weiner, an expert on appraisal methodology, and the trial slowed to its previous pace.

Weiner told Jossen that he had never examined any of the Warhol artwork (not even photographs of the artwork), had only "briefly" looked over sales records but had "definitely not" analyzed them, and that in fact his knowledge was "restricted to documents provided to me by Christie's." Even so, Weiner said he attacked the subject of appraisal methodology "with missionary zeal" and contended that the Christie's appraisal was accurate and reliable. On rebuttal, Jossen got Weiner to admit that he had "no way of knowing" if Christie's took into account the sometimes substantial discrepancies between their appraisal prices and the actual sales records. Should an appraiser consider such discrepancies? "By all means they should," Weiner said.

The next morning, the foundation called its second witness, Stephen Weil, an art dealer who years ago had testified in a case involving the estate of the sculptor David Smith. As it happened, Weil had worked as a dealer for the Smith estate immediately following the artist's death. The point Weil wanted to make in the Warhol case was simple: The discount Christie's applied should have been even greater because there was so much Warhol artwork and because, according to Weil, the vast amount of that artwork was available before Warhol's death and had not been sold. When Jossen asked Weil if he was aware of the fact that $100 million worth of Warhol art had sold since Warhol's death, Weil seemed shocked. Likewise, when Jossen made the point that the size of the Picasso estate seemed to enrich its worth, Weil, a dealer since the sixties, said, "I'm not aware of the size of the Picasso estate." Finally Jossen read from the decision in the Smith case—a case, like the Warhol case, in which the use of blockage discounts was hotly debated. In that decision, the judge harshly criticized Weil for selling off a number of Smith's sculptures at ridiculously low prices. In fact, Weil had so little faith in the art he was selling that he valued the entire Smith estate in 1965 at around $700,000. In 1993, Jossen pointed out, *one* piece of Smith sculpture sold at auction for $816,000.

. . .

Later that day Hayes called his last witness, Will Goetzmann, an econo-mist. Goetzmann had not been available until that afternoon—the reason the foundation, against its repeated protests, had been forced to call its first two witnesses. In his testimony Goetzmann argued that on average during the twentieth century the return on art investments hovered at about 17 percent, a figure substantially higher than the return on investments in the stock market. Hayes rested his case.

It was at this juncture in the trial that Jacob made a request for a direct verdict—a little-used motion for the judge to throw out the case. Hayes had not proven his point, Jacob said; he had offered no evidence that would discredit the Christie's appraisal. Samuels joined in Jacob's mo-tion, as did the attorneys for the estate.

Preminger asked Jossen to respond. Jossen stood. "This is in the nature of a contested accounting," he said. "I believe the evidence is plain and more than ample to deny the motion for a direct verdict. Not only have we offered substantial evidence but there is evidence to question the validity of the Christie's appraisal as well as the motivations of the people involved, including not only individuals at the foundation but people at Christie's."

"I agree with you," Preminger said. "The motions are denied."

The foundation called its next witness, William Baumol, another econo-mist, who was paid a fee of $56,000 by the foundation for writing an affidavit and appearing in court. The most memorable moment in his testimony came after he had offered a detailed (if convoluted) discussion of the difference between the art market and the stock market. Appar-ently unaware of what her own witness was just saying, Jacob said, "Will you explain the difference between art and the stock market?"

Preminger looked at Jacob, obviously puzzled. "He just did," Prem-inger said.

"May I agree with Your Honor," Baumol said teasingly. "I have become a hostile witness."

From there, Baumol went on to make the point the foundation was counting on. "Art is probably not a good investment," he said, "and this is probably true of a large portfolio as well." Baumol had earned his $56,000, but at least one of the lawyers for the estate and the foundation felt differently. "We know we're heading for a collision with the judge," the lawyer said after court that day. "We just don't know how bad the collision is going to be."

The foundation called Elizabeth Hahn, who evaluated the Warhol prints for Christie's. Adam Rowland, a young, studious attorney who in many ways masterminded the actual execution of Hayes's case, cross-examined the witness for Hayes. Rowland led Hahn to admit that she was "not sure who her client was," that she never made an effort to determine who her client was, and that, while she had spent thirty hours preparing her deposition for this case, she had spent only twenty hours examining the thirteen thousand to fourteen thousand prints. She maintained, however, not only that the 75-percent blockage discount applied to the total price she had put on the prints—$29.8 million—was appropriate but that it was correct to have applied a further 20-percent across-the-board reduction on a reappraisal. Samuels and Jacob questioned Hahn; then on re-cross Hayes took over the questioning himself, hitting Hahn with one question after another until she revealed that she—a high-ranking administrator in Christie's contemporary art department—had so little interest in Warhol's work that she had not even attended the Museum of Modern Art's retrospective, perhaps the most noteworthy show to open in New York in 1989.

Finally, on the afternoon of December 8, Martha Baer took the stand. Just as Jeffrey Hoffeld had provided the cornerstone of testimony for Hayes, Baer was to be the star witness for the foundation and Christie's. After all, she had been in charge of the entire Warhol appraisal, a job for which during one six-month period alone she had billed the foundation over $50,000. But Baer now had a serious problem: Gillies had testified that he knew so little about the business dealings concerning the appraisal that Baer had to offer more or less the same kind of testimony or she would make Gillies look as if he had not been telling the truth. Jossen started with some general questions.

"Are you proud of the appraisal?"

"Yes," Baer said.

"Is it the most thorough appraisal you have ever done?"

"Yes, it is."

"I take it, then, that you have confidence in the methodology that Christie's applies in its appraisals?"

"Yes."

But Jossen had few easy questions. He brought up an October 1992 meeting at which Baer had said that the Warhol appraisal—one of the most difficult she had ever attempted—contained figures that were subjective. Did she say that? "No," Baer answered, "I did not. I don't believe."

So Jossen showed her a memo in which she was quoted as saying that "the figures are . . . very subjective."

Still, Baer was unwavering. "I don't recall saying that," she contended. " 'Subjective' would not be a word I'd use to characterize our appraisal."

"Then is the memo erroneous?" Jossen asked.

"Yes."

Next Jossen addressed a series of sales made by the d'Offay Gallery in London that brought prices far out of line with the figures Baer had put on these same canvases. Though Baer had appraised *Dennis Hopper* at $45,000, it sold for $85,000; *Frederick the Great* had been appraised at $80,000 but sold for $135,000; *Life Savers* was appraised at $50,000 and sold for $65,000; and *Double Hamburger* sold for $400,000, a quarter of a million more than Christie's appraisal. In addition, these appraised prices were reduced by an additional 20 percent in the reappraisal.

Did Baer contact any dealers when she was conducting her appraisals? Jossen wanted to know.

"No."

"Did you talk to [experts like] Kynaston McShine?"

"No."

"Did you use sales information from dealers?"

"Yes," she said, though it became apparent that in establishing her figures she relied only on sales records from Christie's and Sotheby's and only from the London and New York offices of those companies.

Next, when Jossen questioned her about her client, Baer said that she took her instructions from Fred Hughes, that for a long time she "didn't understand how divided" the sides were, and that she did not realize there was a serious dispute between the parties until six months ago. Even though many art world insiders had known about the disagreement between the estate and the foundation from as far back as 1990, Baer claimed that she had no idea there was any conflict over the very appraisal she was conducting.

"Did you even know who your client was?" Jossen asked.

"I was told the client was the estate."

Then why, in an April 1990 memo to her, did Lash refer to the *foundation* as the client? Jossen wanted to know.

"Mr. Lash obviously did regard the client as the foundation," Baer said.

As for the August 9, 1990, meeting in which Hayes confronted her, Baer remembered that Hayes was "obviously angry . . . at both our unit values and our use of blockage discount," but she recalled nothing else from the meeting, not even Hayes's heated discussion of the Mapplethorpe appraisal.

Jossen queried Baer about an October 4, 1990, meeting she had with lawyers from Carter Ledyard.

"I don't remember that meeting. But apparently I was there. Somebody says I was."

"What were you doing at a meeting with lawyers for the foundation in October 1990 without any representatives from the estate?"

"I didn't feel that they were two different entities. I was not zeroing in on that."

Finally Jossen brought up a May 14, 1992, meeting concerning the value of the Polaroids, which Baer had priced originally at a nickel each.

"I don't remember these meetings," Baer said, "but I'm sure they took place."

Jossen had finished with Baer for the day. The woman in charge of the Christie's appraisal could not remember meetings she had attended, conversations she had had, advice she had given. She had not made a good impression.

On her second day of testimony, Baer admitted that "blockage discount *has* to be considered" in all cases. With Warhol, the discounts were up to 90 percent, but to Baer they were perfectly reasonable. When Jossen finished with Baer, Samuels began his questioning. He was preparing to ask a question about how a fair market value appraisal affects an executor's commission when Jossen objected and Preminger sustained.

"Mr. Jossen asked the same question *six times*," Samuels said, pointing at Jossen.

Preminger looked at Samuels in disbelief. "Is that an objection, Mr. Samuels?" Preminger said.

"To the hypocrisy of Mr. Jossen's objection, Your Honor."

"Mr. Samuels," Preminger said, "that is not an appropriate comment to be made by the office of the attorney general in a trial. Do you have any further questions?"

He did, but only a handful. Then, dejected, he sat down.

At last, Jacob got to question her star witness. She had Baer establish that 1988 and 1989 were good years for the Warhol art market, but Baer went on to say that she didn't "know if [the market] will ever get back to 1988 and 1989 levels." For this to happen, the art would need "a lot of marketing," since after 1988 and 1989 "people lost confidence in Warhol." On re-cross, Baer told Jossen that the May 1990 sales represented Warhol's "last gasp." She seemed unaware that this period she was referring to was the time Gillies took over as the foundation's president.

Finally Baer was finished. When Preminger called the attorneys to her bench for a sidebar, she announced that because of the holidays she was recessing the trial until January 12, 1994, a little over a month from the seventh anniversary of Warhol's death.

. . .

When the trial resumed in the new year, the foundation called Rick Wester, who was credited with appraising Warhol's photographs for Christie's even though he was brought in only after an associate had done most of the work. In addition, the work he *did* do was not reflected in the appraisal. According to Wester, he suggested raising the value of the 19,879 black-and-white photographs from one dollar to five dollars each. That would have put their value at a little over $99,000. On the Christie's appraisal, though, the price had not been changed, and they remained appraised at $19,879.

"Why was that figure not changed on the appraisal?" Jossen asked.

"That doesn't reflect the work that I did," Wester said.

"I'm sorry, what did you say?"

"I said that doesn't reflect the work that I did on it."

"This was supposed to reflect your work but it doesn't. Is that what you are telling us?"

"Yes," Wester said. "That's what I'm saying."

"It's a mistake," Jossen said.

"Yes," Wester admitted.

As its last witness, the foundation called André Emmerich, a New York art dealer. Emmerich, who was paid $4,000 a day to testify plus $3,500 for preparatory work, said that he believed Baer's large discounts were conservative—"modest, low," he called them. Had he been doing the appraisals, he would have discounted the total even more. Emmerich felt his position was justified because, compared with other artists, Warhol was a "particularly risky" investment. "I would have a more pessimistic opinion of the enduring value of Warhol," he said. And why? Because "by definition, what's fashionable today is old-fashioned tomorrow." He thought it likely that Warhol's work would fade into obscurity because Warhol's subjects—celebrities like Marilyn Monroe and Elvis Presley—would eventually be forgotten. Even the Coke bottle would be redesigned, he speculated, decreasing the value of Warhol's many renderings of it. To this notion, Frank Harvey would later reply with a quote printed in *The Wall Street Journal*: "Who the hell is Mona Lisa?"

Emmerich, who years earlier had employed Martha Baer before she went on to work at Christie's, picked up his attack on Warhol during his second day on the stand. "I don't think comparing Warhol to Picasso makes any sense at all," Emmerich contended. "Picasso's reputation is unique in this country but also worldwide. . . . Warhol didn't create a body of work that was as unique as Picasso's."

"Is that an opinion generally shared in the art community?" Preminger asked.

"That's a subject of hot debate," Emmerich admitted.

To date, the foundation's entire case had been an exercise in cynicism. The foundation had used Warhol's money to hire Carter Ledyard (in anticipation of and during the Hayes trial, the foundation paid the firm, according to press reports, well over $2 million), which brought in witness after witness to discredit the reputation of Warhol as an artist and to question the lasting value of his work. Putting Emmerich, well paid with Warhol's money, on the stand to conclude its case was a tasteless moral offense. The trial's testimony ended on this disturbing note.

Preminger recessed the trial for lunch. Afterward, the attorneys offered their closing arguments. Jossen began by stating that he believed Warhol to be worth "in excess of eight hundred million" when he died. Jossen arrived at this figure by adding together the various appraisals Hayes commissioned on the Warhol artwork: $400 million for the paintings, $91 million for the appraised drawings, $40 million for drawings Christie's had not yet appraised, $97 million for prints, and $80 million for the photographs—along with $119 million in real property and cash. According to Jossen, the entire Warhol estate was worth $827 million. These numbers compared sharply with those Christie's put on the same work: $194 million for the paintings, $15.3 million for the drawings, $30 million for the prints, and $16 million for the photographs. Adding up the Christie's numbers, Jossen noted that the total was $265 million, but to this number Christie's applied substantial blockage discounts, which brought the figure down to $95 million. Combined with the $119 million in real property and cash—both sides still agreed on that amount—and some art by other artists, according to Christie's the Warhol estate was worth $220 million.

Jossen attacked Hughes for not testifying (he "would have said very different things about Warhol's reputation") and Gillies because "he came here and basically said, 'I could care less.'" Jossen stopped. "'I don't know and I don't care'—that's what came through in his testimony." As for the attorney general, "they're fond of saying they're the guardian of the people, but where are they on the [required contribution of] five percent? You don't hear about that."

In closing Samuels argued that the judge should wait until the end of the second part of the trial to offer an opinion on the value of the Warhol estate. "You have argued that point and you have not succeeded," Preminger told him.

Jacob's final argument focused on the application of a blockage discount as "a marketplace reality." Preminger finally stopped her too. "I have trouble looking at economic principles subjectively," she said. "I don't begin to understand the workings of the person's mind [who determines the discount]." Finally, in a baffling move, Susan Kohlmann, a lawyer for the estate, argued that the value of an artist's work has nothing to do with that artist's reputation. It was one of the most perverse twists of logic in a trial full of perverse twists of logic.

Preminger thanked all of the lawyers, then called them to the bench. There she told them that because the foundation had asked for an exchange of briefs—a relatively pointless exercise that tends to make a legal process longer and therefore more expensive—Hayes had to submit a brief by January 24. The foundation would have ten days to respond. After that, Preminger would offer her written opinion.

On January 24, 1994, Hayes submitted his posthearing memorandum. In it, he reiterated a number of points made during the trial. The case may have developed because of his disputed legal fee, Hayes admitted, but it also "coincides with the protection of the legacy and value that Warhol deliberately worked to create." In addition, he said, "the proper recognition of value . . . is a matter of public interest" since the charities

Warhol wanted to support were not getting 5 percent of the *authentic value* of the estate each year. Instead, these institutions "have been and are being cheated by the undervaluing of the Warhol art." The foundation was able to place a low value on the estate because "Christie's work in this matter was tainted by a lack of independence and conflict of interest as it sought to curry favor with its 'client,' the Foundation, and particularly its president, Mr. Gillies." The memorandum pointed out that, as of late January 1994, the foundation "has yet to file an annual report for its fiscal year [that] ended 9 months ago in April 1993, and we are unclear what investigation the Attorney General has made or will make. . . ." Hayes ended his memorandum by returning to the trial—and Warhol. "The evidence reinforces that Warhol is one of the most prominent contemporary 20th Century artists, more marketable than his peers . . . and that his art has appreciated through his life and after his death."

In a letter to Preminger dated February 1, David Samuels answered the charge that the attorney general had been lax in his efforts to monitor the foundation and Gillies. "We are relying on the Court's observation on January 13," Samuels wrote, "that the Court was 'not impugning any wrong doing to the Attorney General's office. . . .' " This was the sole charge Samuels responded to; he concluded "that no further submission is required by this office" and so he did not submit a brief.

On February 3 Jacob filed a brief for the foundation. Motivated by the opportunity "to chase a $16 million legal fee," she charged, Hayes had called into question the appraisal done by Christie's, a firm whose long history and vast experience should make its opinion beyond reproach. Jacob described Hoffeld as "an unsuccessful art dealer" and Stulz as "head of Photographs at Christie's years ago." Jacob believed that a blockage discount had to be applied to Warhol's art since "art is a risky investment." The foundation's critics had previously pointed out that this seemed an odd position for Andy Warhol's foundation to take, but Jacob did not believe her argument to be incongruous. "The issue before this Court is not the artistic merit of Andy Warhol and his work," she wrote. ". . . It is not the protection of the Warhol legacy."

. . .

During the months leading up to the trial and during the trial itself, Gillies and other people affiliated with the foundation became increasingly concerned about the press coverage the Warhol foundation was receiving. When my cover story appeared in *The Village Voice* in July 1993—"Who Is Killing the Warhol Legacy?"—Gillies called me up, told me my article was riddled with errors, and asked to meet with me. As we sat in his office at the Factory a few days later, however, he was unable to point out to me any real mistakes; instead he complained that it wasn't the facts themselves that were wrong but the *tone* of the article. As the trial proceeded both Alexandra Peers of *The Wall Street Journal* and Carol Vogel of *The New York Times* wrote thoughtful, objective pieces about the proceedings, though both reporters identified the absurdity: that the Warhol foundation had gone to court to argue that Warhol was not an artist whose work and reputation was going to last—the same criticism Warhol himself fought for years. But Gillies took exception to the fact that Peers and Vogel reported this development. He had heated telephone conversations with Peers, and he had foundation lawyers write a threatening letter to the *Times*. Finally, Gillies retained Robinson Lake Sawyer Miller, the expensive public relations firm headed by Linda Robinson, who was famous for, among other things, having been in *Barbarians at the Gate*, the book that recounted the fall of RJR Nabisco.

On April 14, 1994, several weeks after the final papers had been filed in the first part of the trial, Preminger handed down her opinion. In her decision, a thoughtfully reasoned twenty-five page document, she began by restating the question that had required her to divide the trial into two parts, and then offering a wry reply: "How much is Andy Warhol's art worth? It is difficult, if not foolhardy, to attempt an answer." But in order to consider the merit of Hayes's 2110 petition—now nearly two years old—she had to determine what she regarded as the estate's authentic value.

Before launching into a category-by-category evaluation, Preminger had some general comments to make about the case. "In ascribing unit values," Preminger wrote, "all of the experts for the Foundation presented a negative view as to the marketability of Warhol's art. This view is not supported by the empirical evidence. . . . Warhol is an artist of international prominence. He is widely recognized as one of the world's most important and influential artists. His work has been exhibited and sold throughout the United States and the world. . . . More people visited the Warhol retrospective [in 1989 at MoMA] than those visiting the major exhibitions at MoMA of Picasso, Braque or Matisse."

Yet Christie's did not seem to share this opinion. "They failed to consider," Preminger wrote, "the importance of Warhol as an artist, which is relevant to his staying power and marketability. The weight to be given an appraisal is dependent upon the consideration of precisely such factors." Preminger charged that Christie's "limited the focus of the appraisal to its own auction sales and those of Sotheby's," disregarded "many of its own sales . . . if they did not support the appraisal," and overlooked "innumberable [sic] sales consummated by other auction houses and dealers." For their part, Hayes's experts were found to be not wholly objective in their valuations, and to have "concentrated on retail sales, which inflated some of the values." On the whole, however, Preminger found they "presented more reliable appraisals than Christie's of the drawings, prints, and photographs, considering all of the factors for determining fair market value."

Preminger saved her harshest criticism for the relationship between Christie's and the foundation. Though the company had been retained initially by the estate's executor, "Christie's staff communicated primarily with the Foundation's president, Archibald L. Gillies." Specifically, before the appraisal was finished, Gillies met improperly with Stephen Lash on April 16, 1993. "At the luncheon meeting," Preminger recounted, "Gillies and Lash discussed Christie's role in the appraisal and payment to Christie's for services rendered." Gillies also told Lash about $60 million worth of Warhol art that would be available in June 1994. "Although Gillies was aware that Christie's hoped to obtain that business, neither he nor Lash saw any impropriety in engaging in such a discussion while the appraisal was ongoing." Preminger did. "Courts have frequently disregarded testimony of an appraiser where there appears to be bias or collusion with the owner/taxpayer. While the evidence here does not rise to collusion between the Foundation and Christie's, it does demonstrate a conflict on the part of Christie's in seeking future business from the Foundation at the same time it was retained to render an impartial appraisal."

Preminger also reprimanded Martha Baer, specifically for the way Baer applied blockage discounts to the value of Warhol's art. "She was unable to explain how she chose a discount rate considerably higher than those in the reported cases for an artist concededly more successful and established than those artists. [Therefore,] it seems clear that Christie's discount is too high."

With this in mind, Preminger next documented her value for each category of Warhol art with what she regarded as appropriate blockage discounts applied. For the photographs, she accepted Stulz's valuation of $80 million; she then applied a 20 percent discount, placing the photographs' worth at $64 million. For the paintings, sculptures, and collaborations, Preminger increased Christie's total by 60 percent to $311,708,800, after which she reduced that number by 20 percent to make the category worth $249,367,040. She set the net value of the drawings at $29,575,000, which reflected a 35 percent discount applied to the undiscounted value of $45,500,000. Finally, for the prints, she applied a 30 percent discount to an undiscounted value of $68,624,625, making the prints worth $48,037,238. "Based upon the foregoing," Preminger concluded, "the court finds that the transfer-date value of Warhol's art is $390,979,278"—four times as much as the $95 million price tag Christie's had placed on the art. "Including the non-art assets at the stipulated value of $119 million, the fair market value of the gross estate is $509,979,278."

Preminger's decision represented an unqualified failure for Christie's and the foundation, who were now in the odd position of having to justify the fact that they had defended a price almost $300 million below the value Preminger had put on the estate. On the other hand, the decision was an unqualified victory for Hayes, who potentially stood to gain—if the terms of his contract with the estate were upheld without penalty—more than $5 million in addition to the $4.85 million he had already collected.

The son of poor European immigrants, Andy Warhol moved to New York City in the late forties and became, in just less than forty years, one of the century's most wealthy artists. He may be surpassed only by Picasso, who was worth, as best as can be determined, at least a billion dollars when he died. (Much of that wealth came from Picasso's own unsold artwork.) Unlike Picasso, however, Warhol actively built an enormous business enterprise at the same time he worked as an artist. He became as successful as he did through sheer hard work, an uncanny ability to foresee popular trends, and a willingness to take risks. He *earned* his wealth—and did not apologize for his love of money or the way of life he was able to lead because he had money. He may never have achieved true happiness, a loss that finally makes him a more sympathetic person than the image of himself he projected to the public, but, as an adult anyway, he was not discontented because of any lack of worldly comforts.

Warhol produced a body of work that not only changed the direction of art in this century (by ending the vogue of abstract expressionism and popularizing pop art), but also had a profound impact well beyond the confines of contemporary art. Through his public self and through his paintings and his films, Warhol personified detachment, irony, fragmentation—the hallmarks of postmodernism. Perhaps no other figure has done more to make postmodernist ideas and techniques accessible to the general public than Warhol. And for years, while he did this, he rarely missed a day of shopping.

Then he died. For a time, with Fred Hughes in control of the operations of the estate and the foundation, the overall performance of the Warhol organization remained essentially the same as it was when Warhol was alive. This was not surprising. After all, Hughes, more than anyone besides Warhol himself, helped shape the empire Warhol built.

By the beginning of 1990, Hughes, assisted by Ed Hayes, had generated well over $25 million in cash, which had been transferred to the foundation, as well as another $10 million, which remained in the estate. Though Hughes had spent some significant amounts on expenses (legal bills, administrative fees and salaries, general overhead), he was well on his way toward achieving his goal of amassing a $100 million trust fund that would guarantee the foundation's ability to operate indefinitely. But because of Hughes's illness, because of legitimate business disputes, and because of base catalysts such as greed and ambition and outright pettiness, the Warhol organization began to unravel as Hughes, Hayes, and Gillies found themselves mired in a bitter three-way dispute.

Money evaporated from the estate. Under Gillies, administrative costs at the foundation soared, leaping from an average of $400,000 a year during 1987, 1988, and 1989—when Hughes and Hayes were in charge—to $5 million a year during 1990, 1991, 1992, and 1993. (Gillies certainly had veered from the advice he had given Hughes at that first lunch years ago when he told him the key to good management was to keep costs low!) While costs skyrocketed at the foundation, income shrank. As a result, the more than $25 million in the foundation bank accounts began to disappear. By the end of 1993, only $6 million remained; even so, Gillies did not stop spending. Sadly, the enormous effort that had been exerted to build up nearly half of the $100 million trust fund was wasted. Almost all of that money was gone or owed, and the likelihood of anyone coming forward to liquidate judiciously the remaining assets, which were also dwindling, was slim. With so much money being spent and so little revenue being generated, with the main players locked in a seemingly endless futile struggle, it appeared likely that the destruction of the Andy Warhol Foundation for the Visual Arts would be inevitable. Only taking drastic steps could prevent this from happening, steps no one seemed willing to take.

11

NOT LONG BEFORE PREMINGER HANDED DOWN HER DECISION, I WENT TO A meeting late one afternoon with the attorney general, G. Oliver Koppell. At the end of 1993, Robert Abrams, who seemed much more interested in running for the United States Senate than in being New York's attorney general, resigned from office. Koppell took over in January. The Warhol trial had been reported extensively in the press throughout the fall, but Koppell was unaware of even the fundamental details of the dispute. He seemed to know only the facts that had been provided him by David Samuels, who joined us for the ninety-minute meeting, which presumably was meant to be a bit of a Warhol primer and a public relations gesture.

As we sat in his office that afternoon, I was charmed by Koppell, who was hospitable and pleasant, though I could easily detect an authoritative slant to his personality. I was also concerned by his apparent lack of knowledge of the case—surely one of the most high-profiled his office had had to deal with since he had taken over as attorney general. He did not know that in the course of their legal battle with Hayes, the Warhol foundation had paid out millions of dollars in fees to several law firms, among them Winthrop, Stimson; Donovan Leisure; and Carter Ledyard—probably as much (or more than) Hayes would have settled for back in 1992. He did not understand the way the relentless stream of negative publicity created by the foundation had affected all Warhol-related enterprises, such as the Warhol museum and the Warhol art market. He did not even seem to be aware of the fact that during the trial there had been extensive testimony about the improper meetings the foundation had taken with Christie's. Koppell knew only this: He was absolutely opposed to Hayes getting any more money—under any conditions. It was my opinion that in opposing Hayes's 2110 petition Koppell's office had ignored highly questionable behavior on the part of key foundation representatives.

Days later, when the judge issued her opinion, the attorney general's press secretary released various statements indicating that the attorney general's office was going to launch an investigation into the management of the foundation. The attorney general wanted to know, it was said, more about the nature of the improper meetings the foundation had taken with Christie's. In addition, he was going to consider whether Preminger's opinion would affect the amount of money the foundation would be required to give away each year to charities under the 5 percent rule. However, in the weeks following the attorney general's announcement, there was no evidence whatsoever that anyone from the attorney general's office was investigating any aspect of the operations of the foundation. As they had for years now, staff from the attorney general's office was content to allow the Warhol foundation to conduct business in almost any fashion it chose. By allowing this kind of behavior to go unchecked, the attorney general's office was profoundly negligent in its charter to monitor organizations like the Warhol foundation.

Soon after my meeting with Koppell, I learned that the board of directors of the Warhol foundation had scheduled a meeting. Immediately I wrote a letter to the board asking them if I could attend the early part of the meeting in order to ask them some questions about the general management of the foundation. In particular, I wanted the board to explain spending such huge sums on professional services—between April 1992 and April 1993 the foundation had paid some $1.5 million in legal fees and just under $400,000 in accounting fees—and other budgetary items, including salaries and stipends. Though Gillies had an annual package worth somewhere near a quarter of a million dollars, including his salary, pension plan, and expense accounts, the foundation had gone from having a cash position of over $25 million in early 1990, when Gillies became president, to less than $6 million by early 1994. I wanted to know why Gillies had abandoned the business plan Hughes and Hayes had put into place, choosing to deplete the foundation's cash supply instead of continuing to build it up, and why the board had let him. I informed the board that I would show up at the Factory on the morning of the meeting and wait until a vote was taken on whether or not they would see me.

When I arrived at the Factory that morning, movers were packing the building's contents in anticipation of the foundation's move to new offices in SoHo that Gillies had recently rented. Though staying in the Factory would have been economical—the building was paid for—and maybe even sentimental—it represented the one last link to the world Warhol had created while he was alive—Gillies was determined to move out as soon as the building had been transferred over from the estate. It was almost as if Gillies was anxious to situate the foundation in a neutral space. In the process he could also rid himself of Hughes. Fred always had an office in the various incarnations of Warhol's Factories since the late sixties, but Gillies made it clear to him that there would be no room for him in the new offices.

On this morning, the Factory lobby was a scene of controlled chaos. All of the canvases had been taken down from the walls and packed into crates. The stuffed dog, there for years, had already been removed—shipped to the museum in Pittsburgh where it would soon be placed in the museum's library. And the life-size cardboard cutout of Warhol, which had been standing on the tiny balcony overlooking the lobby as if the ghost of Warhol himself were still hovering over the Factory's comings and goings, had been packed away. In only a matter of days, everything in the Factory would be moved out. All that would be left behind was the huge hand-painted sign that dominated one full wall of the lobby. "I never wanted to be a painter," the sign said, quoting Warhol. "I wanted to be a tap dancer."

Before the meeting began, an announcement was made that I wanted to address certain questions to the board, and after some resistance a vote was taken. Not surprisingly, my request was turned down. The vote was unanimous. One member summed up the board's decision. "We will not be dictated to by a journalist." The rest of the board agreed.

Preminger issued her opinion on the value of the Warhol estate not long after the board meeting. It was a harsh indictment of the foundation, for which Gillies and the board had to assume full responsibility. Gund announced that she was thinking about resigning; otherwise, the board did nothing. In fact, instead of taking constructive action, the board members continued to endorse Gillies, who began a public assault on Preminger's abilities as a judge. The board also allowed Gillies to bolster Carter Ledyard, who had lost the first half of the trial, by hiring a second law firm to represent them in the litigation. Gillies and the board chose Skadden, Arps, Slate, Meagher & Flom—one of the most expensive law firms in New York. At the firm, the foundation's main lawyer would be Thomas Schwarz, a corporate law specialist who bills out at $475 an hour. Still, despite its poor representation of the foundation, Carter Ledyard was not fired. Instead, to keep up the fight against Hayes, the foundation was now paying two firms. It may not have mattered much anyway. In the weeks after she issued her opinion, Preminger indicated that there would not be traditional live testimony in the trial's second part. She wanted each side to submit a brief on the merits of Hayes's legal services; then she would award him his fee. Still, this did not keep Schwarz from filing a motion appealing Preminger's decision on the value of the Warhol estate and a second motion asking Preminger to recuse herself from the case.

Before the trial could continue, however, a truly clarifying event occurred: As scheduled, in mid-May, the Andy Warhol Museum opened in Pittsburgh.

While fireworks exploded over the Allegheny River at midnight on Saturday, May 14, the Andy Warhol Museum opened its doors to the public. And what a reaction from the public! Outside the museum, people jammed the streets, forming two different lines that ran for blocks. City fire codes demanded that only a fixed number of visitors could be allowed in the museum at any given time. Crowds of people stood outside in the middle of the night waiting to be admitted—as many as ten thousand people or more.

The large open lobby of the museum was filled with a variety of Warhol self-portraits, both paintings and photographs. Visitors were encouraged to take the elevator to the seventh—and top—floor of the 88,000-square-foot former warehouse. There, lining all four walls in a continuous sequence, was Warhol's *Shadows*, on loan from the de Menils' Dia foundation for a year. One of Warhol's few abstract efforts, the series was shown off extremely well by the floor's vast unencumbered space. The five floors below were each divided into large rooms that documented the stages of Warhol's career: His pop art work from the sixties, numerous examples of his portraiture, and selections from the series he did during the seventies and the eighties. Especially noteworthy in the sizable collection—Mark Francis, the museum's curator, had put on display 500 of the museum's 3,000 pieces of Warhol art—were an enormous *Mao*, on indefinite loan from the Chicago Art Museum; versions of *The Last Supper*; a room full of *Jackies*, *Marilyns*, and *Lizes*; and another room that contained numerous selections from Warhol's fifties drawings, several of them stunning nudes of young men rendered in a simple, elegant style.

For the Friday night opening, 1,100 people paid $300 each to attend a black-tie dinner in a huge tent that had been erected behind the museum. The audience was a cross-section of the different circles Warhol moved in: Roy Lichtenstein, Francesco Clemente, Dominique de Menil, and Anthony d'Offay from the art world; Dennis Hopper and John Waters from Hollywood; Mary McFadden from the fashion industry; Tama Janowitz, Bob Colacello, and John Richardson from the literary world; Anne Bass, Nan Kempner, and Molly Wilmot from the world of high society; and Ultra Violet, Billy Name, and Baby Jane Holzer from Warhol's inner circle, at least the one he had in the sixties.

In the cavernous tent, 110 tables had been set, each with a centerpiece of a brightly lit neon sculpture of Warhol. The sculptures were for sale, of course—at $400 apiece. By nine o'clock, when Fred Hughes made his entrance, the tent was jammed with people, many of whom were milling about from table to table. As he was wheeled into the tent by an attendant, one person after another came forward and leaned down to shake his hand or kiss him on the cheek. It was a slow procession because of the many well-wishers. At one particular moment, Dennis Hopper rushed to Hughes to give him a long hug in the light of numerous flashbulbs. Finally arriving at his table, Hughes was seated only a short distance from Gillies, whose presence at the function was all but over-looked. Ed Hayes had declined to attend, not feeling it appropriate.

Speeches were made by Robert Casey, the governor of Pennsylvania, and Teresa Heinz, whose husband, Senator H. John Heinz, had helped line up development money for the museum before he died. Thomas N. Armstrong III, the director of the museum, spoke to the audience as well. All in all, it was not a party that Warhol himself would have been impressed by. Still, he would have attended, mostly because Warhol would go to *any* party, as long as he knew celebrities were going to be there.

"I loved Andy," Molly Wilmot, the Palm Beach and Saratoga society figure who was escorted to the black-tie dinner by Denton Cox, was heard to comment that evening. "I wouldn't have missed this opening for the world." Unfortunately, some celebrity friends who knew Warhol didn't attend. Many wondered why the list of no-shows included Rich-ard Gere, Bianca Jagger, Calvin Klein, Grace Jones, and Diana Ross, some of whom had indicated that they would make the trip to Pitts-burgh. Just as disturbing, many of Warhol's closest friends and col-leagues did not attend the ceremonies either. This is how Brigid Berlin, who had worked for the foundation after Andy's death, only to be fired a little more than six months before the museum's opening, explained her decision not to go: "I hate Arch Gillies. I hate them all at the foundation. They're jerks. They don't know what they're doing. Andy loved beautiful people. I'll tell you one thing. None of the people at the foundation are beauties. I have nothing against the museum. I just won't be in the same room with Arch Gillies."

Berlin's comment underscored a problem that the museum and Armstrong had encountered. Because of the enormous amount of negative feeling the Warhol foundation had generated over the past several years in its public dispute with Hayes and with its somewhat less public spats with many of Warhol's friends and associates (Berlin was only one), raising funds for the museum was difficult. To start the project—to buy the building, to pay for the renovation, to hire a staff—just under $15 million was needed. Most of the money came from four sources: $6 million from the Commonwealth of Pennsylvania, $5 million from the various endowments of the Heinz family, $2 million from the Warhol foundation, and $1 million from Henry Hillman, a Pittsburgh philanthropist. That money had been raised some time back, though—before much of the recent controversy began. After that initial capital campaign, however, Armstrong was able to raise only $1 million of a $20 million endowment fund he felt he needed to run the museum. So, when the doors to the museum opened, it was already in financial trouble. With a separate $1.3 million operating budget, Armstrong had about a year to raise much of the $19 million required to keep the museum going. Otherwise, the Carnegie Institute, which assumed responsibility for the day-to-day management of the museum, would have to cover the daily expenses or shut the museum down.

Closing the museum would be not only a major embarrassment but also unfortunate, for there is interest in the museum. In the first twenty-four hours the Andy Warhol Museum was open, 22,000 visitors passed through—almost one thousand people an hour.

On Sunday afternoon, as the crowds lined up to go inside the museum, I decided to drive out to Warhol's grave. Near the cemetery I noticed what was all too obvious: Warhol had been buried in one of the most run-down, decidedly lower-middle-class neighborhoods in Pittsburgh. For all of his adult life, Warhol had worked tirelessly—compulsively— to better himself, to get rich, to make his place in the art community and the New York social scene. He had been so ashamed of his past that he would frequently lie to people about where he had been born, claiming states as remote as Hawaii as the site of his birth. He disliked his personal heritage so intensely that he rarely went home to Pittsburgh. Yet now he had been brought back to be buried in a neighborhood not unlike the one he had grown up in so many years ago.

I walked through the cemetery, which is located on the side of a long sloping hill, until I found Warhol's grave. Just above it were the graves of his mother and father. When his father died in 1942, Julia had chosen to bury him in this cemetery, which was the final resting place for many families who had emigrated to the United States from Eastern Europe. Now, with Andy beside them, the family was reunited in death.

On the grave of Marilyn Monroe admirers leave flowers, just as they do poems on the grave of Sylvia Plath and packs of Chesterfields on the grave of James Dean. But on the grave of Andy Warhol admirers do not leave such ordinary objects of affection and remembrance. Besides a Campbell's soup can and a Brillo box, I saw lying under a small stone a single dollar bill. I wondered if it was an oddity, left by a singular fan. I reached down and picked up the Brillo box to see if anything was inside. It was full of money.

ACKNOWLEDGMENTS

This book grew out of three articles that I wrote about the estate and the foundation of Andy Warhol: "What Happened to Andy's Treasures?," which appeared in *New York* magazine on January 27, 1992; "Who Is Killing the Warhol Legacy?," which *The Village Voice* ran on July 20, 1993; and "Let Us Now Appraise Andy Warhol," which *ARTnews* published in its March 1994 issue. I would like to thank the editors who worked on these articles—Tom Prince at *New York*, Lisa Kennedy at *The Village Voice*, and Milton Esterow, Steven Henry Madoff, and Robin Cembalest at *ARTnews*.

For their contribution to the preparation of this book, or the articles that led to it, I would like to thank Frank Andrews, William Avery, Richard Barr, Brigid Berlin, Richard Bernstein, Victor Bockris, Sam Bolton, Leo Castelli, Pamela Clapp, Bob Colacello, Virginia Regan Coleman, Denton Cox, Martin Cribbs, Linda Cummins, Charlotte Fischman, Vincent Fremont, Peter P. McN. Gates, Brendan Gill, Archibald L. Gillies, Agnes Gund, Pat Hackett, Frank Harvey, Edward W. Hayes, Jean Hayes, Steven Hayes, Susan Hayes, Jeffrey Hoffeld, Frederick W. Hughes, Tama Janowitz, Robert Jossen, G. Oliver Koppell, Benjamin Liu, Gael Love, Jack McCann, Christopher Makos, Ron Marsenison, Taylor Mead, Sylvia Miles, Glenn O'Brien, Stuart Pivar, Myrna Post, Paige Powell, Mark Rennie, Adam Rowland, David Samuels, Thomas Schwarz, Paul Scott, Jay Shriver, Emily Todd, Whitney Tower Jr., Amanda Vaill, Janet Vallella, Molly Wilmot, Andrew Wylie, Tom Wolfe, and Bobby Zarem. I am indebted to Mary Loving for her advice and support and to Elizabeth McBride for her constant friend-ship.

I was also helped by reading *Warhol* by Victor Bockris, *Holy Terror* by Bob Colacello, *The Andy Warhol Diaries* edited by Pat Hackett, *Warhol* by Carter Ratcliff, *Edie* edited by Jean Stein with George Plimpton, *Famous for Fifteen Minutes* by Ultra Violet, *The Philosophy of Andy Warhol* by Andy Warhol, *POPism* by Andy Warhol and Pat Hackett, and *The Painted Word* by Tom Wolfe.

I am grateful to Leon Friedman for his advice, his legal expertise, and his willingness to take the actions that he did. I would also like to thank Margaret Tufts, who assisted me with library research, and Ellen Horan, who researched the photographs for this book; Tom Kazar, who helped me through two demanding books; Maura Wogan and Martin Garbus at Frankfurt, Garbus, Klein, & Selz; Marcy Posner and Krystal Hall at the William Morris Agency; Howard Rosenman at Brillstein-Grey; and Diane Reverand, Heather Kilpatrick, Beth Pearson, Sharyn Rosenblum, and Nicky Weinstock at Villard Books. In addition, I want to acknowl-edge James Stein, whom I am fortunate to count as both my agent and a friend, and Julie Grau, an editor with style, intelligence, and, that dying commodity, integrity.

PHOTO CREDITS

Warhol with Brillo boxes: Fred W. McDarrah

Pop party: Fred W. McDarrah

Edie Sedgwick: Film still reproduced with the permission of The
  Andy Warhol Foundation for the Visual Arts, Inc. Copyright
  © 1993 The Andy Warhol Foundation for the Visual Arts.

Valerie Solanis: UPI/Bettman

Warhol with Leo Castelli: Roxanne Lowit

Dominique de Menil; Warhol with Fred Hughes; Hughes and
  Paloma Picasso: Courtesy of Frederick Hughes

Warhol with masseur: Christopher Makos

Warhol with Pope: Courtesy of Frederick Hughes

Warhol with Stuart Pivar: Christopher Makos

Paige Powell and Benjamin Liu; Warhol with Tama Janowitz:
  Patrick McMullan

Warhol with Dolly Parton and Sam Bolton: Pat Hackett

Warhol with *The Last Supper*: Christopher Makos

Pallbearers: Sam Bolton

Gravesite: Victor Carnuccio

Paul and John Warhola: AP/Wide World

Halston and Liza Minnelli: Christopher Makos

Yoko Ono: UPI/Bettmann

Dr. Denton Cox: Courtesy of Dr. Denton Cox

Fiesta Ware and cookie jars: Sotheby's/Sygma

Jewelry: R. Maiman/Sygma

Warhol's townhouse; Sotheby's warehouse: Frederick Charles

London pop singer: UPI/Bettmann

Ed and Susan Gilder Hayes; Fred Hughes and Bruce Cutler: Dustin Pitman

Hughes and friends: Patrick McMullan

Ed Hayes, Richard Merkin, Tom Wolfe: Neil Selkirk

Judge Eve Preminger: Author's collection

Arch Gillies: Cori Wells Braun

Ed Hayes gives opening argument; Surrogate Court, January 1994: Faye Ellman

ABOUT THE AUTHOR

A former reporter for *Time* magazine, PAUL ALEX-ANDER has written for *The New York Times Magazine, The Nation, New York, Premiere, ARTnews, The Village Voice,* and *The Guardian.* He is the author of *Rough Magic,* a biography of Sylvia Plath, and *Boulevard of Broken Dreams,* a biography of James Dean. He lives in Manhattan with his daughter.